Father Iwa... (and his per...

with many gratit... for enro... n and

GEORGE R. EDWARDS is professor of New Testament at Louisville Presbyterian Seminary. He has written for the scholarly press on the Dead Sea Scrolls and the New Testament and will bring out a book in this area in 1964.

NORMAN K. GOTTWALD has been professor of Old Testament at Andover Newton Theological School for eight years and has previously taught at Columbia University. He is the author of the text "A Light to the Nations, An Introduction to the Old Testament."

WILLIAM KLASSEN is associate professor of the New Testament at Goshen College and has lectured at the Menninger Foundation and at Garrett Biblical Seminary. He is co-editor of the book "Current Issues of New Testament Interpretation."

CLINTON MORRISON is professor of New Testament Literature at McCormick Theological Seminary. He is editor of "Biblical Research" and author of the book "The Powers that Be: Studies in Biblical Theology."

PAUL PEACHEY is a sometime professor of sociology at Eastern Mennonite College, now on leave as executive secretary of the Church Peace Mission. He is lecturing on sociology at the University of Maryland.

OTTO A. PIPER is professor emeritus of New Testament at Princeton University and author of a number of books, the most recent: "Biblical View of Sex and Marriage."

JOHN EDWIN SMYLIE is professor of Church History and Chaplain at Occidental College

KRISTER STENDAHL is Frothingham Professor of Biblical Studies at Harvard University. He is co-author of "The Scrolls and the New Testament."

JOHN J. VINCENT is a Methodist pastor, one-time Secretary of the World Council of Churches Commission on the Lordship of Christ. He is author of the book "Christ in a Nuclear World."

LIONEL A. WHISTON is professor of Old Testament at Eden Theological Seminary. He is a former president of the National Association of Biblical Instructors.

BIBLICAL REALISM CONFRONTS THE NATION

BIBLICAL REALISM
CONFRONTS
THE NATION

**Ten Christian Scholars Summon
the Church to the Discipleship of Peace**

••

Edited by PAUL PEACHEY

Published in association with
The Church Peace Mission by

Fellowship Publications

Distributed by
Herald Press, Scottdale, Penn.

Printed and bound
by Sowers Printing Company,
Lebanon, Pennsylvania

CONTENTS

Identification of writers:

GEORGE R. EDWARDS is Professor of New Testament Language and Literature in Louisville Presbyterian Theological Seminary, Louisville, Kentucky

NORMAN K. GOTTWALD is Lowry Professor of Old Testament in Andover Newton Theological School, Newton Centre, Mass.

WILLIAM KLASSEN is Associate Professor of New Testament in Mennonite Biblical Seminary, Elkhart, Indiana

CLINTON MORRISON is Professor of New Testament in McCormick Theological Seminary, Chicago, Iilinois

PAUL PEACHEY formerly taught sociology and church history in Eastern Mennonite College, is now Executive Secretary of The Church Peace Mission, Washington, D. C.

OTTO A. PIPER is Emeritus Professor of New Testament in Princeton Theological Seminary, Princeton, New Jersey

JOHN EDWIN SMYLIE is Associate Professor and Chaplain in Occidental College, Los Angeles, California

KRISTER STENDAHL is Frothingham Professor of Biblical Studies in Harvard Divinity School, Cambridge, Massachusetts

JOHN J. VINCENT is a New Testament theologian and is Superintendent of Rochdale Mission, Rochdale, England

LIONEL A. WHISTON, JR. is Professor of Old Testament in Eden Theological Seminary, Webster Groves, Missouri

INTRODUCTION

In a recent publication, John C. Bennett observes that "there has been a noticeable silence in this country about the ethical issues involved in the nuclear arms race and in the possibility of nuclear war."* Policy decisions of the nuclear age hinge rather on political and military calculations, on technological and economic feasibility. In contrast to some earlier periods of Western history, eternal verities or moral urgencies today appear to have little more than ritualistic relevance.

The factors behind this imbalance doubtless are too complex to yield to any quick or simple solution. But one point at which the issue comes to sharp focus is our rapid transition from the American Protestant cultural synthesis into an era of cultural pluralism. So profound and revolutionary is this shift that numerous reactions against it can be discerned on the national scene, not the least of which is the religious response. Viewed *sociologically*, it may be said that in the dominant response of the churches, the culture-*ratifying* consequences of biblical faith eclipse its more fundamental *innovating* impulse. Thus in a time that cries out for prophetic vision and pioneer deeds at the frontier between the old and the new, the energies of "religion" are expressed more characteristically in resistance to the new world struggling to be born.

Viewed *theologically*, the problem is one of uncertainty con-

---

* *Nuclear Weapons and the Conflict of Conscience,* New York: Scribner's, 1962, p. 7.

cerning the content and the authority of the imperatives of the Christian faith when confronted with insistent national demands. "Christian" values, perhaps largely because of the earlier outer success of Christianity, are so diffuse in the national ethos that to many, both inside and outside the churches, gospel imperatives and the national ethos are scarcely distinguishable. Indeed, likely the vast majority think of Christianity primarily as "values" or "principles," resident now in the ethos and institutions of our society, rather than as the continuous incursion of grace, the new possibilities that recurrently break through the "natural" possibilities of the ethos.

Modern American Protestantism has been dominated successively by the social gospel movement, by the Fundamentalist, and later, the Neo-orthodox reactions, and by the struggle between them. These movements were informed in part by authentic but contrasting notes of biblical faith, the one by an insistence on the immediate relevance of the Kingdom, the other by the awareness that its realization in the larger social order is not directly possible. In the emergence of these movements, constructive as they may have been at some points, somthing integral in the gospel broke apart which, Humpty Dumpty-like, all the king's theologians have not been able to reassemble. Camouflaged behind this struggle, however, the prostitution of church by nation went largely unnoticed. Today the issue can no longer be evaded. At a time when Christianity on the world scene represents a dwindling minority a spiritual and theological reconstruction in the domain of church-in-relation-to-nation can be no longer postponed.

Among the varied theological currents of recent decades one of the more important has been a recovery of biblical theology. Spiritual and theological developments combined with the growing textual and archeological resources have brought the world of biblical faith closer to us, more than at any other time since the Reformation. Accordingly, early in 1962, the Church Peace Mission invited a number of biblical scholars to address themselves to the definition of biblical imperatives as they relate to the claims of the national ethos. These scholars, most of whom for reasons of time had to adapt studies already taking shape under their hand, were asked to move as far as their discipline would permit from the technical biblical field toward our problem.

The studies here presented are the result of the endeavor. In June, 1962, these writers were brought together near Washington, D. C., with a number of additional biblical scholars, other theologians, ethicists, pastors and social actionists, for a three-day discussion of the various papers. Following the conference the writers were given the opportunity to revise their essays as they wished, and in this form the seminar discussions are reflected in the present volume. The reader must seek the unity of the symposium in the problem toward which the studies are directed rather than in a common theological viewpoint or in a common conclusion. Given the current insights and disagreements in biblical studies today, what light do they shed on an imperative that must articulate itself with reference to a persistent and inclusively demanding national ethos? What may we expect from the Bible and what may we not expect? Two introductory essays sketch the ethos problem.

This volume is intended for the theologically literate Christian, whether lay or clergy, rather than for specialists. By the nature of the case, however, some technical material had to be included. This can be bypassed by the general reader, while serving nonetheless the interest of specialists.

Our undertaking took us into uncharted seas, and to those courageous enough to risk with us, we tender here our deep thanks.

PAUL PEACHEY

part 1

THE PROBLEM

1

CHURCH AND NATION
IN WESTERN HISTORY

Paul Peachey

THE CONTINUED spiraling of the arms race and the growing clamor from outraged consciences and fearful hearts for the outlawry of war demand with increasing urgency that the churches choose colors. Both individually, and communally through the churches, Christians, of course, have long demonstrated great concern about the problem. But their expressions lack both consensus and authority. From their witness it is not at all clear whether the Christian imperative calls for the limitation of war—a position from which, given the exigencies of the moment, support of nuclear "deterrence" might nonetheless be extrapolated, or for the elimination of war—a position that, if taken essentially, means total renunciation of war whatever the outer course of events. Amidst this uncertainty, one gains the impression that the churches seek to bet on both horses, with the result that it is left to other forces to shape the events of our time.

One is reminded of those agonizing months between the outbreak of war in Europe, and America's entry into the conflict to turn it into World War II. During this time, in a 1940 editorial, the editors of Fortune Magazine wrote:[1]

> There is only one way out. . . . The way out is the sound of a voice, not our voice, but a voice coming from something not ourselves, in the existence of which we cannot disbelieve. It is the earthly task of the pastors to hear this voice, to

11

cause us to hear it, and to tell us what it says. If they cannot hear it, or if they fail to tell us, we, as laymen, are utterly lost. Without it we are no more capable of saving the world than we were of creating it in the first place.

That voice, however, was not forthcoming and the result is only too familiar.

Once more similar pleas can be heard but from people who hardly expect the churches to speak. Thus the late Albert Camus, disillusioned with Christianity and communism alike, waited merely for a grouping of men who would refuse to be dogs. The late C. Wright Mills concluded that the clear test of man's Christianity was the ability to say an unequivocal "No!" to nuclear weapons. Similarly Hobart Mowrer, still somehow related to the church, concludes that "if theological thought forms can no longer offer a cogent and persuasive plan of salvation, the challenge clearly passes to secular disciplines."[2] Kingsley Martin is driven to say, "We listen to Archbishops as we listen to politicians and agree or disagree on political grounds. When they try to relate what they say to the teaching of Christ, we blush. . . ."[3] Or there is the trenchant criticism of the philosopher Walter Kaufmann, once a Christian, who regards theology as simply the attempt to get "around the Sermon on the Mount without repudiating Jesus."[4]

It must be recognized at the outset that many indictments of the churches reveal deep misconceptions on the part of those who make them. People, whether in the Church or outside, who expect the "Church" to wield a superhuman wisdom or authority, to cut through the tragic knot of the international conflict that threatens our momentary destruction, gravely misunderstand both Gospel and Church. For the authority and wisdom of the Church lie alone in the Lord to whom she witnesses and to whom she responds in obedient faith. She is not here to exercise the suzerainty of an absent God. To be God's *witness* and God's *vicar* are fundamentally different matters. That they are recurrently confused is the fault of both Church and world. Thus Christians have neither the power nor the mandate to mediate

12

programmatically between Washington and Peking, nor to compel the two cities to come to terms. But they are answerable for a clear response to the Gospel, which response by its very nature illuminates the basic issues underlying the conflict of these two cities.

But it may also be asked, and asked legitimately, whether indeed the Gospel is directed to these issues. Does the Gospel, as a message to which men must respond individually, perhaps provide mere individual deliverance from a collective condition that is beyond redemption? Indeed, could it be that to prevent the disruption of the Church's ministry of inner individual deliverance, her members must be prepared to do "the necessary," e.g., to wipe out the Kremlin or the Forbidden City? Is it at all legitimate to await anything from Gospel or Church beyond the assurance that, if we respond to God's proffered salvation in Christ, we may end even a nuclear holocaust, "safe in the arms of Jesus"?

Without attempting to answer these questions explicitly, this essay assumes, in part contrary to their implications, that inner and outer life are inseparably at stake in the divine seizure of man entailed in the Gospel. This means that, while neither Gospel nor Church can give the expected answer to falsely formulated questions, there is clarity and unity in the Gospel imperative, also on the question of war. This is not to ignore, however, the enormous problems of biblical interpretation that confront us—and to these the essays of the present volume bear testimony. It is to argue rather that much of the confusion originates outside the Gospel, in our own traditions and misunderstandings.

A major source of confusion is doubtless the fact *that in the churches of America the Christian ethical imperative has been so fully assimilated to the national ethos that the majority of church people can scarcely distinguish the two and, in time of national crisis, do indeed mistake the "logic" of the latter for the former.* Precisely because Christianity has profoundly shaped our civilization, that civilization itself tends to become the autonomous repository of ultimate values. "Religion" is reduced to an idealistic sentiment whose function it is "to keep America strong."

Ends and means are hopelessly confused. Even for Christians, the logic of national "survival" usurps priority over the demands of the community of grace.

It is our task in the present paper to describe briefly how this confusion has arisen in Western Christianity, and to assess its implications. John Smylie, in the following essay, analyzes the problem in its American form.

I

On a bluff overlooking downtown Brussels looms the massive *Palais de la Justice,* symbol of the majestic achievements of Western jurisprudence. Dwarfed on the square before it, yet threatening, as it were, its very foundations, stands a monument to Belgium's World War I dead. Inscribed on its base is the classic motto: *Salum patriae suprema lex*—the salvation of the fatherland is the supreme law.

Unwittingly thus, architect and sculptor, in this impressive setting, have conspired to expose the Achilles heel of Western morality. For while it is the glory of the West to have secured the dignity and rights of the citizenry in objective legal codes, in the external relations among the very states that guarantee these codes domestically, might still makes right. The nation itself stands outside the requirements of the code, which limits its citizens individually. Where national "honor" or "survival" are threatened, the code itself may be broken through. "To kill a public enemy or an enemy in war," wrote Euripides in a play long ago, "is no murder."[5] "My country, right or wrong!" is still the maxim according to which the American schoolboy learns his patriotism. As a result, anarchy forever lurks at the fringes of the ordered national community. Katyn Forest, Dachau, and Hiroshima testify to us in the still of the night that the great rival political systems of our time may be more alike in their tribal idolatry than different in their virtues.

Despite recurrent blood baths into which this anarchy has plunged us, war has enjoyed an honored place in the history of our civilization. Not only is it glorified in the ideology, the romance, and the legends, which shape our national conscious-

14

ness, but in the formulation of national policy it is often viewed as a positive factor in economic and technological development.[6] The consolidation of minor social groups into larger unities seems always to depend in part on conflict, on the challenge and confrontation of other collectives. War, as the extreme form of conflict, characteristically appears as a force in the achievement of national self-determination. William James, in a famous appeal, called for a constructive "moral equivalent to war." Yet even in this appeal he hailed war as "the gory nurse that trains society to cohesiveness."[7] Almost intuitively, great statesmen sense the delicate balance between domestic unity and foreign danger. A consumate example was Bismarck's precipitation of the Franco-Prussian War in 1870 at the propitious moment when only the challenge of a common outer enemy was needed to give his recalcitrant Germanies their final nudge toward unification. Closer to our own experience is the familiar ebb and flow of Western unity as the threat from the Soviet bloc rises and wanes.

At the same time, however, war has been a costly luxury in Western history. Thus the apologists for war as a constructive factor have not gone unchallenged. Critics such as Arnold J. Toynbee and J. U. Nef hold rather that war has been the proximate cause of the downfall of civilizations.[8] The progress of civilization has been possible only insofar as war has been held in abeyance. War may hasten certain technological developments, but in other respects it monopolizes resources and deflects energies that are urgently needed in constructive tasks. Repeatedly whole societies have lost the flower of their manhood, from which loss only slow recovery was possible. And none of these losses speaks to the loss of the victims themselves.

On balance, then, our society displays an ambivalent attitude, a contradiction never resolved. War is both glorified and abhorred. Its roots are extremely complex, and it is not surprising that throughout the centuries men have often viewed it with fatalistic resignation. Though viewed with terror, war is periodically embraced as a great national purgative, as a momentary release from purposelessness. Indeed, Robert Nisbet sees the real tragedy of modern war, not in its physical destructiveness, but in the fact that its regimentation tends "increasingly to become invested with the attributes of moral community," that we endow it "with the moral satisfactions ordinarily denied to the individual."[9]

This ambivalence toward war is institutionalized in instruments for its containment or limitation. Destruction, with its ultimate anarchy, cannot rage indefinitely. Accommodation must once more be achieved, if only because of the exhaustion of the belligerents. Other needs and forces operating within and between human groups indirectly and unconsciously place effective limits on the anarchy of militarism. With the growth of nations, the advance of technology, and the increased rationality of social organization, war became increasingly destructive. Ironically, the very revolutions which brought us modern democracy brought also, with the introduction of citizen soldiery, the age of total war. Indeed, protagonists of conscription argue that democracy and universal military service are inseparable.[10]

As the scope and the destructiveness of war have increased, however, the indirect containment of war proved increasingly inadequate. It is thus no accident that movements to avoid war, and more recently, to outlaw it completely, date from the generation of wars unleashed by the French Revolution.[11] Nevertheless formal limitations were attempted already in ancient times. One of the most celebrated devices in Western history was the *Pax Romana*, a peace achieved by the ability of one nation to impose a political and economic order upon a broad community of nations. When this order decayed, and no central authority remained with means to coerce, during the Middle Ages there developed in its stead, "a common ideology, propagated throughout Christendom by the clergy, which gave support to principles of justice." But this framework likewise collapsed. More recently the order has been reversed. Materially we are one world, but "many diverse nationalities, each demanding sovereignty, and the absence of a universal religion" militate against the acceptance of a common sense of justice.[12] Accordingly the quest has turned, to a search either for principles of "natural law" which might provide the basis for at least universal convention, if not for world government, or, barring such agreement, for practical arrangements that would substitute adjudication for the demon of war.

The nineteenth century seemed encouraging enough. From the Congress of Vienna in 1815 until the outbreak of World War I, European conflicts were limited in time and scope. The movements for the peaceful settlement of disputes bore tangible fruits in conventions such as the Hague Tribunal established in 1899, and the Geneva Convention. Scientific and technological advances, abetted by notions of evolution and progress, encouraged the hope that man had at last evolved beyond the tooth and claw stages of civilization. Man now possessed both the wisdom and the resources, it was believed, to have done with war.

World War I dealt this hope a staggering, yet by no means crippling, blow. Quickly the war was interpreted as the war that would end all war. The optimists were not wrong, but only one conflict ahead of schedule. The belief that war could be outlawed revived. There was to be an Indian summer of peace in which leading nations signed the Kellogg-Briand Pact (1928), on the surface renouncing war as an instrument of national policy. A few years later thousands of clergy signed pledges that they would never again support a war. But only for a moment! The world was quickly plunged into the winter which has not yet ended.

II

To many people, the mushroom clouds tht rose over western Japan in August, 1945, signaled a turning point in history. Events meanwhile demonstrate that indeed, something profound has transpired. But what is the nature of this turning point? Does the nuclear age differ only *quantitatively* from what has gone before, or *qualitatively?* Far from being merely academic, this question lies at the heart of all foreign and military policy. It is unresolved, precisely because strong arguments can be mustered for either point of view. Nor can an early unequivocal answer be expected. In the past men have failed notoriously to assess their own time properly, and in our age we are hardly endowed with any new burst of wisdom.

That the changes in the coming of nuclear weapons are merely *quantitative* may be argued, for example, on the basis that "wars before the atomic age have been destroying God's creation."[13] Likewise it may be argued that obliteration bombing with conventional bombs in World War II achieved results as devastating in Tokyo or Dresden as that of the A-bomb in Hiroshima. Indeed, as Robert Batchelder has shown, it was our prior acceptance of obliteration bombing by "conventional" means that calloused us to accept Hiroshima and Nagasaki.[14] More important to some people than the nature of the revolution in weaponry is the fact that such a revolution does not of itself alter the structure of nations or the nature of power. Power still arbitrates, and as always, vacuums invite disaster. Given the dynamic character of international communism, the enhanced dangers of modern weaponry are thought simply to heighten the urgency that the West maintain its armaments lead. The magnitude of international problems has changed but not their nature.

On the other hand, however, it can be argued, fully as convincingly, that nuclear weapons constitute a *qualitative* change, with *qualitative* political consequences as well. War now is thought to destroy more than any possible gain from it; therefore it is declared obsolete. John J. McCloy, architect of the new national Arms Control and Disarmament Agency, wrote recently: "Today we are approaching—if we have not already reached—the era of ultimate weapons . . . which . . . have become so destructive in their power that they can or could encompass the end of mankind itself. It is said that even more destructive weapons lie ahead . . .", the consequences of which are still incalculable. But "whatever the balance of probabilities in this respect, the situation today is such that mankind must face up to the necessity of eliminating war as an acceptable arbitrament of international disputes." These are the words, not of a demagogue, but of a man who spent a lifetime supporting defense efforts. When challenged by dubious congressmen in a House committee hearing in 1961, it became clear that precisely his experience and knowledge drove him to this conclusion.[15]

We shall not presume to answer here the debate as to whether the revolution entailed in nuclear weapons is *quantitative* or *qualitative* in nature. We cite it rather to underscore the agony of our time, and to suggest further that considerations more basic than the technological must ultimately determine the course we pursue. Practically the distinction merges in the urgent need for an immediate and profound moral and political revolution among mankind such as history hardly encourages us to expect.

At stake is not merely the question of national policy, but our total existence and values. The struggle between the power blocs is for "keeps," and everything is to be sacrificed to it. One system or the other must triumph; both cannot. Accordingly, in the Soviet system, wars of "liberation" have been rationalized; in our system, "deterrence" or wars of "defense." Each is aghast at the callousness of the other—we at the Russians in Budapest or at the Chinese in Tibet, they at us in Hiroshima. This is not to equate the virtues or the vices of the two systems—there are important differences—nor yet to pronounce a plague on both houses. But whether Dachau or a Russian slave camp differ morally from the bombing of Hiroshima is a question that must be pondered long and earnestly. Perhaps we react to the former with greater horror, first because it is an enemy deed, but then also because the deliberate terror of man-to-man in the concentration camp is something our mind can visualize. The Hiroshima bombing, by contrast, seems remote and impersonal, the "clean" operation of a pilot, soaring against an azure sky, returning home unscathed.

In the frantic search for a way out, two impulses are met. On the one hand, there is the uneven growth of world community, materially already a fact, politically, much less so. Yet despite set-backs, there is progress, both in the development of regional consolidations, and in the growth of political world instruments. Perhaps this growth is analogous, as so many people have long hoped, to the unification of smaller units into nations, at earlier stages of development. On the other hand, while the optimism of the turn of the century to inspire the effort is lacking, it is undergirded by an unprecedented sense of urgency, by the aroused "fear" and "conscience of mankind." Indeed some crusaders hope devoutly that fear may yet accomplish what other compulsions have thus far failed to do. A few days after the Hiroshima bombing, Robert Hutchins, Chancellor of the University of Chicago, declared in a radio broadcast, "remember that Leon Bloy (French novelist, d. 1917) . . . referred to the good news of damnation, doubtless on the theory that none of us would be Christians if we were not afraid of perpetual hell-fire. It may be that the atomic bomb is the good news of damnation, that it may frighten us into that Christian character and those righteous actions and those positive political steps necessary to the creation of a world society, not a thousand or five hundred years hence, but now."[16] *The Bulletin of the Atomic Scientists* was founded in 1946, according to the editor, Eugene Rabinowitch, as "part of the conspiracy to preserve our civilization by scaring man into rationality."[17]

Fear, certainly, is a noble instinct which belongs to the divinely-given human endowment. Furthermore, the necessity for men to cooperate despite all differences is today hardly subject to dispute. Christians should be the last to scoff at the efforts of men of whatever persuasion to effect frameworks of cooperative existence among diverse systems and values. Radical actions for peace, however futile, and however much lampooned by critics, are bound to become increasingly significant.

Nevertheless it must be recognized clearly that fear is an uncertain quantity, that if forced to stand alone, it will lead more quickly to irrationality than to rationality. If the debate concerning the implications of nuclear weapons cannot lead of itself to a solution of the problems they pose, neither can fear. We are driven rather to face the ultimate questions of human existence in political decision with a directness that has been ignored for centuries. Edward LeRoy Long, Jr., stated the issue well, when he wrote a few years ago, "When two nations, both of which are atomically armed, are pitted against each other, a decision for or against the use of the bomb cannot be made on calculative grounds, since none of the historical alternatives is to be preferred over the other." Rather, at this point only "ultimate religious obedience" remains.[18] *But what is the imperative that defines this obedience?* It is the obscurity of this imperative that occasions the present symposium.

III

Few problems have been as perplexing in Christian history as that of war. On the one hand, when viewed in the perspective of the character, the example, and the word of Christ, war evokes a verdict that is simple and clear. Whatever use may be made of the Bible to justify war otherwise, no attempt to do so in terms of Christ himself has ever stood up. On the other hand, however, the churches traditionally, and during most of their history, all but universally, have supported or condoned war. And they have often done so in genuinely good faith that they enjoyed biblical sanction in the course they pursued. Indeed, so well have the churches accommodated to the militarism of the Western nations, that many non-Western people profess to see a genetic connection between Christianity and militarism.

Stated extremely, such a view, of course, is erroneous. As Arnold J. Toynbee well points out, war in Western history is a tradition that far antedates the rise of Christianity.[19] Any criticism of the militarism of the West must recognize that the Gospel has often exercised a restraining influence on the belligerency of Europeans. Yet, whereas Christian influences conquered gradually one social ill after another, war has so far proven itself invincible. Accordingly, Christianity and the churches have accommodated themselves to it. Theologically this accommodation was expressed in the doctrine of the "just war." This doctrine "attempted to provide rules and regulations for the conduct of war, which was understood to be a legitimate instrument of policy if conducted according to these rules." In practice, however, the doctrine became instead "a too easy sanction for war."[20] Instead of a restraint upon war the doctrine became its rationalization.

The concept of the "just war," however, must be viewed in its historical setting. Probably no one today can appreciate fully the profound impression that the "conversion" of the Roman imperial government made upon the fourth century Church, exhausted as she was by bitter persecution, nor yet, on the other hand, the deep shock sustained by the Christians of the following century when Rome fell to the Goths. These impressions led to contradictory concepts in the history of the Church, both eloquently illustrated in Augustine, Bishop of Hippo. In response to the incursion of the Goths, Augustine wrote *The City of God,* a treatise that repeatedly has called men back from the identification of the eternal Kingdom with passing regimes. Out of the former, however, there emerged a secondary view of Church and State that in Western history was to eclipse the more basic philosophy of *The City of God.*

This second view appears dramatically in Augustine's correspondence with the Roman tribune in North Africa, Count Boniface, around the year 417 A.D. In the course of a united campaign of Church and empire, instigated by Augustine, to settle finally the vexing Donatist schism, Boniface apparently was reluctant as a Christian to exercise the coercion for which the policy called. Augustine, however, urged him forward into the fray. The aloofness displayed by New Testament Christians toward civil rulers, he writes, stemmed from the fact that these were still pagan! Meanwhile, *ordo temporum volvebatur,* the temporal order having revolved, the Scriptures predicting that the kings of the earth should some day fall down and worship God (Psalm 72:11), are beginning to be fulfilled. Who therefore, *mente sobrius,* in his right mind, would hinder these, now Christian, rulers from exercising their power on behalf of the Church, the more so since even pagan rulers such as Nebuchadnezzar were called upon to legislate concerning true worship? Each member of the Church in any case has his gift, the one to battle in prayer against invisible enemies, another by physical means, against visible enemies.[21]

This letter which, as Augustine indicates elsewhere, summarizes his views on the Donatists,[22] contains embryonically, fifteen centuries of Christian history. Admittedly, in fairness to Augustine, it represented a minor theme in his thought, born of a desperate situation. Nonetheless it expresses the clear belief that the "conversion" of the Emperor constituted in some manner an eschatological event, whereby the civil government, in New Testament thought and heretofore regarded by the Church as belonging to the fallen "world," outside the Church, had been transposed into the realm of redemption. Church and state now could stand shoulder to shoulder, achieving the divine purpose, battling against the twin threat of heresy and barbarism, a view further elaborated by Ambrose, Bishop of Milan, and other later writers.[23] Augustine also coined the famous interpretation of Luke 14:23, ". . . compel them to come in," as the authorization for coercing church membership. Thus Fr. van der Meer, a contemporary Dutch Catholic historian, writes that Augustine "must be regarded the true father of the Inquisition."[24]

This secondary line of interpretation became the classic view of the churches, triumphing over the more profound biblical views set forth in *The City of God*.[25] More than a thousand years later, for example, Heinrich Bullinger, successor to the Swiss reformer, Zwingli, in Zurich, quoted the letter of Augustine against the Anabaptist criticism of the reformers' militarism and invocation of the civil ruler in the formation of church polity. Bullinger based his arguments on both Luke 14:23 and Isaiah 49:23 ("And kings shall be thy nursing fathers, and queens thy nursing mothers"). If already heathen kings could exercise the death penalty in religious matters, argues Bullinger, much more are Christian regents entitled to do so.[26]

Out of this background, and undergirded by just war concepts assimilated from Graeco-Latin antiquity, was fashioned the classic Christian approach to war.[27] In its logical simplicity, it exercises strong appeal, and breathes an air of sober "realism." Given the dynamics of interacting human groups in a fallen world, sooner or later unjust aggression will be committed. The group or nation so wronged may turn back the aggressor in self-defence. Not only is war in such circumstances permissible, hence "just," but it may be a positive duty. (The moralist, interestingly enough, is fortunately usually on the side of the "innocent" party.) By the same token, however, wars out of base motives were outlawed, and instances are not altogether lacking where a bishop was able to bring a belligerent prince to heel by "religious" restraints.

This approach to war seemed to comport fully with the biblical view of God, man, and history. Man is a sinner who must be restrained. Wrongs must be redressed if order is to be maintained. "Whoso sheddeth man's blood, by man shall his blood be shed" (Genesis 9:6). The ruler is "the minister of God" who "beareth not the sword in vain" (Rom. 12:4). War admittedly is evil, but in the fallen world it is inevitable. The Gospel of Christ operates within this framework, it is assumed. The restoration and redemption to which it tends may be experienced in personal foretaste, but the alteration of the structure of history, when swords will be beaten into plowshares, is an eschatological hope rather than an historical expectancy. And accordingly, Charles Lowry could write but recently as a Christian churchman, "The only answer to naked, lawless power is counter-power. . . . Far from declaring, in accordance with some theologians in their most recent pronouncements, that we will never initiate nuclear war in any form, that is just what under present circumstances we must be willing to do." This, "of course," does not apply to "person-to-person contacts with Communists in peaceful circumstances" where "the ethic of Jesus applies." This approach Lowry regards, in contrast to "idealism," "the older tradition of Christian realism."[28]

To this doctrine and practice in the Church, however, there has been recurrent dissent. Sensitive Christian spirits, alone and in groups, have protested this dichotomy between personal and social ethics, claiming that "just war" doctrine overrides whole segments of biblical teaching. So certain has the "Church" been of the rectitude of her position, however, that she not only ignored their witness, but suppressed the dissenting practise, or at least consigned it innocuously to the monastery. Out in the world no dissent was tolerated and, as the persecution of sixteenth-century sectaries showed, when the Reformation suppressed the monasteries, dissent had no place to go.

The suppression of the pacifist witness, however, meant the impoverishment of "Church" and "sect" alike. Pacifists eventually withdrew to the fringes, content to seek asylum, rightly incurring the accusation that they contracted out of responsibility.

The "Church" became apostate as she professed to fight, Christian nation against Christian nation, "for God and country." For the doctrine of the "just war" had been fashioned over the mold of the Empire, which ideally represented an ecumenical order, holding at bay the incursions of barbarians, Christian here, pagan there. But when the empire was dissolved into competing nation states, each arrogated to itself the sovereign attributes of the former empire. Thus, if in some measure a case for a "just war" could be made in a barbarian-molested empire, that case collapsed when the enemy was an equally "Christian" nation, and yet this difference was hardly noted; the old habits remained.

Surprisingly, nonetheless, attempts have been made recently to dust off the doctrine of the "just war." American defence policy is said to have reached its present fatal impasse precisely because we have strayed from classic just-war policies. For "the doctrine of the just war, which many thought had been rendered obsolete by weapons of indiscriminate destructiveness and theories of total war, is now seen to have new relevance." Precisely the limits intended by the just-war doctrine would demand the abandonment of "counter-population" warfare, which is the essence of total war, and a return to "counter-forces" operations only. The same writer, Paul Ramsey, argues that "there is a perennial truth in the just-war doctrine which in every epoch of our human history Christian love, of its own inner logic, will be impelled to affirm and renew as proper Christian action." That is, the doctrine is "a deposit or creation of the Christian love ethic itself, and not merely the result of an independent natural-law reason."[29] Some policy makers likewise are giving renewed attention to this concept of warfare, though there are schools of disagreement in the Department of Defense. The recent emphasis on conventional armaments in American policy, and on guerrilla warfare, though based on prudential considerations, reflects nonetheless the influence of this line of thought. War must be reduced once more to usable proportions.[30]

That the doctrine of the just war has thus been raised to view for Protestants who long assumed it, but too rarely recognized or understood it, is to be welcomed. But the result must surely be the opposite from what its protagonists intend. Quite apart from the theological problems to which we must attend in a moment, the practical difficulties are insurmountable. The strength of the "counter-forces" argument hinges on its "realism," on its recognition that war may indeed be controlled but, judged by the record, hardly eliminated. A policy that recognizes its necessity, but imposes proper limits, is viewed as preferable to a "utopian" scheme, which expects the disappearance of war, but in its unrealism, invites the very thing it would avoid.

But the question now before us is whether it is "realistic" to expect, in the total confrontation of power blocs in the cold war, that either bloc would in the end capitulate to the other without seeking recourse in every resource that science and technology place at its disposal. Can it be expected that either bloc, when the struggle enters its climactic phase, will fight deliberately at a technologically obsolete level? Moreover, does not a return to mere "counter-forces" warfare, to a "just-war" policy, presuppose the sort of gentlemen's agreement among the powers that is possible only when a common world view is shared, such as was the case among medieval or eighteenth-century European powers? And so we are compelled to ask whether the proposed revival of the "just-war" doctrine, actually pertains to the world of the 1960's, or whether it is not rather merely a sort of exercise in games theory. In any case, it is noteworthy that Paul Ramsey, the foremost Protestant spokesman for this viewpoint, nowhere in the end actually renounces every resort to nuclear weapons.

IV

When we survey the theological legacy of the classic "Christian" view of war, we discover serious perversions of particularly three major Christian doctrines; *eschatology*, *ecclesiology*, and *soteriology*.

1. The *eschatological* perversion. The Augustinian view, in the Donatist controversy, that civil government had been baptized into the Church, paved the way for the eventual identification, in Thomas Aquinas, of the Church with the Kingdom of God. Whatever the status of office holders, which is a separate

question, the New Testament foresees no such transformation in this "age." However constructive governments may be, however much they may serve as a "minister" of God, they always belong to the passing order which stands somehow in revolt against God. This fact does not exclude all overlap of interest or of personnel between "Church" and "state," nor does it portend necessarily a pitched battle between the two societies. But it does preclude the intrusion of political or military instruments into the sphere of grace. It precludes the Church's sanctification of ungodly deeds by the state, and conversely, the use of the instruments of the state for the direct prosecution of the aims of the Church.

The supposed transposition of civil government into the realm of grace, however, was to have disastrous consequences in the history of the Church. Arguing that eschatology had been fulfilled *politically* but not *ethically*, state churches put enthusiasts to the sword who argued in reverse terms that in the *Church* there was an *ethical* fulfillment which, however, was not yet realized *politically* in the world. The Church now tended, perhaps inevitably, to become socially conservative. The maintenance of the Kingdom, supposedly realized in her hierarchical and sacramental order, took precedence over her expectancy for the coming Kingdom in the midst of the ever new problems she faced. Proponents of Christian anti-Communist crusades today, unfortunately can find all too much precedent in Christian history for their action.

2. The *ecclesiological* perversion. The shift in eschatological perspective entails inevitably also an *ecclesiological* perversion. However the New Testament may conceive the nettlesome relationship of Church and world, within the inclusive purpose of God they are tangibly distinct entities. The Church serves or saves the world in surpassing it. But particularly after the Theodosian edicts of about 380 A.D., which outlawed pagan religions and made Christianity compulsory, Church-world relations became hopelessly blurred. Confronted with a church embracing a mixed multitude of "sinner" and "saint" alike, Augustine developed the familiar, now Protestant, scheme of the

visible-invisible church. In practise, however, the putative eleva-
tion of the state meant instead the lowering of the church. As
Dietrich Bonhoeffer well said, "The claim of the congregation
of the faithful to build the world with Chrisitan principles ends
only with the total capitulation of the Church to the world. . . ."[31]

The results again were disastrous and sometimes bizarre. For
example, during the "Augustinian" Swiss Reformation the sectaries were lampooned for their legalism, namely their attempt
to constitute the congregation on the basis of committed and
disciplined believers. Yet soon city governments in Zurich and
Geneva, faced with the decay of public morals, and coached by
the official churches, found themselves enacting sumptuary legislation that touched at times on the very matters that the sectaries
had made the subjects of congregational discipline. Similarly,
Franklin Littell observes with regard to American prohibition
laws, that "politicians in the churches attempted to secure by
public legislation what they were unable to persuade many of
their own members was either wise or desirable."[32]

What this means with regard to the Church's witness on war
was well put recently by the Jewish philosopher, Martin Buber,
when he was queried concerning the ineffectiveness of Christian
appeals against nuclear weapons. Says Buber concerning the
framers of Church appeals and pronouncements:

> They were not committed; they only said what *other* peo-
> ple—those in governments and the General Staff of armies—
> ought to do. They never stated what the authors of these
> appeals would do *themselves,* nor to what they committed
> themselves. . . . And it is only when a man commits himself
> that others really listen to him."[33]

3. The *soteriological* perversion. One of the most instructive,
yet least explored phases, of Western Christian history is the
transition from the early Church motif of the "open grave," as
the central symbol in faith and life, to that of the "cross." However complex the factors in this development, the partial assumption by the Church of the burdens of empire, as the old Roman
order decayed, was clearly decisive. Moreover, the Roman legal
mentality was ready at hand to foster a *forensic* rather than a

victorious view of the atonement. The brooding Gothic spirit, with its sense of suffering, completed the transformation of the victorious Gospel into a tragic view of life and history. "It can be said that the appeal of the passion, the martyrdom of Christ, has never been so deeply felt as in medieval religion," writes Gustaf Aulén.[34] Luther, rightly incensed at Tetzel's answer to the problem of guilt, poignantly stated in the latter's couplet, "As soon as the coin in the coffer rings, the soul from purgatory springs,"[35] failed to see that the real problem lay in his formulation of the question that man faces. Gandhi may have been a better theologian at this point when he observed autobiographically, "I do not seek to be redeemed from the consequences of my sin. I seek to be redeemed from sin itself."[36]

That is to say: a Church which presupposes a mistaken notion of eschatological fulfillment, and which includes within her fold populations without faith or commitments, is bound to reduce the good news of deliverance and renewal to the mere word of forgiveness and justification in the midst of continued defeat. For a time, the conditions of modern life, particularly in America, seemed to belie the tragic view. In the face of rapid scientific and technological progress the Social Gospel restored the note of confidence, but superficially and prematurely, without due regard for the cross. Reinhold Niebuhr rightly sounded the note of recall. But the "tragedy" of this theologian of tragedy is that he led back, not to *Christus Victor*, but to the Gothic Christ. As Donald Meyer has well said, "The grace to which Niebuhr was pointing carried no positive guarantees for politics, for society, or for history. It was not a resource that, supplementing the virtue and intelligence of men, guaranteed the Kingdom. It was a resource that consoled men for the fact that the Kingdom was an impossibility in history. . . ."[37]

Beneath the weight of such a heritage, can the authentic biblical note be recovered? Arnold J. Toynbee observes that it is uncommon for the creative responses to two or more successive challenges in the history of a civilization to be achieved by the same minority. Success in the meeting of one challenge leads to the "idolization of the ephemeral self."[38] Is Toynbee right in this instance? Is the creative imperative of Christian faith too encrusted in the forms of an earlier day to speak compellingly in this desperate hour? Are the prophets of doom right?

There are signs of hope. A generation of Niebuhrian judgment has alerted us to the perils of our tribal idolatry. World War I already convinced Niebuhr that "religion can be effective only as it resists the embraces of civilization."[39] The experiences of these dark decades have disabused us of the illusions that the Kingdom will be won in our technological progress and cultural evolution. In the realm of faith and ethics the focus has shifted far, perhaps too far, or on questionable premises, from objective propositional systems to real men and their commitments in living situations. Social science, sometimes arrogantly or pedantically, but occasionally prophetically, has exposed further the fallacies and foibles of culture religion.

But the picture is that of the swept room, described in Matthew 12. Demons have been cast out, yet the room is still void. The astute analyses of numerous Niebuhrs are effective as brooms, but they provide no creative imperatives. Whatever else may be required, this vacuum is an urgent call to the biblical scholars of our day. Fortunately they are equipped with better resources than ever before. What can we await from them?

It may be that the growth of international independence, reinforced by the aroused conscience and fears of mankind, may yet avert the destruction that so darkly threatens us. Certainly among Christians one should hear of no disdain for this possibility, nor of any quest for churchly prerogatives in this matter. The incarnation of our Lord drives us to take the struggle of men on the purely human level with utmost seriousness. Jesus himself would not break the "bruised reed" nor quench the "smoking flax" (Matthew 12:20). But it may also be that we shall fail, indeed, that we are already doomed. Nevertheless in the biblical perspective, however God may work through proximate causes, or however important the specific tasks in which men may labor, destiny always turns on ultimate spiritual-moral issues, on faith and unfaith. It is the elucidation of these that we await.

Church and Nation in Western History

FOOTNOTES

[1] "War and Peace," *Fortune*, January, 1940, p. 26f.

[2] O. Hobart Mowrer, "The 'New' Psychological Liberty," *The Christian Scholar*, XLIV/3 (Fall, 1961), p. 219.

[3] Kingsley Martin, in a review of J. Middleton Murry's, *The Betrayal of Christ by the Churches*, quoted by G. H. C. Macgregor, *The Relevance of the Impossible*, London: Fellowship of Reconciliation, 1941, p. 64f.

[4] Walter Kaufmann, *The Faith of a Heretic*, New York: Doubleday, 1961, p. 246.

[5] Quoted by Hugo Grotius, *The Rights of War and Peace*, tr. by A. C. Campbell, Washington and London: M. Walter Dunne, 1901, p. 325.

[6] Cf. Friedrich Nietzsche's statement *(Thus Spake Zarathustra)*, that civilization grows only "by acts of violence and nothing else," in Irving L. Horowitz, *The Idea of War in Contemporary Philosophy*, New York: Paine-Whitman Publishers, 1957, p. 35; also Werner Sombart's view that war fostered the modern economic system, R. A. Preston, et al., *Men in Arms*, New York: Frederick A. Praeger, 1956, p. 13f.

[7] William James, "The Moral Equivalent of War" (1910), *Essays on Faith and Morals*, New York: Longmans, Green & Co., 1943, p. 322f.

[8] Preston, et al., *op. cit.*, p. 15; J. U. Nef, *War and Human Progress*, Cambridge: Harvard University Press, 1950.

[9] Robert A. Nisbet, *The Quest for Community*, New York: Oxford University Press, 1953, p. 43.

[10] *Backgrounds of Selective Service*, Washington, D. C.: The Selective Service System, 1947, 1949, pp. 3-9.

[11] Norman Angell, "Peace Movements," *Encyclopædia of the Social Sciences*, New York: Macmillan, 1933, 1959, pp. 41-48.

[12] Quincy Wright, *The Role of International Law and the Elimination of War*, New York: Oceana Publications, 1961, p. 17.

[13] Sir Thomas Taylor, Robert S. Bilheimer, *Christians and the Prevention of War in an Atomic Age*, London: SCM Press, 1961, p. 10f.

[14] Robert C. Batchelder, *Irreversible Decision*, Boston: Houghton Mifflin, 1962, p. 211.

[15] John J. McCloy, "Balance Sheet on Disarmament," *Foreign Affairs*, Vol. XL/3 (April, 1962), pp. 339.

[16] Robert M. Hutchins, *America and the Atomic Age*, Chicago: University of Chicago Press, 1951, p. 14.

[17] Eugene Rabinowitch, quoted by Robert Batchelder, *op. cit.*, p. 245.

[18] Edward LeRoy Long, Jr., *The Christian Response to the Atomic Crisis*, Philadelphia: Westminster Press, 1950, p. 81f.

[19] Arnold J. Toynbee, *Christianity Among the Religions of the World*, New York: Scribner's, 1957, p. 67.

[20] Taylor, Bilheimer, *op. cit.*, p. 12.

[21] Augustine, "ad Bonafacio," Ep. CLXXV (c), alias 50, J. P. Migne, ed., *Patrologia Latin*, Paris, 1845, Vol. XXXIII, pp. 855ff.

Roy Joseph Deferrari, Ed., *The Fathers of the Church*, New York: Fathers of the Church, Inc., Vol. XXX, 141-199, ep. 185, tr. by Sister Wilfrid Parsons.

F. van der Meer, *Augustine the Bishop*, London and New York: Sheed & Ward, 1961.

[22] Deferrari, *op. cit.*, p. 160.

[23] F. Homes Dudden, *The Life and Times of St. Ambrose*, Oxford: At the Clarendon Press, 1935, Vol. II, p. 538.

[24] *op. cit.*, p. 95.

[25] Cf. Martin Schmidt, "Biblische Begründungen für die Konstantinische Staatskirchenordnung im Laufe der Geschichte," *Der Evangelische Erzieher*, Frankfurt/Main: Verlag Moritz Diesterweg, XI/3 (März 1959), pp. 67-72.

[26] Heinrychen Bullinger, *Der Widertouffern ursprung/fürgang/Secten* . . . , Zurich, 1561, p. 144.

[27] Roland Bainton, *Christian Attitudes Toward War and Peace*, New York & Nashville: Abingdon, 1960, Ch. II.

[28] Charles Lowry, "Perspective of the Power Struggle," *Christianity Today*, Vol. VI/16 (May 11, 1962), p. 765.

[29] Paul Ramsey, *War and the Christian Conscience*, Durham: Duke University Press, 1961, pp. 9f, xix.

[30] Robert Osgood, *Limited War*, Chicago: University of Chicago Press, 1957. Batchelder, *op. cit.*

Thomas E. Murray, Nuclear Policy for War and Peace, Cleveland & New York: The World Book Publishing Co., 1960.

[31] Dietrich Bonhoeffer, *Ethics*, tr. by Eberhard Bethge, New York: Macmillan, 1955, p. 41.

[32] Franklin Hamlin Littell, *From State Church to Pluralism*, New York: Doubleday Anchor, 1962, p. 120.

[33] Quoted by Helmut Gollwitzer, "Christian Commitment," *Therefore Choose Life*, London: International Fellowship of Reconciliation, 1961, p. 33.

[34] Gustaf Aulen, *Christus Victor*, New York: Macmillan, 1951, p. 97.

[35] Roland Bainton, *Here I Stand*, New York & Nashville: Abingdon, 1950, p. 78.

[36] M. K. Gandhi, *The Story of My Experiment With Truth*, Washington, D. C.: Public Affairs Press, 1954, p. 155f.

[37] Donald B. Meyer, *Protestant Search for Political Realism 1919-1941*, Berkeley & Los Angeles: University of California Press, 1960, p. 239.

[38] Arnold J. Toynbee, *A Study of History*, (Somervell Abridgement), New York: Oxford University Press, 1946, 1958, Vol. I, p. 307f.

[39] "What the War Did to Change My Mind," *Christian Century*, Vol. XLV (Sept. 27, 1928), in Meyer, *op. cit.*, p. 220.

2

THE CHRISTIAN CHURCH
AND NATIONAL ETHOS

John Edwin Smylie

▪▪▪

I N WHAT SENSE, or in what measure is it true that American Christianity has been wrongly assimilated by the national ethos, thereby impairing the integrity and witness of the churches? Conversely, where and in what measure has the relationship been an authentic one?" [That is the not-so-modest question assigned for this paper.[1]] The problem is interestingly stated both in its assumptions and the directions it points. It assumes American Christianity and the national ethos have been assimilated. That comes as news to no one. Our generation takes for granted that empirical religion mirrors and is mirrored by its ethos. It assumes correctly that in talking about American Christianity the word "church" has to be used in the plural. There is no such thing organizationally as the American church in the singular. The suggestive prospect which the question raises, perhaps only as an after thought and formally (as if Aristotelian contraries require that every wrong be chaperoned by its right), is that such assimilation can have positive and authentic elements.

Thus far conversation about culture religion in America has failed to provide for the possibility of authentic elements in the assimilation of Christianity and the national ethos. Commentators point scornfully to deficiencies in American religious life: its ecclesiastical individualism, its failure to distinguish between the Christian way and the nation or class, its lack of churchly discipline and its inability to witness effectively on crucial political and social issues like integration and the bomb. These failings are obvious and sad. Praise God for prophets-in-academic-clothing who use scholarship to destroy inflated notions of ourselves by pointing to our failures and inconsistencies.[2] But historical and sociological iconoclasm, like all iconoclasm, rarely takes accurate measure of what it destroys. Critical formulas about culture religion in America, for all their contribution to pathology of religion, have inadequately accounted for what is impressively, although perhaps accidentally, healthy about American Christianity and its influence on public life. Any thesis that does not account satisfactorily for that vitality, generosity, zeal and resilience which distinguishes American from European Christianity, and American from European nationalism is, to say the least, incomplete.

This chapter offers a tentative, un-documented and speculative interpretation, which might explain the process of assimilation and prove useful in setting the stage for a discussion of kerygma and ethos in the nuclear age.

I

A preliminary observation concerns the American experience and understanding of the church. Church life in America has been *denominational* in theory and in structure. English in origin, the idea of a denomination, unlike the idea of the sect, carries no implication of negative value judgment. The denomination is not exclusive and separate like a sect. "The group referred to is but one member, called or denominated by a particular name, of a larger group—the Church—to which all denominations belong." "No denomination claims to represent the whole Church of Christ."[3]

Peculiar circumstances in seventeenth-century England made this denominational theory socially possible and politically necessary. In Britain there arose the anomaly of an established and jealous Church of England alongside a tolerated Protestant pluralism. Nonconformists claimed to major in personal holiness and doctrinal and ecclesiastical apostolicity. The Church of England enjoyed national unity, ties with similar churches through the world, and apostolicity resting upon episcopal genealogy. In this division of the notes of the church, the good of England seemed furthered and the integrity of English Christianity at least formally preserved. Since then Christianity in England has had its brains in Westminster, its voice at Canterbury, its limbs extending into every parish of the United Kingdom and its blood purified by a throbbing nonconformist heart.

Once it had been proved that more than a single religious organization could live in a given political entity, Calvinism's definition of the local visible church made denominations permissible theologically and ecclesiastically. If the litmus test of a true local church asks only if the apostolic word is truly preached and heard and the apostolic sacraments properly administered,[4] local congregations or groups of congregations can pass formal inspection without much difficulty. In the process other marks of the church, especially its unity and catholicity, receive little attention.

England exported Calvinism to America packaged in a Protestant pluralism. Whatever understanding of the church lay behind seventeenth-century colonial experiments—especially Covenant congregationalism in Massachusetts, which tried to maintain religious unity within a given political entity, the first amendment of 1791 forbidding a national establishment assured the triumph of denominationalism in America. The result? There are many churches here but no such thing ecclesiastically as *The Christian Church of America.* American Protestants have their general assemblies, associations, conferences, and conventions. They take associational business and responsibilities seriously, sometimes too seriously. But no one takes these assemblies so seriously as to pretend that they are *the* Church in America, that they are for this country what the Convocations of Canterbury and York are for England and the General Assembly for Scotland, or that they represent the first estate in America comparable to the clergy of feudal France. No churchly organism has evolved in American life that can speak as the Christian Church either to the nation or to other national churches. The Evangelical Alliance had enthusiasm but no corporate integrity.

The National Council of Churches, which might appear to supply the need, is dependent upon denominational support and defensive before its own constituency.

This denominational experience has been devastating for attempts in American Protestantism to understand the church theologically. While American churchmen were neat and tidy about apostolic word and sacraments, they had little or no experience of the community of the redeemed as the One Holy Catholic Church. In a word the denominational church as they knew it was not for them the New Israel of God's elect. It was voluntary society, perhaps the most important among others, but hardly the organ through which God made his ultimate historical demands and offered his fullest earthly rewards. Did this experience of the church as denomination affect the American Protestant experience of and attitude toward the nation?

II

The suggestion of this chapter is that at the very time the denomination as nineteenth-century Protestant Americans knew it failed to function fully as the church, the nation came more and more so to function. In turn American Protestants endowed the nation with churchly attributes. The nation became more than a political unit of life headed by a civil magistrate whose chief end was the preservation of life, law, justice and order. Specifically American Protestants endowed the nation with three theological notes.

1. The nation became the primary agent of God's meaningful activity in history. Hence Americans attributed to it a catholicity of destiny similar to that which theology attributes to the universal church. The nation bore and embodied values, goods and purposes which it had to share with every other people. The Americanization of the whole world was the obvious goal of history. The nation became the chosen people of God replacing the community of the redeemed as New Israel.

American Christians came by this notion from two sources. Old Testament patterns portrayed a political people bound to each other and to God by past covenants. Also influential during the nineteenth century were romantic philosophies of history that looked to the future as the key to world meaning and made nations the most significant units of historical life.[5]

Puritans tried to create a New Israel in Massachusetts Bay Colony. Acceptance of the congregational covenant was necessary for full participation in the political community. Behind this scheme lay a high sense of cosmic purpose. The settlers had come to create a wilderness Zion that would solve the unresolved problem of the Reformation—How to organize a new church and a new society on biblical principles? Eventual awareness that seventeenth-century England and the rest of the Protestant world had solved the same problem in rather different ways, ignoring Massachusetts altogether, brought bitter disappointment.[6]

During the great awakening Jonathan Edwards speculated that Americans were to be the great missionary people of the world. His attempt to interpret the awakening in terms of ultimate purposes has been dismissed as a cosmic rationalism of a local revival.[7] The missionary constituency of nineteenth-century American Protestantism did not dismiss it so lightly. By then the colonies had become a new nation to which the same feelings of religious destiny had been transferred with perfect ease.

Romantic philosophies of history appeared in the United States early in the nineteenth century. They described the progress of the world in terms of a succession of nations moving from east to west and bringing progress, freedom and civilization. These exhilarating interpretations of God's role in history provided an understanding of destiny oriented to the future. As the westernmost nation in the temperate zone the United States was the world's last great nation. It embodied all ultimate values and would disseminate them to the rest of the world. Thus even the missionary movement was not merely a denominational or interdenominational matter. Foreign missions was the foreign policy of the nation. Even theologians like Philip Schaff, who had high doctrines of the church, believed America was uniquely chosen to further ultimate historical values.

It is interesting that the sin of schism does not weigh heavily upon the consciences of American Christians. Denominations have never had such ultimate historic value that their lives could not be sacrificed to other commitments. Thus the history of Presbyterianism in this country is the story of not-so-gentlemanly schisms followed shortly by more-gentlemanly reunions. The sin of secession from the nation, however, upon whose shoulders rested ultimate historical values and purposes, was intolerable. People sacrificed everything to preserve the nation: family, denomination, party, and business. The struggle was all the more fierce because southern Christians endowed the Confederacy with competitive values for which they claimed like ultimacy. It may be possible roughly to identify the southern ideal of national destiny with the narrow interpretation of past political covenants, and the northern with a broader interpretation more hospitable to the extreme claims of romantic nationalism which looked to the future.

The legacy of this transfer to the nation of purposive functions, universal and catholic in scope, is great. Protestant America is reluctant to believe that any other agent of history except the United States can carry forward God's purposes in the world. Every group, from religious sect to United Nations and the World Council of Churches, which claims to possess truth and to serve purposes not its own, is suspect of the ultimate sin of being un-American. Mormons for decades were un-American simply because they lived as if the Church of the Latter Day Saints embodied values that the nation did not. They acted as if they really were the continuation of ancient Israel. Roman Catholicism, acting as if it were the true bearer of historical meaning, automatically came under suspicion. Only the nation can bear universal purposes and have ultimate historical meaning.

2. The nation assumed another function of the church when it became the primary society in terms of which individuals, Christian and non-Christian alike, found personal identity. The nation was the one unity that absorbed all pluralities and in connection with which full personal life was realized. The melting-pot motif meant not only that Europe's diversities were coming to America, but that in America they would melt. The resulting mass would have a rich but homogeneous unity with English

color and Protestant adhesives. All denominations, races, classes, and sections would be subsumed under a single nation. Certainly the nation was pluralistic. But each element in the pluralism was expected to submerge itself in the larger unity with all deliberate haste. No peculiarity was allowed to claim priority at the expense of the whole. This was essentially a continuation of seventeenth-century English pluralism which preserved national unity. Thus individualism and pluralism in this country should never be stressed to the neglect of that overriding unity and homogeneity which seems to make everything the same here.

The sense of corporate unity in which all pluralisms are submerged might well be tested by asking our older citizens still under the influence of nineteenth-century educations which of the following labels describes them most completely. Presbyterian, Roman Catholic, Mennonite, or Quaker by denomination? Missourian, New Yorker, or Virginian by state? Italian, Scot, Irish or German by national origin? Middle, lower, upper by class? Westerner, Southerner, Easterner, Northerner by section? Or simply—I am American? I suspect that the last would be chosen as the label of true identity. In the term "American" most would find their corporate identity.

Thus the unity which theology would localize in Christ and his church was actually realized in the American experience in the nation. Since the Civil War and with successive amendments to the Constitution, it can be claimed at least legally and formally that in America there is neither East or West, North or South, neither Jew nor Greek, male nor female, slave nor free, for all have united in the one great community called America.

The public school system forged this unity. That system has been Protestant in religious outlook but nationalistic in the sense of corporate identity which it fostered. Some of the most vivid memories of my days at Horace Mann Public School in St. Louis, Missouri were learning to toot the bugle for the pledge of allegiance to the flag and reading a patriotic manual called *Man Without a Country* by the Unitarian pastor Edward Everett Hale. That little text (still in print and used in public schools) impressed me indelibly with its teaching. Philip Nolan, the key figure in the tragedy, ruined his life in pretending he could find meaningful personal identity apart from his nation.

Recent talk about pluralistic America perplexes older Protestants. The pluralism now under discussion is not a friendly pluralism within assumed unity, but a hostile pluralism which does not share common religious or democratic pre-suppositions. If this hostile pluralism becomes normative, it will destroy overarching national unity. Some Roman Catholics admit that they would be just as happy if all religions in America had educational systems supported by the state on a nonpreferential basis. This view appears un-American to older Protestants because it makes the demands of a church instead of a denomination, demands which are embarrassing in terms of ultimate loyalties.

This puts Protestants on the horn of a dilemma. The public school system is essential for the health and unity of the nation with which they are completely identified. If this hostile pluralism becomes normative denying all religious content in public schools, Protestants will have no alternative but to create their own parochial schools with state aid, the same state aid they wish now to deny Roman Catholics. Most of all Protestants resent having to contemplate a choice between nation and denomination. They have never taken their denominations that seriously as units of identification and are in no position to do so now.

3. The nation became the primary community in terms of which historic purpose and identity were defined. It also assumed a churchly function as the community of righteousness. Theologically the church is the primary community of sanctification where men individually and corporately strive for perfect obedience to the will of God and holiness of life. Traditionally, holiness of life had been a main concern of Calvinists and radical reformers, the two groups that dominated American religious life. It is still so for some closed religious communities. But the more Americanized these communities became, the more they became just other denominations, the less able were they to preserve discipline.

The results of this transfer are obvious in modern American mythology. In our literature and drama it is the federal agent who appears as the ultimate opponent of evil and supporter of good in society. Consider the myth of the Federal Bureau of Investigation. The "feds" are more component than local and state officers. But more important, its agents are untouchable, angelically immune to temptation. We canonize J. Edgar Hoover as the national saint charged with preserving national morality. The only organ in American society today that comes close to fulfilling the functions of Geneva's consistory, is the congressional investigating committee. Every so often we experience a national catharsis as we observe witness after witness spell out his sins in a situation that is nothing less than confession under oath.

The same mentality that makes a hero of the federal agent (Marshall Dillon on the post-Civil War frontier, and Elliott Ness during Prohibition), that participates vicariously in televized congressional hearings, is revolted by the caricature of a Calvin in Geneva, or a Mather in Massachusetts. It is somehow acceptable to think of the nation's responsibility for keeping people on the narrow path. But the church is not to meddle. Protestants would be horrified if the local congregations began to act in a disciplinary capacity.

At the same time church discipline was declining in the nineteenth century, America experienced a revival of classical ethical theory under the influence of Idealism and Romanticism. Many clergymen eagerly adopted the thesis that the political body, in this instance the federal government, was the basic community of moral endeavor.

In the United States efforts to bring in the Kingdom of God became efforts to Christianize the statute book. One of the early prophets of the Social Gospel, George Herron, claimed that if the Kingdom of God were to come on earth at all, it would have to come through the state. The history of social reform in this country follows a consistent pattern. Begin with a voluntary society initiated by "religious" persons. Agitate until the national community enacts laws securing the desired reforms, and assumes responsibility for enforcement. Thus after the Federal Government assumed responsibility for the slaves and freedmen, the limited role of denominational and interdenominational societies led to their decay and abandonment. To this day most Protestant laymen think initiative in correcting racial inequity rests with the federal government rather than the churches. Prohibitionists likewise assumed that once the eighteenth amendment was on the books federal coercion would achieve what Protestant churches had long failed to attempt through religious discipline.

III

In the popular experience of denominational life during the nineteenth century, certain traditional notes of the church were lacking. By default, and in a measure, the nation became the community of historical purpose, unity and moral endeavor. In turn, American Protestants transferred churchly attributes and loyalties to the nation. If this suggestion comes near the historical facts, and that has yet to be proved, we may have a clue to our present confused scene and the direction in which we ought to work.

Separation of church and state, of ecclesiastical and governmental organizations, about which we have boasted with some justification, has not at all meant separation of religious and national communities. To the contrary the national community became the unit of real religious involvement and commitment. It made demands and offered rewards of an ultimate nature. In the American experience failure to be a member of a particular denomination, to "belong to a church," was in no way equivalent to being a non-Christian, much less a heathen. There was something about being simply an American which had religious connotations. No wonder it is difficult to distinguish the Christian way from the nation's way!

In diagnosing our present situation, we would be much misled were we to concentrate merely on the negative results of this process of assimilation. Some results, through incongruous, have been salutary. Occasionally the nation has in fact played the church more than the denominations! Detractors accuse the nation of moral hypocrisy. True enough. But hypocrisy is a theological sin which does not exist apart from prideful pretension.

On occasion America has in fact acted as if God were the ruler of history and nations, and as if this people were elected to peculiar tasks of service. The nation has pursued high purposes in many areas of the world, it has brought a certain unity out of disparate immigrant groups, it has grown in outward moral improvement. And it has done these things precisely at the federal level.

Contrast the temper of political morality in this country at the national with the local levels. One tends to take influence peddling for granted in city halls and state houses. Obvious offenders are elected again and again to local office. But let a Sherman Adams carry on a naive flirtation with a Bernard Goldfine at the national level, and the result is ignominious retirement. Americans have few qualms about the economic imperialism of its large corporations in small countries. But we have an uneasy conscience about a Federal military base like ours on Okinawa. We simply have not the clarity of self-understanding to admit to ourselves and others publicly that we as a nation control the island by right of military conquest over a past enemy and intend to stay there as long as national interest demands. That kind of talk would be bad for public relations, but it would also jar our own high ideals of national disinterestedness, which seem necessary because we have merged the religious and national communities. It is estimated that Federal expenditures in the Philippines during America's experiment in imperialism cost more than they profited the nation. Is there really the possibility of a benevolent imperialism in an immoral society?

This relative Christianization of the nation makes for difficulty now. Are we yet speaking and acting in light of what the denominations have been trying to rediscover since the 1930's? I mean the fact that the nation is still not the church and never will be, and that the church can never be only the nation. Admittedly, the Lord of the church is also Lord of the nation. That was the theological presupposition that made it possible for Protestants to treat the nation as the church when the denomination stopped acting like a church, and which makes it necessary always for the church to see in the unpretentious political community its strongest ally.

But is Protestantism behaving as if the existence of a true community of the redeemed in Christ, which is loyal to apostolic witness, which does have ultimate purposes to pursue as a community in history, which does unite all men, and which strives toward sanctification in this life—as if the existence of such a community makes any difference in a nuclear age? Pacifists traditionally talk as if they cannot understand why the nation does not act like the church. Do they think they will be taken seriously in an increasingly secular society? Other spokesmen tell us social groups further immorality rather than morality. This reverses the assumptions of classical and romantic idealism which claimed morality comes only with the group.

We have yet to take seriously the rediscovery of the church and to think it through. The nation is not the church. That is clear enough. Perhaps now we can move to the unresolved questions. What is the universal church? How is it to express itself organizationally in a national context where denominational experience has robbed the church of any corporate significance? How in that context should the church as church and individual Christians as individuals bear witness to their international and supranational unity in Christ?

FOOTNOTES

1 Paul Peachey, Executive Secretary for the Church Peace Mission, set this topic as an introductory paper for the conference which was composed primarily of Biblical scholars. The intention was to give some historical background to the American scene, in the context of which the seminar occurred.

2 Franklin Littell's *From State Church to Pluralism* is designed homiletically to disillusion American Christians about their distant and near past that they may act intelligently today.

3 Winthrop S. Hudson, *American Protestantism* (Chicago, 1962), pp. 33-48.

4 John Calvin, *Institutes,* IV i 9.

5 Perry Miller, "From the Covenant to the Revival," in *Religion in American Life I, The Shaping of American Religion,* especially pages 361-368.

6 Perry Miller, *Errand Into the Wilderness,* (Cambridge, Mass., 1956), pp. 1-15.

part 2

OLD TESTAMENT PERSPECTIVES

3

GOD AND THE NATIONS:
A STUDY IN OLD TESTAMENT THEOLOGY

Lionel A. Whiston, Jr.

RADITIONALLY THE OLD TESTAMENT is viewed as a somewhat provincial collection of writings whose interests are largely confined to the private affairs of Israel. Yet the most superficial reading of ancient Near Eastern history makes it self-evident that to have lived in Palestine in biblical times meant to dwell at a crossroads of international forces, ranging all the way from the Balkan-like complex of minor states surrounding Israel to the great power struggles of Egypt, the Mesopotamian powers and the Persians.

I

Equally international are the horizons of the Old Testament itself. As early as Genesis 10 there are inserted the J (Gen. 10:1b, 8-19, 21, 24-30) and P (Gen. 10:1a, 2-7, 20, 22, 23, 31, 32) tables of the nations in which the nations of the world are seen as ethnically linked in a complex genealogical system. The record of God's people may be said to have begun with Abraham (Gen. 12-25), but repeatedly the traditions assert that God will make of Abraham, as well as of Isaac and Jacob, and of his descendants "a great nation," a great nation which from the beginning is to be seen in relation to the other peoples of the world, for "by you shall all the families of the earth bless themselves." (Gen. 12:1-3, *et al.*) Nor should this statement be lightly regarded, for it is rooted firmly in J, the oldest of the literary sources of the Pentateuch, and quite probably the tradition extends even further into Israel's past.

The God of Israel is seen at work throughout the career of Joseph in Egypt (Gen. 37-50). The crucial Exodus event sees a contest between Yahweh and variously the gods, magicians, Pharaoh and armies of Egypt (Ex. 1-15). In the wanderings in the wilderness Yahweh leads his people to victory in battle over Amalekites (Ex. 17:8-16), the Canaanite king of Arad (Num. 21:1-3), Amorites (Num. 21:21-32), Og of Bashan (Num. 21:33-35) and the Midianites (Num. 31:1-54). The conquest involves Yahweh's defeat of the many peoples who comprised the population of Canaan, battles which continue into the book of Judges. In the battles with the Philistines, who replace the Canaanites as the enemies of Israel and its God, Israel's God is increasingly known as "Yahweh Seba'oth" which W. R. Arnold[1] used to translate as "Yahweh Militant" and which is more frequently rendered today as "The Lord of Armies."

Prophets like Elijah, Elisha and Micah report God's will and judgments in Israel's relations with its neighboring nations. The book of Amos, the first of the canonical prophets, which opens with a comprehensive indictment and threat of doom upon the nations surrounding Israel (Amos 1:3–2:3), claims that Yahweh's authority extends as far as Crete and Cush (perhaps the Upper Nile region) (Amos 9:7). In each of the major prophets there are large collections of oracles against the nations, and the prophet Jeremiah is given the charge to be "a prophet to the nations" (Jer. 1:10). For the Second Isaiah writing in the days of the Exile, the nations of the world in all their pomp and circumstance are as a "drop from a bucket" or "the dust on the scales" and, in language reminiscent of Genesis 1 (a kind of creation in reverse), "All the nations are as nothing before him, they are accounted by him as less than nothing and emptiness" (Isa. 40:15, 17).

When we move into the post-exilic community we find a polar movement in which on occasion nations are welcomed into the community of Israel (Isa. 56:6-7; Zech. 8:20-22, *et al.*) and on other occasions the Jewish community withdraws from all such contact (Neh. 13:23-30) or rejoices in the wrath of God being visited upon its enemies (Obad.; Isa. 63:1-6). On the one hand, voices like those of Ruth and Jonah remind the Jews that God's redemptive purposes include all nations; on the other hand, a book such as Esther implies the destruction of the enemies of God's people. But in either case, the sovereignty of God over all peoples and nations is recognized.

Perhaps the point is here being belabored, but it must be made forcibly. Our time is so much under the influence of evolutionary hypotheses of history that it assumes that the concept of a God active, effective, and sovereign among and over *all* nations and peoples upon the face of the earth must by definition be a late development. To be sure, obviously there is a development in Israel's thought about the relationship of God with the nations of the world, and such a development can be traced. However, in its essential form, this sovereignty of God is found in the earliest expression of Israel's faith both in the way in which it recounts its history and in its liturgies. Even at the risk of repetition, it must be emphatically stated and re-stated that from the very beginnings of biblical faith, God was recognized by his people as Lord of all nations and peoples.

II

Since Israel saw itself and its God involved in the affairs of the nations of the world, it quite naturally developed a vocabulary to express these relations. Accordingly, it is not surprising to find the Old Testament employing a number of terms and phrases to describe the nations and their relations with Yahweh and his people Israel. Of these expressions, two words carry connotations which are particularly significant for the purposes of this paper: *'am,* usually translated as "people," and *goy,* usually translated as "nation." What we have said above about the prominence of nations and peoples in Old Testament thought is strengthened when we find that the word *'am* is used about 1,800 times in the Old Testament and that *goy* appears approximately 555 times.

As the translation "people" and "nation" implies, both of these words carry their own weight of connotation, yet on occasion their use gives the impression of being interchangeable. The two words are sometimes used as synonyms in the parallelism characteristic of Hebrew poetry.

"Behold, I will lift up my hand to the nations [*goyim*]
and raise my signal to the peoples ['ammim] . . .
(Isa. 49:22; cf. also Gen. 25:23; Isa. 1:4.)

Moreover, in the covenant promises of Genesis and elsewhere we read that God will make the descendants of the patriarchs into "a great nation" *(goy)*, and yet "by you all the families ['*ammim*] of the earth will bless themselves" (Gen. 12:2-3, *et al.*). Here the people of God are being described as a "*goy*" and the nations of the world are being described as '*ammim,* seemingly the exact antithesis of their original meanings.

While to the contemporary lay reader such usage may give the impression that the two terms are interchangeable, yet to the Old Testament authors each of the two words carried its own distinctive connotation, a fact which has been for some time known to Old Testament specialists.[2] The kind of ambiguity found in the passages cited above is quite characteristic of biblical writers. Here, as is so often true of biblical thought patterns, words are not primarily used to express objective static denotations, but rather they are intended to express the perspective of a particular moment. That is, '*am* and *goy* are two words bearing different connotations which may be used to describe the same collective social unit. Either of these words, depending upon the occasion, may be used to designate Israel, a nation other than Israel or the nations regarded collectively. The biblical writer's choice of word is always deliberate. The interchangeability of these two terms is, therefore, only apparent.

One basic clue to the fundamental difference of these two words may be found in the following observation: The characteristic Old Testament designation of Israel is the "people *('am)* of God." On the other hand, the expression "nation *(goy)* of God" is *never* employed. Thus we can speak accurately of "the chosen people," but never of "the chosen nation." This is of more than casual theological importance both in understanding the Old

Testament and in understanding the role of the church in the world today.

The basic meaning of *'am* is a group which is held together on the basis of kinship, whether this be the family in an immediate sense or whether the idea of kinship be extended to the larger social grouping of community, tribe or nation. Hence, one may be born or adopted into an *'am,'* or an *'am* may develop into a mighty nation *(goy)*, but an *'am* cannot be "made" or "founded." The usual English rendering of *'am* as "people" is acceptable, but it must always bear with it the connotation of a community or communities linked together by their common ethnic inheritance. Whether the point of reference be Israel, a foreign nation or a group of nations, the connotation remains the same.

On the other hand, *goy* is used without any such connotation of ties of kinship. As was mentioned above, one can speak of the *'am* of Yahweh, but not the *goy* of Yahweh. Similarly, while *'am* may be used as a compound in personal names (usually indicating some form of relationship between a god and his worshipper), this may not be done with *goy*. As Speiser has said, "A *goy* can be made *('asah)*, established *(nathan)*, founded *(sim)*, or the like . . . *Goy* comes rather close to the modern definition of 'nation.'"[3]

Thus *'am* refers to the qualities of culture, language, religion and ethnic origins which make a community feel itself "kin" and *goy* refers essentially to the structuring of a society as a political unit. "People," although not fully adequate, is probably the best rendering we have of *'am* into English, but "nation" is a reasonably satisfactory translation of *goy*.

Thus from one perspective Israel is essentially an *'am* in its social solidarity and in its elect relationship to its God. Likewise, it is properly regarded as a *goy* as it becomes a great nation under its kings. It is of importance to recognize that the nations of the world are *goyim* in terms of their political power, but they are also *'ammim* in their common life. Accordingly, although it is not common, one does read at one and the same time of "nations and peoples" where reference is made to the same group or groups.

He [Nebuchadrezzar] and his people ['am] with him, the
most terrible of the nations [haggoyim]. . . .
(Ezek. 30:11; see also Gen. 25:23; Isa. 1:4; 49:22)

In the light of these comments it becomes of relevance for our
purposes to examine the way in which Genesis 10 and 11 speak
of mankind. In the Tower of Babel narrative we are told that
"the whole earth had one language." Further, Yahweh comments,
"Behold, they are one people ['am] and have one language" (Gen.
11:1, 6). For the Old Testament, mankind is regarded as one related group in the primeval period before the nations were established.

In the preceding chapter (Gen. 10, especially vv. 5, 20, 31f.)
we are given a genealogical table of all the nations of the world
in terms of their common descent from Noah in Japhethitic,
Hamitic and Semitic divisions. Five times these divisions are
clearly recognized as national and are called *goyim,* but the entire context of the chapter by its use of genealogies shows the
common relatedness and ancestry of all nations. Even further,
the context of nationhood is described as "in their lands, each
with his own language, by their families *(mishpehotham),* in their
nations *(goyehem)."*

The point to be made here is that on the basis of Israel's language for nations and peoples it cannot be claimed that there
is any fundamental distinction qualitatively to be made between
Israel and the nations of the world. There is, of course, the difference of election, and this makes all the difference. Nevertheless, the words of Amos ought not to be forgotten.

> "Are you not like the Ethiopians to me,
> O people of Israel?" says the Lord.
> "Did I not bring up Israel from the land of Egypt,
> and the Philistines from Caphtor and the Syrians
> from Kir?"

(Amos 9:7)

The essential kinship of all humanity under God is clearly stated
in Genesis 10 and 11. What is implicit in such passages becomes
explicit to a later writer.

God and the Nations

> And he made from one [blood][4] every nation of men to live
> on all the face of the earth, having determined allotted pe-
> riods and the boundaries of their habitation. . . *(Acts 17:26)*.

From this perspective, *goyim* and *ammim* appear together in
striking fashion in Deut. 32:8.

> When the Most High gave to the nations [*haggoyim*] their
> inheritance, when he separated the sons of men, he fixed the
> bounds of the people [*ha 'ammim*] according to the number
> of the sons of God.

Thus, not only does the Old Testament from its very opening
pages recognize God as the Lord of all nations, but it likewise
recognizes all nations as being regarded by God as intrinsically
kin to one another.

III

The purpose of the two preceding sections has been to suggest
that any view of the Old Testament is too narrow which sees in
it only the relationship of God and his chosen people and which
ignores the prominent role given to the relationship of God with
the nations. In this and the following two sections we will set
forth three Old Testament developments of the relationships of
God with the nations. Our first concern is with the war-like character of Israel's God as he is portrayed in a number of passages
in the Torah and the Former Prophets.

The modern mind is often taken aback by the apparent blood-
thirstiness of Israel's God. It finds abhorrent the instructions given
Israel to exterminate utterly the inhabitants of Canaan (Deut.
7:1-5, 17-26) or its enemies in battle (I Sam. 15:3). Obviously,
there can be no denying that Israel regarded God as its leader
in battles.

In recent years, under the heading of "holy war" there has been
a considerable discussion of warfare in ancient Israel.[5] Because
Israel was wholly the people of Yahweh, no social institution
could be separated from its own distinctive religious character.
All of life, including the waging of war, took place under the
leadership of Yahweh. It was not that Israel fought for Yahweh,
but rather that Israel's God fought for Israel, delivering it from

its enemies and giving the nation victory. Accordingly, up to the time of the monarchy, there grew up certain ceremonies and procedures by which Yahweh's battles should be carried out. Included in these was the *herem* in which the enemy and all that was his was regarded as dedicated to another God and was, therefore, profane before Yahweh. Thus, in theory, all the population and its property were to be totally destroyed, although in actual practice there were various modifications.

We cannot and ought not to gloss over the militancy of Israel, particularly in the period before the monarchy, but which in actual fact is found throughout the Old Testament. No theoretical argument for pacifism can be built upon the pages of the Old Testament as a whole. However, neither should we say that the Old Testament regards God as *essentially* a war god. That is, we must put the motif of God the warrior within its larger context. Part of this context is the historical situation of the ancient world and the specific historical situation of this tribal confederation struggling for a place and way of life. We ought to be no more surprised at the role played by military institutions in ancient Israel than we are at the similar role found in our own day.

More central for our purpose here is the recognition of how fully Israel's military life is placed within a theological frame. For example, it does not occur to the preservers and shapers of Israel's traditions and faith that God is not involved in her history. As in former days in the Exodus from Egypt, so now in the present, whenever that present may be, God is still at work to save his people. Had not God made promises to the fathers of the former times? Had he not acted to deliver his people out of Egypt? The God of Israel was a faithful God, keeping covenant troth and would not fail his people. Israel's God is revealed as a Lord of armies because he is faithful to the word he swore to the fathers and to the covenant he has entered into with his people.

Further, the Canaanite nations in their worship of other gods, which took the form of the baal worship of the fertility cult, were hideously shocking to the stern morality of a desert nomadic people. Before a holy God, such peoples were profane and wicked beyond measure. Hence there can be no intercourse between Israel and the Canaanite, whether of inter-marriage or interplay of cultures, for "you must utterly destroy them, and show no mercy to them" (Deut. 7:2).

Rather than point self-righteously to the primitive qualities of Israel's war-like God, we do much better if we point out where Israel was strong and modern man tends to be weak. Notice the theological accents in the following passage from Deuteronomy.

> Do not say in your heart, after the Lord your God has thrust them out before you, "It is because of my righteousness that the Lord has brought me in to possess this land"; whereas it is because of the wickedness of these nations that the Lord is driving them out before you. Not because of your righteousness or the uprightness of your heart are you going in to possess their land; but because of the wickedness of these nations the Lord your God is driving them out from before you, and that he may confirm the word which the Lord swore to your fathers, to Abraham, to Isaac, and to Jacob
> *(Deut. 9:4 f.)*

Note here that the character of God as a warrior is of comparative unimportance. The chosen people are reminded in blunt terms that they have no claims of merit ("righteousness") by which they can demand that God give them the land. Rather the imperative behind the action of God is twofold. First, the holy and almighty Lord of history will not tolerate the "wickedness" of the nations. Before a holy God, sovereign in history, they must be "utterly destroyed." Second, the God of Israel is a faithful God, and therefore will fulfill in history his promises.

We must be most careful that we do not judge Israel entirely in the light of our own time. Central here are motifs such as "justification by the faithfulness of God" or the holiness and faithfulness of God. Here is the solid substance of ancient Israel's faith in God which still speaks today.

IV

It is common practice to approach the relations of Yahweh with the nations by way of his chosen people and how through them Yahweh will bring all peoples unto himself. This area constitutes the theme of the next section. Here we wish to consider what the Old Testament has to say about the direct relations between Yahweh and the nations. To a certain degree this must be a form of abstraction, for no part of the Old Testament can be severed completely from a consideration of the covenant people. But admitting this, there are still some things to be observed.

It is not uncommon for the Old Testament to set forth God's actions in history toward the other nations in terms of his mighty acts of grace. The career of Joseph in Egypt is, to be sure, focused toward God's people, but as the story is told, not only Israel, but also the Egyptians come to know God's power. The master of Joseph recognized that "the Lord was with Joseph" (Gen. 39:3) and Pharaoh says of him, "Can we find such a man as this, in whom is the spirit of God?" (Gen. 41:38). In the midst of famine, all of Egypt and, for that matter, "all the earth" (Gen. 41:57) bought grain of Joseph and were saved from starvation.

In the Psalms the nations can be invited to praise God.

> "Praise the Lord, all nations!
> Extol him, all peoples!   *(Ps. 117:1)*

Or, the nations are viewed as coming together to worship God in his sanctuary because of God's great acts in creation and history.

> There is none like thee among the gods, O Lord,
>   nor are there any works like thine.
> All the nations thou hast made shall come
>   and bow down before thee, O Lord,
>   and shall glorify thy name.   *(Ps. 86:8 f.)*

The prophets speak frequently of how all the nations will come together in peace to worship the Lord at Jerusalem (Isa. 2:2-4; 11:9; Zech. 8:20-22; Isa. 66:23; *et al.*). These prophetic passages do not explicitly state why the nations come to worship God, for their stress is placed upon eschatological fulfillment rather than explanation. Presumably, however, they come to worship because they have come to know Israel's God by his actions in history.

Thus we can say that in portions of the Old Testament the nations are overwhelmed by God's gracious acts and as a result of witnessing his actions they turn to him. However, it is more characteristic of the Old Testament to see God's work in history as terrifying acts of judgment in which the nations, too late, in a "moment of truth" come to know "that I am the Lord."

Yahweh is seen in combat with gods, rulers and armies of the nations, from which battles he emerges victorious. The entire Exodus account should be read not only from the perspective of the deliverance of a people, but equally from the perspective of a god who makes himself known as God. Moses is told,

> And the Egyptians shall know that I am the Lord, when I stretch forth my hand upon Egypt and bring out the people of Israel from among them. *(Ex. 7:5)*

The account of the capture of the ark by the Philistines with the subsequent overturning of the image of Dagon and plague (I Sam. 5-6) does not explicitly talk about making God known. However, it is quite evident that the narrative carries the same theological atmosphere as the Exodus event and that here God reveals himself to the Philistines as a dread god. Within this context, we may read the words of Solomon's dedicatory prayer.

> . . . may he [the Lord] maintain the cause of his servant, and the cause of his people Israel, as each day requires; that all the peoples of the earth may know that the Lord is God; there is no other. *(I Kings 8:59 f.)*

In varying and striking ways, the prophets describe how God makes himself known directly to the nations. The book of Jeremiah represents the prophet as commissioned to be "a prophet to the nations" (Jer. 1:5) even to the extent that he is required to announce to the neighboring nations God's great judgments in history (Jer. 27:1-4). At the close of Micah we read of how

> nations shall see and be ashamed of all their might . . . they

shall lick the dust like a serpent . . . they shall turn in dread
to the Lord our God, and they shall fear because of thee.
(Mic. 7:16 f.)

A startling passage in Isaiah describes how

the Lord will make himself known to the Egyptians. . . . And
the Lord will smite Egypt, smiting and healing, and they will
return to the Lord. . . . *(Isa. 19:21 f.)*

In Third Isaiah the enemies of God, extending as far as the
coastlands (probably a synonym for the most remote regions of
the earth), will receive Yahweh's wrath and requital

So they shall fear the name of the Lord from the west,
and his glory from the rising of the sun. . . . *(Isa. 59:19)*

But it is in Ezekiel that the theme of the nations coming to
know God as God receives fullest expression. In chapters 26-32
the expression "they [or, you] will know that I am the Lord" is
used more than thirty times of various nations. Ezekiel couches
this in the form of a legal lawsuit (Hebrew, *rib*).[6] The literary
form of these oracles shows clearly the development of thought.
The *rib* is introduced by an opening phrase, usually "Thus says
the Lord," revealing the identity of the accuser. The statement
of the indictment is introduced with the conjunction "because"
(Hebrew, *ya'an*). Sentence is then pronounced and announced,
introduced by "therefore" (Hebrew, *laken*). The final result and
goal of the lawsuit is given at the end, "Then they (or sometimes,
you) shall know that I am the Lord."

Because of its brevity, Ezekiel's *rib* directed against Moab provides a good example of this pattern of thought. The four divisions of the *rib* indicated above are here underlined to show the
movement of thought within the oracle.

Thus says the Lord God: "Because [*ya'an*] Moab said, 'Behold
the house of Judah is like all the other nations,' therefore
[*laken*] I will lay open the flank of Moab from the cities on
its frontier, the glory of the country, Bethjeshimoth, Baal-
meon, and Kirathaim. I will give it along with the Ammonites
to the people of the East as a possession, that it may be
remembered no more among the nations, and I will execute

judgments upon Moab. Then they will know that I am the Lord." *(Ezek. 25:8-11)*

Thus we see that Israel regarded the power and glory of its God's activity in history as so dramatic and awesome, that the nations of the world must inevitably come to know Yahweh. A number of passages show the nations, overwhelmed by Yahweh's majesty, recognizing him as Lord or coming to worship him spontaneously apart from Judgment. However, by far the greater number of passages show God at work in history to punish or destroy the nations because of their indifference or hostility to him and his people. In these acts of judgment the nations come to know that Yahweh is indeed Lord of all nations. Whether to save or to destroy, the effect is the same—as a consequence of their witnessing God's actions in history, the nations come to know him.

V

In the preceding section we sought to show ways in which the nations came to know directly the God of Israel as God. It remains in this section to show how God reveals himself as God to the nations by means of his actions in history through his chosen people Israel. Once again, as before, our starting point must be the election promise of J found in Genesis 12:1-3 and echoed elsewhere in Genesis.

> ". . . And I will make of you a great nation, and I will bless you, and make your name great, so that you will be a bless-ing. I will bless those who bless you, and him who curses you I will curse; and by you all the families of the earth will bless themselves." *(Gen. 12:2f.)*

The problem arises: how will the families of the earth be blessed by the descendants of Abraham? By and large, the Old Testament answer to this question seems to be in the form of witness. On the one hand, the nations will witness the acts of sal-vation performed by God for Israel and the nations will be over-whelmed with awe and believe. On the other hand, Israel itself shall be a witness; an eye and ear witness of God's saving acts and a witness in the sense of bearing testimony to what Israel has heard and seen. This witness takes two forms, a negative and a positive.

1. *The negative witness.* In a number of passages, Old Testament writers regard God as being compelled to act to save or to show mercy upon his people "for his name's sake," or as some have punned, "for his fame's sake," i.e., for the sake of God's own reputation he must act.

When Yahweh is angry with his people for their sin with the golden calf and is about to destroy Israel, Moses remonstrates and says in part:

> ". . . Why should the Egyptians say, 'With evil intent did he bring them forth, to slay them in the mountains, and to consume them from the face of the earth'?" *(Ex. 32:12)*

An even stronger statement is given in Deuteronomy:

> . . . lest the land from which thou didst bring us say, "Because the Lord was not able to bring them into the land which he promised them, and because he hated them, he has brought them out to slay them in the wilderness."
>
> *(Deut. 9:28)*

As one might suspect, it is Ezekiel who gives this theme its strongest and most biting expression.

> ". . . But I had concern for my holy name, which the house of Israel caused to be profaned among the nations. . . . And I will vindicate the holiness of my great name, which has been profaned among the nations and which you have profaned among them; and the nations will know that I am God, says the Lord God, when through you I vindicate my holiness before their eyes. . . . Then the nations that are left round about you shall know that I, the Lord, have rebuilt the ruined places, and replanted that which was desolate."
>
> *(Ezek. 36:21, 23, 36; cf. vv. 16-36)*

Regardless of whether the people of God remain faithful or faithless, it is of the utmost importance that God be made known to the nations as a God of faithfulness and power. Therefore, through God's dealings with Israel is he known to the nations.

2. *The positive witness.* We have seen that the negative witness focuses on the unfaithfulness of the chosen people. It is more characteristic of the Old Testament to find this witness to the nations originating in the chosen people within a context of Israel's faithfulness and God's grace. Hence we read in Exodus:

> "Behold, I make a covenant. Before all your people I will do marvels, such as have not been wrought in all the earth or in any nation; and all the people among whom you are shall see the work of the Lord; for it is a terrible thing that I will do with you."
>
> *(Ex. 34:10)*

This "terrible thing" is, of course, a matter of perspective: terrible from the point of view of the nations; wonderful from Israel's standpoint. More explicit is the statement attributed to Rahab of Jericho.

> "I know that the Lord has given you the land, and that the fear of you has fallen upon us. . . . For we have heard how the Lord dried up the water of the Red Sea before you when you came out of Egypt. . . . And as soon as we heard it, our hearts melted, and there was no courage in any man, because of you; for the Lord your God is he who is God in heaven above and on earth beneath."
>
> *(Josh. 2:9-11)*

This context gives us an insight into the interpretation of the closing petition in Hezekiah's prayer offered when Assyria threatened Jerusalem.

> "So now, O Lord our God, save us, I beseech thee, from his hand that all the kingdoms on earth may know that thou, O Lord, art God alone."
>
> *(II Kings 19:19)*

Despite traces of this theme in the prophets and Psalms, it is in Second Isaiah that this teaching finds its fullest formulation in which God is portrayed as working through his servant people, Israel, for the redemption of all nations. Second Isaiah's purpose is to give comfort and expectation to the people exiled in Babylon. One major way he accomplishes this is by relating

Israel's suffering in exile to God's world-wide purposes of redemption. God is now about to reveal his glory so that "all flesh shall see it together" (Isa. 40:5). This will take place through the agency of Yahweh's servant, Israel[7] (Isa. 44:1, 21). Serving as the witnesses of God in a vast court scene involving all the nations (Isa. 43:10; cf. 43:1-13), Israel shall be a "light to the nations" (Isa. 42:6; 49:6) and as a "covenant to the people" (Isa. 42:6; 49:8). How will this take place? So greatly shall the servant Israel prosper and be exalted, that the nations shall be struck dumb with amazement as they recognize that this nation which they thought despised by its God and politically dead in exile, is now the greatest of all nations (Isa. 52:13—53:12). Confronted by such an overwhelming witness and demonstration in history, how can the nations help but recognize God as God: there can be no other. Consequently,

> Behold, you shall call nations that you know not,
>> and nations that knew you not shall run to you,
> because of the Lord your God, and of the Holy One of Israel,
>> for he has glorified you. *(Isa. 55:5)*

In this panoramic theology of history we find Old Testament thought at a zenith, yet intellectual honesty will compel us to make at least one reservation. Involved in this picture of the mighty God at work to deliver his people and bring all nations to him is a form of exclusive nationalism and a justification of religious rewards in the form of prosperity and political power. For example:

> "Kings shall see and arise;
>> princes, and they shall prostrate themselves;
> because of the Lord who is faithful,
>> the Holy One of Israel, who has chosen you."
>>> *(Isa. 49:7f.)*

> "Kings shall be your foster fathers,
>> and their queens your nursing mothers.
> With their faces to the ground they shall bow down
>> to you, and lick the dust of your feet. . . . "
>>> *(Isa. 49:22f.)*

Yet despite this one reservation, and it is a major one, we still have here a magnificent statement of how God's mighty acts of deliverance to and through his chosen people will bring all nations unto him. Old Testament thought at its finest always sees beyond the God of judgment to the God whose purpose is the redemption of all men and nations.

VI

The purpose of this chapter has been to examine the relationship between God and the nations as found in the Old Testament. In so doing, this chapter has sought to establish five propositions.

1. The Old Testament from its very beginning to its close and from the earliest traditions to the latest writings assumes that all nations are subjects of God's concern. The nations exist under his sovereignty and are subject to his purposes for all mankind.

2. Two terms applied by the Old Testament to social groupings are of particular concern to this study. '*Am* is used by the Old Testament writers to represent the essential kinship of a group and *goy* to represent the idea of nationhood. Both words are often used to refer to the same groups, for it is the perspective that determines the diction. The Old Testament has no prejudice against a people becoming a nation. Fundamental, however, is the requirement that a nation or the nations should recognize their common kinship in their common origin and their common life.

3. The manner in which God is portrayed in war-like guise presents great difficulty to the modern reader. What is here needed is a recovery of the perspective within which the militant actions of God are expressed; namely, that the people on whose behalf God acts are not in and of themselves righteous, and that the motive-springs of God's conduct are his implacable opposition as a holy God to the wickedness of the nations and his faithfulness to his promises made to the fathers. Therefore, he must act, and Israel described his actions in terms of its own

cultural limitations. How else could God's activities be understood?

4. It is perilous to be regarded as a nation in God's world, for while on occasion his actions extended toward the nations are gracious in character, more commonly they are, in the fullest sense of the words, awful and terrible. Regardless of the cost, God is determined that all men and all nations shall know that he and he alone is God.

5. The way to the salvation of the nations rests through the witness made to them by the people of God. In its highest expression this witness involves suffering even to death on the part of the people of God for the redemption of the sins of the nations.

No brief resumé could hope to encompass the entire breadth of what the Old Testament has to say about God and the nations. What stands above is only a sketch in which an attempt has been made to stress five facets which have relevance when applied to this nuclear age. Such implications would undoubtedly be developed by each individual, each in his own fashion.

Such variety of application should occasion no distress. All too often our use of the Bible is altogether too wooden. We insist upon shaping it into a crystal ball, a precise blueprint or applying it to our world with our own rigid prejudices. We need to be reminded that God's word is a lively word, flexible and surprising. We need to be shaped to it rather than shaping it to fit our purposes.

One caveat needs to be stated. There are those who would equate the United States with the chosen people of God, while others would identify the role of the United States with that of the nations of the Old Testament. Either of these extremes seems to me naive and unwarranted. Obviously, the Church as the New Israel constitutes the people of God in Christendom. Certainly the biblical faith has permeated our culture to a remarkable extent so that to a certain degree it is proper to understand Christians, churches or the Church as a part of the people of God, particularly if we recognize ourselves to be living under grace rather than by works. Equally obviously the United States plays a role in the world as a nation, not unlike the nations of the Old Testament. Certainly the United States is quite unlike the fusion of church and state that was ancient Israel. Certainly much of its national life is structured apart from the will of God and the United States is summoned before God in the same fashion as the biblical nations.

In brief one may say that to the extent that the biblical faith has permeated our culture, to this extent is it proper to understand ourselves as a part of the people of God. Likewise, to the extent that our society has taken on the pattern of the nations who live unto themselves, to this extent we share in the nature of the nations and shall, under God, be involved in his fearsome and terrible acts by means of which the nations are returned to him who originally made all men to be one people.

In the light of what has been said above, what applications of the five propositions of this chapter may be made to our time?

1. *All nations are subjects of God's concern.* There is no room for myopia in the biblical faith. It is only in the compartively recent past that the United States has been able to shake off the shackles of isolationism. Had we understood our biblical heritage better, this would have happened long, long ago. Even today, many people would rule out certain nations or groups as being beyond the pale of God's concern. This cannot be defended biblically. He who has said that "the earth shall be full of the knowledge of the Lord as the waters cover the sea" (Is. 11:9) requires of us that we abandon all provinciality and understand the role of *all* nations and peoples upon earth in terms of God's purposes for them.

2. *Political groupings are both "people" and "nations."* The very pattern of the Hebrew language and the traditional narratives of Israel make it clear that social units under one political grouping are to be regarded from a double perspective. At one and the same time they are both "peoples" and "nations."

This implies that there is nothing sinful per se in a people under God becoming a great nation. In fact, this is a major part of the promises made by God to Israel. It is when the excesses of nationalism make the nation forget its kinship with all other peoples that the nation comes under the judgment of God. An awareness of this double nature of nation and people may so enlighten us so that nationalism does not become the Tower of Babel of our age. A nation must be a people under God and dwell in the world as a people among peoples. The alternative is God's judgment in history.

3. *The militant actions of God and his motivations have modern relevance.* All too often we rationalize the biblical word and place it under our domination. In so doing we evade the real heart of scripture. Piously we reject what we call the Old Testament God of wrath and battles and with clear conscience we evade the sting of God's word. If before a holy God, our nation stands convicted of the same forms of wickedness that the biblical nations practiced, then we stand under the same judgment. If we find ourselves living in a time of the shaking of the foundations and yet remain faithful to our God, we have reasons for trust and a peace that passes understanding. Such trust does not originate in the hope that God will go into battle for us, for to hope for this is to shape God in an image of our own making. Our trust and peace come from our confidence that God is faithful to his promises. There is thus placed upon us the responsibility of gaining a greater knowledge of historical situations in interpreting the events of the past, present and future. Such an undertaking must be oriented to the holiness of a holy God and the faithfulness of a faithful God.

4. *All nations shall know the Lord is God.* We are here reminded that as the United States lives as a nation among nations in tensions of hot and cold wars there is being brought upon us the judgments of a sovereign God. It is God's will that shall be done on earth. The existence of tensions and estrangements among nations is both the revelation of national sin and of divine judgment. Therefore, before it is too late we must become more and more aware of the ways in which we have abandoned or never achieved the life of a people of God and the ways in which we are enmeshed in the life of a nation whose existence is structured apart from God. Over us like a sword of Damocles hang the words, "Behold, days are coming, saith the Lord."

5. *The people of God will be a witness to the nations.* Here we are confronted with an either/or dilemma. Are we, as members of an affluent society, going to continue to identify our existence with that of a particular nation? Or, shall we move into the life of the people of God to which we are called? If it be the latter, this means there is placed upon us the necessity of suffering for the healing of the nations. We must think through clearly what it means to be a witness of God to the nations in our present situation and to what forms of suffering we have been called.

Looming over and beyond all that we have said are the vast purposes of God, the father of all men, by whose will men have been gathered into peoples and nations. It is his will that is being unfolded in history. He has called us to participate in the working out of that will in order that all the nations may become one people and that his peace may abound.

FOOTNOTES

1 William R. Arnold, *Ephod and Ark, A Study in the Records and Religion of the Ancient Hebrews* (Harvard Theological Studies, III; Cambridge: Harvard University Press, 1917, pp. 142-148).

2 Leonhard Rost, "Die Bezeichnungen fuer Land und Volk im Alten Testament" in *Festschrift Otto Procksch* (Leipzig, 1934), pp. 125-144. A more recent, and hence up-dated, discussion is given by E. A. Speiser, " 'People' and 'Nation' of Israel," *Journal of Biblical Literature,* 79 (1960), pp. 157-163.

3 Speiser, *op. cit.,* p. 160.

4 The word "blood" is here placed in brackets to indicate the presence of a textual problem. The RSV omits it.

5 Cf. Gerhard von Rad, *Der Heilige Krieg im Alten Israel* (Abhandlungen zur Theologie des Alten und Neven Testaments, 20; Zuerich: Zwingli Verlag, 1951). For a full discussion in English with bibliography, cf. Roland de Vaux, *Ancient Israel* (New York: McGraw-Hill, 1961), pp. 258-273, 537. Inasmuch as the term "holy war" has a history of its own in Western culture and may lead to some inaccurate surmises, the expression will not be used again in this work.

6 The *rib* is also used in similar fashion against the nations in Isaiah 41. Verses 1, 5, and 20 are particularly relevant to this discussion.

7 This writer accepts the identification of the Servant as the people of God in exile in Babylon.

4

PROPHETIC FAITH AND
CONTEMPORARY INTERNATIONAL RELATIONS

Norman K. Gottwald

T HE HEBREW PROPHETS have long been recognized as sharp
critics of the social order and their teaching has had a profound effect upon Christian Socialism in England and the Social
Gospel in the United States. The related prophetic concern for
international order has not received equal attention. It is the
intent of this study to examine the prophetic attitude toward
international relations and to assess its relevance for today.

PRESUPPOSITIONS

At the outset it is necessary to formulate certain presuppositions concerning the relation of church and nation, the prophetic
character of the church, and the propriety of speaking of ethical
principles. These presuppositions cannot be argued at length but
they must be stated as clearly as possible.

Church and Nation

1. It is recognized that church and nation are two separate
"orders" or "realms" whose roles and mandates cannot be inter-
changed or confused and yet which are intimately related in
that both are under the will of God and all members of the
church are also members of a national body. This statement does
not intend to endorse any particular historic Christian view of
the relation of church and world or of church and state, but it
is obvious that, on reflection, it would be close to some historic
views and perhaps incompatible with others.

2. While church and nation are separate loci for God's work, the Christian church observes the widespread activity of God in the whole of human life and, therefore, in faithfulness to its understanding of God, the church cannot attempt to limit the sphere or the scope of the divine activity.

3. Although the Christian sees God's work everywhere, he does not expect non-Christians to see the same reality except as they become a part of the redemptive center, the church, and thus the church does not attempt to impose its own insights, ethics, or political dicta upon non-Christians.

4. God often deals with men and with nations other than directly through the redemptive community of Israel or the church. This is explicit in the Noachian covenant with pre-Hebrew man (Gen. 9:8-10) and in the Pauline assertion that when non-Jews do what is right "they are a law to themselves, even though they do not have the law (of Moses)" (Rom. 2:14). It is also apparent in many biblical passages which implicitly claim that a wide knowledge of God is available to man without special revelation (Amos 2:1; 9:7; Isa. 1:3; Jer. 8:7; Matt. 5:44-48; 7:11; 19:3-9; Luke 12:57; 14:8-10; Acts 15:28-29; Rom. 12:17; I Cor. 11:13-15; I Pet. 2:12; 3:16).[1]

5. The church, in fidelity to God the Creator, has the basis and the mandate to speak to men and nations without reference to the special redemptive criteria which she herself knows but solely with respect to what God requires of his creation. This mandate rests upon an impressive body of biblical witness to God's work with men and nations in creation and providence and not only in the special and familiar biblical sense of God's use of outsiders for the chastisement and restoration of Israel or the church. Without endorsing any particular historic view of "natural law," it is evident that something of the sort must be presupposed to explain this solid testimony.

Prophetic Role of the Church

1. In assessing the relevance of Old Testament prophecy for our situation, one must simply accept the fact that the New Testament stands between us and the prophets of ancient Israel

in such a way that we can never directly appropriate Old Testament prophecies. The reconstitution of the church and world in Christ is the touchstone for all Christian use of the Old Testament. Attempts to equate alliance politics in the ancient Near East with alliance politics today, to identify Babylon with Nazi Germany or Soviet Russia, or Israel with the United States or the West, generally ignore the shattering impact of the New Testament which creates the church as a new reality in the world and thus as the basis for another type of politics.

2. Prophecy is a biblically-rooted reality broader than the use of the Hebrew and Greek words for "prophecy" and "prophet."[2] Prophecy is one way of expressing the biblical testimony about God's constant use of humanity to reveal himself and his purposes.

It has often been claimed that prophecy is negligible in the New Testament, yet even a study of the linguistic evidence shows that prophecy was in fact a pervasive and potent factor in the early church. Jesus called himself unequivocally a prophet (Mark 6:4//Matt. 13:57-58; Lk. 14:33-34) and the first believers so thought of him (Acts 3:22; 7:37). Prophecy is widely attested to as an activity in the early church, but no single office can be confidently delineated. Prophecy is sometimes described as foretelling (Acts 11:27-28; 21:7-14), but more often it is speech addressed "to men for their upbuilding and encouragement and consolation" (I Cor. 14:3; also Acts 15:30; Rom. 12:6-8; I Cor. 12:6-8; I Cor. 12:10, 27-31; 14:3; I Thess. 5:19-20). Prophecy is, in truth, more a power than it is an office and, while some men are noted as prophets, the humblest members of the community may prophesy so long as order is observed (I Cor. 13:2; 14:29-32).

Prophecy in both covenants is primarily the embodiment of God's will in human life, by word and deed, from which it follows that faithful prophetic activity today does not imply the duplication of a biblical office but rather the faithful execution of a perpetual function of the church whenever it really listens to its Lord.[3]

3. Prophecy is an activity of persons *within* the people of God and it is an activity *of* the community itself, both in ancient

Israel and in the church. The single prophetic figure speaks to and acts within the empirical community on the basis of its highest traditions and his own experience of God. The community itself, by its existence and by its message, speaks to the nations. While the understanding of Israel as a prophetic word or sign is recessive or non-existent in much of the Old Testament, it is crystal-clear that the New Testament picks up and transforms the one strong motif in ancient Israel of the obligation of the people of God to the nations. Thus to be the people of God is to nourish prophets within the fellowship and to listen to them in order that the people as a whole may be a prophetic sign on earth.

4. The prophetic function of ancient Israel as the people of God is taken up by synagogue and church and not by any particular theocratic or pseudo-theocratic state, such as modern Israel or the United States of America. When the single prophet or the church as prophet speaks to the nation or the state it speaks not to the covenant people but to man under the aspect of creation. Whatever the church then says to man in society and to man within the state cannot be based on the assumption that the society and the state are answerable to Christian faith or to a Christian ethic. What the church declares is addressed to the knowledge of the right which is written into man's nature. It speaks to and seeks to awaken that latent sense of the right which it believes God the Creator has put in every man. It is a sense of right before which society and state are judged. But to short-circuit this process by speaking to the nation with explicit Christian norms is to betray the biblical foundation of the church's prophetic function, for it pays too little tribute either to Christ and his church or to the wider world which God made and in which He is continually active.

5. The prophetic church has the double task of *internal prophecy* and of *external prophecy,* and the one is impossible without the other. Internally, the church must encourage and heed her own prophets who by word and deed recall her continually to God's purpose for her. Externally, the church, aware of God's wide concern for his world, must summon the state

(and all of the natural orders and structures) by her word and deed—and not least in the daily vocation of her members—to listen to that voice which God puts in all men to speak his truth to them. It is apparent that the most obvious elements of the church's prophecy, her ecclesiastical pronouncements and political lobbying, are of small effect unless they are deeply rooted in a prophetic preaching and teaching ministry and supported round about by the steady vocation of many Christians well-versed in and deeply committed to the several orders and structures to which the church addresses herself.

Ethical Principles

The prophetic clues to international relations may appropriately be called principles. They might also be designated axioms, guidelines, directives, insights, motifs, perspectives; but principle remains the clearest English term for this purpose. By the manner in which the principles are expounded it should be evident that I am not treating abstract rules which took precedence over persons and events or were consciously formulated and codified by the prophets. I am treating rather certain fundamental tendencies and directions in their thought about the political responsibility of man before God.

PRINCIPLES

Divine Transcendence and Immanence

The root belief of the prophets we may describe as the principle of divine transcendence as the point of origin and divine immanence as the means of sustenance for the communion between God and man. God is "above" church and world but "in" them both. This is the radical monotheism of biblical faith, the intensely practical belief that "God is active in all events."[4]

The nearest that prophecy came to stating this as a principle is perhaps the assertion of Isaiah of Jerusalem in connection with Yahweh's plan to break Assyria because it had plundered the nations with arrogance and rapacity:

This is the design designed for all the earth;
And this is the hand stretched over all the nations.
For Yahweh of Hosts has designed and who shall frustrate it?
And his hand is stretched forth and who shall deflect it?

(14:26-7)

The prophets did not say that God was Lord *only* of those persons and nations who acknowledged him according to Hebrew religious tradition. The reality of Yahweh's rule was a fact observed in the life of every nation. Nations were "condemned" or "vindicated" in his sight not chiefly with reference to their treatment of the Hebrews but primarily with reference to a sense of right relations planted indigenously within all peoples.

Thus the prophetic assessments of national conduct cut across all the existing religious, political, and ethnic lines. A pagan people could be judged for wronging another pagan people, as when Moab desecrated the royal dead of Edom (Amos 2:1). A pagan people could be judged for wronging the Hebrew people, as when Assyria plundered Judah (Isa. 10:5-11). The Hebrews could be judged for wronging a pagan people, as when Judah rebelled against Nebuchadnezzar (Ezek. 17:1-21). One Hebrew state could be judged for wronging its sister Hebrew state, as when Israel and Judah launched wars of aggression against one another (Hosea 5:8-12). All partisan judgments were immaterial to the one question: How is Yahweh at work in these events and how have people violated or obeyed his will?

There can be no Christian attitude toward international relations that fails to be oriented by this fundamental truth, a truth which at one stroke eliminates such trite but shockingly perennial conceptions as "My country right or wrong" and "God is on our side," including the current version that he must be for us against "those godless communists." All of our self-righteousness and ideological pretensions are called into question. Because we are able to demonstrate that other nations practice different forms of Christianity from ours, or other world religions altogether, or are even officially atheistic, does not mean that we automatically fall heirs to the championship of God's cause. In the mélange of shifting guilt and opportunity among the na-

tions today the moralist is aghast. From the playbill the on-
looker is hard put to it to determine who are the good characters
and who are the bad ones, for the roles often change and none
seems wholly good and none wholly bad. If we are looking for
precise means of ranking the nations, often we cannot be more
certain than that God is at work in and through each nation. Yet
that in itself is a great deal for from such a belief flow important
implications.

Concentration of Political Responsibility

The second clue is an inference from the first and I shall call
it the principle of the concentration of political responsibility.
God speaks to nations primarily with respect to themselves and
their own responsibilities. Again and again in prophecy the awful
severity of the attack upon Israel and Judah shocks us into dumb
amazement. Yet we miss the whole force of the attack if we
think that objectively speaking the Hebrews were the world's
worst sinners. Rather the nub of the prophetic attack is the de-
cisiveness of those matters over which the listeners have control.
No single uniform international obligation lies upon all nations
with equal weight. Each nation stands in a unique situation and
is responsible in differing degrees and at varying points in the
affairs of nations. For some, the obligations take one form and
for yet others, the obligations assume quite different shapes and
substances.

A nation repents only of its own wrongs and corrects only its
own misdeeds. This doubtless strikes us initially as so much sentimental nonsense, but it is at this point that nations must begin
their maturation. It was true not only of the Hebrew people for
whom the special belief in the covenant with Yahweh made con-
tinual self-correction imperative. It was equally assumed that the
immediate neighbors, Damascus and Tyre, and the more distant
imperial powers, Assyria, Egypt, and Babylon, could understand their crimes of barbarism in war, slave-trading and de-
portation of captives, and the breaking of treaties. All these crimes
were seen to root in a false sense of self-mastery and an ego-
centric mania to control history which stood condemned before

the bar of public conscience even among pagan peoples who are instructed in the rudiments of international conduct by a kind of veiled presence of God.

Similarly today prophetic faith calls each nation to a fundamental self-examination. This may be justified in Western democracies on the theory that a majority of citizens still accept the Jewish-Christian tradition. But it is fully justified in all nations—Christian, non-Christian, or atheistic—on the theory that each people has an inescapable responsibility for its own life and conduct. Therefore, even in a land with complete separation of church and state or in a land without historic Christian traditions, the prophetic challenge to self-examination is not only relevant but imperative.

Is one nation more guilty than another? In given situations it is possible to discern greater or lesser guilt. Yet precisely as in broken or threatened marriages, the legalistic apportionment of guilt in international affairs is generally incapable of touching the deeper problems. The chief prophetic question is not: Am I more or less guilty than another? but rather, How can I respond to God's will in this situation, bearing in mind the guilt in which I am involved and the opportunities which lie at my disposal? Far from implying a double standard of judgment for nations, such a view accepts and acts upon the single standard in the only way possible—by putting it into effect in one's own nation. It is in fact evading it altogether and resorting to a double standard when the West puts off national acceptance of responsibility in certain areas until the communists or the neutrals accept the same responsibility. This is to disregard God by assuming that he can be obeyed or disobeyed at will and that his counsels can prevail only if a quorum of the nations can be found to heed him. But can God's will be so disposed?

In practice, this prophetic conviction summons nations to correct injustices and to develop resources over which they have control. In particular, nations must strive to avoid the rationalizations which regard similar behavior as innocent in themselves and their friends but as hypocritical and even malicious in their enemies. Numerous examples from the Cold War come readily to mind, for instance, political propaganda and nuclear testing, both of which we consider hostile acts in the communist case but simply neutral defensive actions in our own case; and of course the communists see us in reverse image. This rigid self-protecting symmetry of fear and guilt devours and assimilates to itself all facts and feelings which would deny or qualify it. And so only with great effort can a nation keep itself sensitive to the unexpected good in its enemies as well as to the undesired evil in itself and its friends. Any serious attempt to implement this principle would mean the death of propaganda as it is now generally understood, the wilful and systematic misrepresentation of one nation in a good light at the expense of another in a bad light, even when such misrepresentation is rationalized as self-defense.

Personalization of Political Responsibility

Yet another implication of the principle of divine transcendence and immanence is the principle of the personalization of political responsibility. God's expectations of men as individuals and as nations, while not co-extensive and identical, are continuous and of the same order insofar as they involve the same persons subject to the same Lord. This does not compromise the distinction between Christian ethics and "natural" ethics. It simply asserts that the similarities in the ethical obligations of the *individual* in personal relations and the same person in social and political groups are primary and the dissimilarities secondary. It also asserts that the similarities in the ethical obligation of a *Christian* in personal relations and the same person in social and political groups are primary and the dissimilarities secondary. In either instance, whether one works from Christian ethics or from natural ethics, any variation—especially any lessening of ethical behavior in large groups—must prove itself by some more intrinsic criterion than the "difficulty" of doing what is right.

The prophetic claim on life was a total claim. The prophet insisted on a continuum of responsibility extending from the individual through the corporate realms. As the individual

Israelites had no warrant for restricting Yahweh's will to his inner feelings or to his conduct toward his friends alone, so the Israelite people had no basis for limiting Yahweh's will to domestic matters such as the cult or the social order, to the exclusion of foreign policy. Nor, if foreign policy were opened to religious considerations, could the loyal Yahweh believer apply those considerations only to friendly nations and not to hostile nations.

Having said this, however, we must carefully note that the prophets did not emasculate political responsibility by dissipating it into a collection of merely individual responsibilities. They understood something of the multiplicity of human roles in social and political affairs. They were not anarchists or egalitarians. They accepted the necessity of political power and political office. The prophets were themselves political non-professionals or, as we might say, "intelligent laymen." Some were close advisors of statesmen, for example, Isaiah and Jeremiah, but they were not approached by kings for the kind of technical information or balanced prudential judgment which many other counselors could supply. None was an official in the sense that he supplied material for national policies or had a voice in formulating or implementing policies. The prophets served government in the manner of a continuing task force which provided, in our terms, a combination of the steady, sharp sniping of a loyal opposition and the soaring, sweeping vision of a properly constituted "committee on national goals."

Crucially illustrative of their respect for the political order was the decision of the prophets not to attempt to replace political leadership with general religious dicta or with other leadership. They criticized policies and practices, but they did not propose anarchy or impeachment as solutions to the misuse of power. In fact, after Elisha's instigation of Jehu's revolt against the house of Ahab, the prophets did not even take a hand in replacing a king faithless from their point of view with a faithful king, although they must have had many opportunities to participate in court plots and intrigues. The prophets recognized that politicians must be trusted to perform their roles and that it was their special task to offer the political leaders the resources of the Yahwistic tradition both in criticism and in encouragement of their office.

It may indeed seem that the kings never had a chance under the terms of the prophetic attack, that they were in fact "damned if they did" and "damned if they didn't." This impression is admittedly heightened by the extreme form of prophetic speech which made it a matter of long-standing convention that judgment be expressed in an absolute and total manner. It is striking, however, that most of the kings showed an extraordinary respect for the prophets, far more than can be explained merely by superstitious awe. The politicians saw in them something more than fumbling crackpots or moralists who could not accept facts. They regarded them as men with a very special task of facing Israel with its total obligation, of laying bare the vast spectrum of its responsibility, of continually organizing the nation's scattered experiences under the unifying word that called them to singular obedience. The kings could not always see their way to incorporate prophetic advice into actual policies, but it is noticeable that they were generally willing and even eager to hear the prophet out.

The prophetic word of the church to national leaders today must also be a word about the totality of the national obligation. It must be a word which distinguishes between the roles of citizens and leaders, but includes them both within the one task of national obedience and which distinguishes between specifically Christian and universally human obligations, but refers them both to the unifying will of God. It must be the word that no one else will speak unless the church speaks it. It is the word about the interests of God and of his creatures in the affairs of nations. It is the word that cuts through form and expedience and strikes unerringly at the heart of deception and indifference. It is the word that must be spoken even when he who speaks it is not at all certain as to which policies should replace the current idolatries of war and propaganda. It is the word that will remind leaders and citizens of what Herbert Butterfield has so well expressed:[5]

When we speak as though there were a separate ethic for the statesman, a peculiar substance called political morality, we are already moving into a world of trick mirrors and optical illusions. The statesman, like the scientist or the poet, will constantly be confronted by the alternative between an act that is more moral and an act that is less moral. But we must not allow that there can be a difference in the quality of the decision in these cases, or a difference in the ethical principles involved.

Today we see a reversal of the general policies favored by the prophets. They were advocates of quietism in foreign policy and activism in domestic policy. When the Assyrian scourge will pass through the land, Isaiah declared, the faithful will have a foundation on which is inscribed the legend: "He who trusts will not be in a hurry" (Isa. 28:16). But the same Isaiah urged upon his people that their calling was to social reform and national renewal, for " 'This is rest; give rest to the weary; and this is repose,' yet they would not listen" (Isa. 28:12).[6] Like the ancient Hebrews with whom the prophets reasoned, we, too, prefer activism in foreign policy and quietism in domestic policy. About 60% of our budget goes toward military rivalry with other nations and this very rivalry lures us into cutting back on the development of our own resources. Our energies are concentrated on security at the one obvious danger point of volcanic eruption while all around us the ground of our national life is cracked and fissured by subterranean domestic tremors. By standing too exclusively *against* something, we have forgotten to stand with sufficient clarity *for* anything.

The parallel between the ancient Israelite and the modern American scenes must not be drawn uncritically, but must be approached through the questions: Are our present domestic and foreign policies taking into account the universal human obligations and needs which political structures must serve? If not, can we learn from the evasions of ancient Israel and the critique of those evasions offered by the prophets?

Programmatic Openness

A further implication of the principle of divine transcendence is the principle of programmatic openness. God speaks to man in his political role with such immediacy that all courses of action must be continually subject to revision in the light of the ever new word of God.

There is in fact a rather distressing lack of unity in the prophetic prescriptions for international affairs. They can be quoted to favor isolationism or internationalism, pacifism or militarism, free enterprise or socialism. A policy of internal revolution urged by Elisha was condemned by Hosea (II Kings 9:1-10; Hosea 1:4-5). A policy of resistance to a foreign power, counseled by Isaiah (37:6-7, 21-32), was replaced by a policy of submission to the foreign power, urged by Jeremiah (27:12-15; 37:6-10; 38:17-18).

Were the prophets actually as unprincipled as they appear? Yes, if we insist on an answer to the question, "What should our nation do now?" for they did not think or write in such a way as to give us any intelligible answer to a policy-oriented question. If, however, we want to ask, "What moment is this in the affairs of nations?" then they offer us amazing resources for preparing our minds and senses to discern the movement of God among the nations and to find our place in relation to it. The prophetic vacillation is not the necessarily worthy openness and flexibility of a statesman. It is rather the openness and flexibility of one who listens for words and signs and who knows that they take different forms in different ages. All principles recede before the one principal that man is engaged as a total being—and therefore also politically engaged—by the God who is his true sovereign.

In place of technical political directives, which we must find for ourselves, we are called to engagement with God and participation in the times. Searching the prophets we must ask: is ours the time of free sovereign action or of subservience and waiting? Is it the time of resistance or of surrender? Or is it perhaps not any single time but a moment in which the various times of human history are superimposed and interlocked in infinite complexity? If so, what does the personal word of the personal God say to political persons? Are they to put their trust

in programs well-suited to habit and tradition or are they to become new persons and to fashion new programs for new times?

We are denied, therefore, the comfort and the fanaticism of
slogans. It is true that the prophets indulged in something very
like slogans. Isaiah could say of patient waiting that "he who
does not believe shall not endure" (Isa. 7:9) and that "in returning and rest you shall be saved; in quietness and confidence
shall be your strength" (Isa. 30:15), and Ezekiel could see in
the pride and punishment of nations the vindication of God "so
that they [the nations] will know that I am Yahweh" (25:11; 29:6;
35:15).[7] The slogans in these instances, however, are not visceral
responses to complex problems; they are rather insights, prophetic
words about a state of mind which men must adopt if they are
to see meaning in events and to help shape those events. All
prophetic catchwords bring the individual element of politics
and international relations to the fore. They do not fog the mind
in making political decisions, but rather provide that perspective
which remains valid in all political decisions, namely, that even
though in aggregations, *man* is after all the stuff of politics.

Yet programmatic openness does not mean vagueness and
perpetual indecision. Politics consists in the definite organization of what is organizable in communal life. This excludes sweeping moralism in place of policy and crude expediency instead of
that human risk which is the essence of all human relations. We
have no choice between absolute love or absolute self-interest in
international relations, any more than in interpersonal relations.
There is a mania for purity in international relations which must
be corrected by the truth of human sinfulness. There is also a
mania for security—especially military security—which must be
corrected by the truth of our impermanence. We cannot be as
pure or as secure as we should like to be, either as men or as nations. If absolute pacifism reaches for too much purity, then our
policy of nuclear deterrence reaches for too much security. The
first political commandment is not purity nor security but responsibility to the Lord of nations and to men in community, not to
theories held in the abstract or by long habit, whether the theory
that force must never be used or the theory that freedom and

justice can really be defended by threatening nuclear injustice and nihilism.

Possessed of the basic belief in God's transcendence and of the implications of self-responsibility and of the continuity of human obligations from the least unto the largest of political roles, assured of the need for continuous revision of policies, with what spirit do we bear our leadership and citizenship obligations?

Disciplined Political Hope

We are to be moved in all that we do by the spirit of disciplined political hope. I speak now more of a spirit than of a principle, more of the tone of our thought and action than of the actual content. We must fight with steady resolve against the two extreme moods that by turn accost us: the uncritical *acceptance* of all political leadership in the name of a false security and the uncritical *rejection* of all political leadership in the name of a false purity—the attitudes which lead us to say either, "Let the politicians take care of that; it's their business, not mine" or "A plague on the whole lot of them; they're a bunch of crooks, the blind leading the blind." We shall, with the prophets, affirm a hope that springs from our knowledge of God and his purposes, and which, at the same time, is content to work for the attainable. "Attainable" is here understood as that which can grow genuinely out of the present situation instead of as a limit imposed in advance by philosophic or strategic pre-judgments, whether utopian or realist. Allowance must always be made for the open-ended nature of history, for the surprise of unpredicted new elements, especially the surprise of "moral man" ceasing to hide behind the immunity of an "immoral society."

Thus we are entitled to hope in international relations, and not merely that natural sentiment toward the future which makes us feel that things must somehow be better this season or this year—if only because they could hardly be worse. Rather, hope springs up because of the actual measure of hopefulness that we see in the coming of God into human affairs and in the demonstrated fruits of peace and order in human life. Such signs appear more often in this world than our taste for the sensational and the perverse will allow us to realize. It is not the hope that we can somehow save the hopeless situation. It is God's world and he has been here first. Neither purity nor security are our chief burdens but the integrity of human life in the light of the transcendent which calls forth our constant endeavors lest it be split so deeply that the variety of human life runs to chaos.

Can we really believe that issues of such vast portent and ramification are affected by you and me? If we cannot, then we have not heard the prophetic word although we may have read the prophetic words; our eyes are shut, our ears stopped, and our hearts made fat. Every German had a calling when Hitler gassed the Jews, but the calling concerned not only resistance to the overt crimes but to the situations that brought Hitler to power and made his reasoning seem eminently patriotic. Every American has a calling with respect to nuclear weapons, but the calling concerns not only the crime of their use but also the ways of thought and conduct which persuade us that preparation for indiscriminate murder upholds freedom and justice. Our calling reaches through the whole of life. It may not occur to individual Germans that the way they lived thirty or forty years ago made it either a little harder or a little easier for the Jews to be gassed. But that was exactly the case. It may not occur to individual Americans that the way we live today makes it either a little harder or a little easier for someone to start a nuclear war. But that too is exactly the case.

He who would allow the prophetic faith to shed light upon international relations faces formidable obstacles. The complexity of issues, in which all certainties of guilt and punishment cease to convince, upsets our security so that, paradoxically, we react by thrusting upon the virtually unknown opponent the burden of evil incarnate. It is an act of primitive propitiation by which we unload our dark uneasy guilt upon the distant and unknown ones who may bear it far from us. But whatever is the case, whether we see no national evils at all or see all evil in the enemy, we miss the summons to self-revision as the precondition of politics. To be sure men have "mixed" religion and politics in reprehensible ways. More often than not, however, when we reject individual responsibility for international relations as "moralistic" or "utopian" we are really saying that we do not want the arduous task of thinking about problems and helping to solve them. Most of all we do not want to admit that we, the individual citizens, constitute the major problem of world order. We do not want or cannot see how to effect the change in ourselves demanded by serious outward reform. Because we are not prepared to disarm our fears and violent urges we are not prepared to work for disarmament. Because we will not stifle our own inordinate greed we are not eager to share a better life with other peoples of the world. Because we will not surrender the illusion that security lies in our control of the future we will not labor for a community of nations in which national sovereignties are held in check for the common good.

Everything hangs upon the "turning," the repentance, which is the key to all prophetic ethics. The same prophet of the exile who hailed the penitent Jew, "let him return to Yahweh, in order that he may be merciful to him" (Isa. 55:7), appealed to the nations of the then-known world: "Turn to me and be saved, all the ends of the earth!" (Isa. 45:22). The repentance of men and the repentance of nations are not identical but they are related and, while the former is the logical precondition of the latter, the two types of repentance must proceed simultaneously. The prophets do not permit us the lame excuse that only when all men are individually converted can anything be done about national repentance. When any individual repents he repents as a political being and to that degree the nation repents. In other words, as Christians and humane individuals recognize their own responsibilities as persons, they simultaneously recognize their responsibilities as citizens and their subservience to the moral obligation which stands over all nations. They must not surrender their consciences to the a-moral, all-knowing state but must rather bring the state into subjection to the moral nature of man. Here the insight of Martin Buber into the prophetic faith will serve us well:[8]

> Prophecy has in its way declared that the unique being, man, is created to be a centre of surprise in creation. Be-

cause and so long as man exists, factual change of direction can take place towards salvation as well as towards disaster, starting from the world in each hour, no matter how late. . . . As in the life of a single person, so also in the life of the human race; what is possible in a certain hour and what is impossible cannot be adequately ascertained by foreknowledge. . . . But one does not learn the measure and limit of what is attainable in a desired direction otherwise than through going in this direction. The forces of the soul allow themselves to be measured only through one's using them. In the most important moments of our existence neither planning nor surprise rules alone: in the midst of the faithful execution of a plan we are surprised by secret openings and insertions. Room must be left for such surprises, however; planning as though they were impossible renders them impossible. . . . Inner transformation simply means . . . that the customary soul enlarges and transfigures itself into the surprise soul. This is what the prophets of Israel understood by the turning in their language of faith: not a return to an earlier, guiltless stage of life, but a swinging round to where the wasted hither-and-thither becomes a walking on a way, and guilt is atoned for in the newly-arisen genuineness of existence . . . the depths of history, which are continually at work to rejuvenate creation, are in league with the prophets.

In sum, the prophetic interpretation of the relations between states rose on religious grounds but was informed by a high degree of political knowledge and a sound respect for political order. The prophets laid the foundations of internationalism in their view of a single God related to all states and not only to the peoples in a special covenant with him. Many urgent contemporary problems cannot be solved directly from the prophetic traditions, for example, the structure of an international organization to bring about effective disarmament and to settle disputes among nations by arbitration. Yet the genuine will to find solutions and to see that there is a higher arbiter than the sovereign state is the root insight necessary to any and all technical accomplishments in the pursuit of peace. The prophet sharply reminds us that the community of man will find its fruition only as I find mine, and that my own fulfilment will be parasitic unless I seek in it the fulfilment of others. This is the "humanism," the "realism," the "totalitarianism," the "socialism" of prophetic faith.

Before our dimly discerning eyes prophetic faith holds the familiar vision of the community of man which shall rise when "all the nations shall ascend to the mountain of the Lord and learn his ways and walk in his paths," when "instruction shall go forth from Zion and the word of Yahweh from Jerusalem and he shall judge between nations and admonish many peoples," when "nation shall not lift up sword against nation nor shall they continue to learn war" (Isa. 2:1-4). In its expectation that all the nations will submit to arbitration from Jerusalem the prophecy hopes for more than we shall probably ever see. Yet another prophecy, perhaps from Isaiah of Jerusalem or one of his disciples within a century of his death, has given us the lines along which we are more likely to see the unity of the human race manifested: "In that day there shall be a highway from Egypt to Assyria and Assyria shall come to Egypt and Egypt to Assyria and Egypt shall worship with Assyria. In that day Israel shall be a blessing, one-third in the midst of the earth, along with Egypt and Assyria, whom Yahweh of Hosts has blessed saying: 'Blessed are my people Egypt, and the work of my hands Assyria, and my inheritance Israel'" (Isa. 19:23-5). To catch the true proportions of this, the most universal word in prophecy, let us cast it into equivalent terms drawn from the current international scene: "Blessed by my people the neutrals, and the work of my hands the communists, and my inheritance the free world." Room must indeed be made for such surprises!

---

[1] For a discussion of the biblical passages cited see C. H. Dodd, "Natural Law in the New Testament," *New Testament Studies*, 1953, pp. 129-42, and A. Wilder, "Equivalents of Natural Law in the Teaching of Jesus," *Journal of Religion* 26 (1946), pp. 125-35.

[2] For a thorough analysis of the linguistic data see the article on *prophētēs* and cognate words in G. Kittel—G. Friedrich, *Theologishches Woerterbuch*

zum Neuen Testament, VI, pp. 781-863 by H. Kraemer, R. Rendtorff, R. Meyer, and G. Friedrich.

3 G. D. Younger, "The Prophetic Function of the Church in Society," *Foundations* 3 (1960), pp. 306-25.

4 C. Gardner, *Biblical Faith and Social Ethics,* 1960, esp. Chap. V; see also Th. C. Vriezen, *An Outline of Old Testament Theology,* 1958, Chap. VI, who contends that "the basis of Israel's conception of God is the reality of an immediate spiritual communion between God, the Holy One, and man and the world."

5 H. Butterfield, *International Conflict in the Twentieth Century. A Christian View,* 1960, p. 16.

6 S. Blank, *Prophetic Faith in Isaiah,* 1958, p. 24.

7 W. Zimmerli, *Erkenntnis Gottes nach dem Buche Ezechiel,* 1954.

8 M. Buber, "Prophecy, Apocalyptic, and the Historical Hour," *Pointing the Way,* 1957, pp. 198, 206-7.

part 3

NEW TESTAMENT PERSPECTIVES

CHRISTOLOGY AND ETHICS

George R. Edwards

I N DISCUSSING the subject of Christology and Ethics the point of primary attention in the New Testament should be the confession of Peter in Mark 8:27-30 with parallels in Matthew 16:13-20 and Luke 9:18-21. The importance of this passage is quite obvious in that 1) Peter's confession is generally identified as the structural watershed of our primary Gospel, Mark,[1] 2) the narrative deals directly with Jesus' identification as the Christ, and 3) to Peter's confession is joined the saying in all three of the synoptic Gospels concerning the disciple's cross.[2]

Perhaps, however, not everyone is conscious of the urgency with which the interpretation of Mark 8:27ff. is pressed upon the church under the auspices of historical criticism. We live in a period of biblical study in which the first three Gospels have been brought into much greater prominence in dealing with the basic christological problem. The Fourth Gospel is viewed not only as later than the Synoptics in its final composition, but it is also believed to embrace a considerably advanced christology as compared to Mark. Even among the first three Gospels, Streeter (and others) can show that Matthew and Luke have elaborated the christological pattern of the second Gospel upon which they depend.[3]

Many Christians feel that the christological question was settled once and for all at Chalcedon in 451. The Chalcedonian formula, having become the traditional Christian answer to the problem of Christ's nature, proceeds then to be the form of christology which is imposed upon the biblical materials, even upon those writings which may embody traditions earlier than Paul. Historians affirm that one distinction between Calvin and Luther was that Calvin's intent was to reconstitute the church in accord with the doctrines he found in the scriptures, while Luther's reform, more moderate in character, was inclined to remove the abuses of the medieval church but not to uproot it in toto.[4] The Calvinistic position was, therefore, the radical wing of the Reformation. Its basic attitude toward biblical theology would presumably suggest that the endeavor to refound (not to say reform) the church would not hesitate to go back earlier than 451 any more than it would hesitate to go back earlier than 1051.

In addition to this feature of Calvinism, we ought also to mention that the direct result of Protestant biblical study since the Reformation is the conception of the priority of Mark to which we have previously referred. In the Protestant tradition, and especially in Calvinism, therefore, we are confronted with a major responsibility to keep systematic theology in tune with biblical theology. The gap between these two areas of faith at this time is so great that one is almost driven into a choice of one or the other without the privilege of embracing both. The conventional method of reading fifth century christology into the Gospel records can hardly be regarded as satisfactory.

THE MEANING OF MARK 8:27 THROUGH 9:1

Let us first examine the handling of this passage in Bultmann's thought. Then we shall take Alan Richardson as an example of an alternative view.

Bultmann discusses the confession of Peter under the subject of the messianic consciousness of Jesus.[5] Bultmann does not feel that the confession of Peter demonstrates the messianic consciousness of Jesus because this whole passage is "an Easter-story projected backward into Jesus' life-time, just like the story of the Transfiguration" which immediately follows in Mark 9. Bultmann strongly urges that "nothing of the might and glory, which according to Jewish supposition would characterize the Messiah, was realized in Jesus' life—not in his exorcisms, for example, nor in his other mighty works." Bultmann further argues that there is no clear indication in the Gospels that Jesus reinterpreted the messiahship to give it a more spiritual rather than political or military connotation. By his reading of the synoptic Gospels Bultmann is assured that the Son of Man sayings which refer to the parousia, the "arrival" or "advent," do not mean that Jesus identified himself with the Son of Man, because he referred to the Son of Man in the third person, as "he." He maintains that these third-person, Son-of-Man, parousia sayings later were transferred to Jesus by the church and were associated with the passion and resurrection in such passages as Mark 8:27–9:1. Butmann does not regard it as credible that Jesus thought that he would be subject to a violent death, raised from the dead, then translated from the earth to await the time when the Kingdom would break in upon men, and when he would return upon the clouds of heaven to perform his real office as the apocalyptic Son of Man. And how are we to understand the predictions of the passion? These are all *vaticinia ex eventu,* prophecies which have been written after the events and made conformable to what had already happened. Bultmann does not feel that the theme of the suffering servant of Isaiah 53 can be traced to Jesus' own understanding of himself as Messiah, but is applied to Jesus by the early church and that not before Luke 22:37.[6]

For an opposing view we may look at Alan Richardson's treatment of Mark 8:27–9:1.[7] He feels that Jesus adopted the title Son of Man because it, unlike the term "Messiah," was not laden with preconceptions which were inconsonant with his mission. So he says:

> They had ready-made ideas about the Messiah, which needed radical correction; that is why Jesus seems somewhat to set aside the title "Messiah" and use instead the designation "Son of Man," into which he could pour a more scriptural content (Mark 8:29-31). Bultmann's view that Jesus never thought of himself as being in any way identified with the eschatological Son of Man follows naturally from his desire to show that Jesus had no Messianic

consciousness at all, in order that faith in Christ might be liberated from all historical questions, such as whether Jesus considered himself to be the Messiah. It is based on modern existentialist philosophy rather than on scholarly consideration of historical evidence, and we need not pursue it here.[8]

In the same place Richardson goes on to affirm that the Son of Man sayings embraced the Suffering Servant theme of Isaiah 53 not merely in the teaching of the church subsequent to the passion and resurrection, but also in the understanding of Jesus himself.

The way that Richardson expresses himself with regard to the predictive powers of Jesus, especially in Mark 8:31 where the prediction of the passion is quite specifically joined to a prediction of the resurrection, is revealing. The same exact sequence of passion-resurrection prediction occurs again in Mark 9:31 and 10:33-34. When Richardson treats these predictions, he uses almost without exception "predictions of the passion,"[9] that is, that Jesus could foresee a suffering for himself. Then he adds the idea of a "triumphant conclusion," which must be taken as the equivalent of the words, "after three days rise again." Richardson's phraseology seems to be an evasion of the blunt assertion that Jesus predicted during his life details of the passion experience as well as the resting in the tomb and the rising again. In the same place where Richardson discusses the predictions of the passion, he shows his own concession to the impact of rationalism when he states:

> We may admit that the form in which St. Mark has written his group of predictions of the passion is affected by his knowledge of the way in which they were fulfilled (especially the details of 10:33 ff.); we may also admit that Jesus did not have a superhuman preview of the future events in detail.[10]

What Bultmann is concerned about in discussing the predictions of the passion and resurrection is whether we are not thereby led into the assumption of supernaturalistic predictions on the part of Jesus. Richardson is certainly not justified in introducing the question of Bultmann's existentialism at this point. Seeing how strongly Richardson's own view is influenced by scientific rationalism in the above quotation, his wholesale attack on Bultmann seems more theatrically apologetic than it is logically justifiable.

We have already observed that the passion-resurrection prediction of Mark 8:31 is followed by two additional predictions (Mark 9:31 and 10:33-34) which have the very same construction and content. It is difficult to avoid the impression that these are formulary, stylized traditions in all three instances. It would also follow from this that the passion prediction patterned so clearly after the Servant of Isaiah 53[11] would tend to stand as an authentic prediction of Jesus as we have received it in the Gospels on the same footing with the prediction of the resurrection. If, moreover, Richardson hesitates to affirm Jesus' superhuman predictive ability with regard to the resurrection in three days, does it not stand to reason that the prediction of the passion after the pattern of Isaiah 53 must be brought under the same question? It may be wiser to leave the matter in the form of a question, but one would be compeled to say that the burden of proof lies more on Richardson than on Bultmann.

Another comment on Richardson's view of the great Markan christological passage is in order. Mark 8:38 refers to the coming of the Son of Man in the glory of the Father with the holy angels. This is the apocalyptic parousia, and it ends the eighth chapter. There is an unfortunate verse division which marks the beginning of chapter 9. The first verse of chapter 9 has to do with the coming of the Kingdom of God in power and the fact that some of those standing there will not taste of death until they see this coming. This verse is actually the conclusion of the parousia passage in chapter 8.

The editors of the Greek text consistently take the view that Mark 9:1 actually belongs to the sense of the eighth chapter rather than the story of the transfiguration which follows. One discovers in Richardson's view of Mark 9:1, however, that he treats this [12] as a prediction of the coming of the Spirit according to the history of the church in Acts 2, rather than in connection with the parousia as the context obviously compels us to take it. If Richardson was faithful to the context, he would be in a severe difficulty indeed, because Jesus' prediction of Pentecost would thus *follow* his prediction of the parousia! Perhaps Richardson so treats Mark 9:1 because to do otherwise would be to invite Schweitzer's understanding of Jesus' unfulfilled apocalyptic expectations. Whatever the cause, Richardson wrenches Mark 9:1 out of its context and makes it a prediction of the Pentecost birthday of the church.

From these observations it follows that Richardson's position is not as independent of Bultmann's presuppositions as he would like for us to believe, especially when his extraneous remarks about Bultmann's existentialism and the untenable exegesis of Mark 9:1 are brought under impartial scrutiny. One may conclude that the major difference between the two writers is in the degree to which they work from the premises laid down at Chalcedon.

The question of the messianic consciousness of Jesus is not the essence of the christological question. Bultmann, in fact, admits that the subject of the messianic consciousness is a very elusive matter at best, that it lies within the domain of the historian, and the historian cannot be the arbiter of faith.[13] If one takes the position that Jesus avoided the title Messiah because it was fraught with so many elements in violation of his mission as servant, he is caught in a semantic cul de sac. That is, Jesus thought of himself as Messiah, but not the Messiah of which everyone else was thinking! It would seem that under such circumstances the word Messiah would have lost its usefulness altogether. The discussion of the christological question needs to take a new direction.

While Bultmann downgrades excessively the importance of Jesus' attitude toward himself, he is certainly on solid ground in advancing the discussion of christology beyond the question of historical facticity and bringing under more direct consideration the believer's experience and life in the christological question. In the passage which treats of the disciple's cross (Mark 8:34-

9:1) we are led to see that to affirm Jesus as the Christ means to commit oneself with a finality which transcends all other considerations. There is, in fact, no "you are the Christ" without "take up your cross." Here is the point at which the interdependence of christology and ethics becomes fully apparent. In the great christological passage in Mark's Gospel the danger of a moralistic ethic uprooted from its religious ground and the danger of a sterile christology which does not touch the essence of human personhood are both overcome.

CHRISTOLOGY AND ETHICS

In Mark 8 the christological affirmation of Peter is brought face to face with its ethical implications: "If any one wishes to follow me, let him renounce self and take up his cross and so be my follower. For whoever desires to save his life shall lose it, but he who loses his life for my sake, and for the sake of the gospel, shall save it." Peter's affirmation of Christ has been one in which conventional expectations of the Messiah remain undisturbed. The demand of Jesus is for new men who have died with him and risen again. Here it would seem that the Markan tradition is cut from the same theological cloth as Romans 6.

The point to be emphasized is that the passage on the believer's cross is so integral to the whole story that we are directed to see here the essential interwovenness of the history of Jesus and the experience of the believer. His cross is our cross, his life is our life, and these two foci of concern echo back in response to one another. This aspect of the confession of Peter should be to us a sign of deliverance from the dry bones of the historical questions which have assailed traditional christology. It should point us to the richly subjective characteristics of christology. It should also assist us in understanding the nature and importance of Christian ethics.

The major preoccupation of New Testament thought in our century has been the eschatological question. At the beginning of it lies the monumental study of Albert Schweitzer in *The Quest of the Historical Jesus*. Schweitzer demonstrated that the Jesus portrayed by nineteenth-century liberalism never did exist.

Schweitzer revealed in his exegesis of the Gospels not a heroic moralist, but an apocalyptic visionary who saw in the signs of the times that God was about to break in upon history with a literal finality that would be seen during the lifetime of the apostles. This is the only fair way to understand those sayings in which Jesus said: "There are some of those standing here who shall not taste of death until the Kingdom of God comes in power." Thus the work of Schweitzer raised thorny problems in the area of christology. But for our purposes in this discussion, Schweitzer is to be seen as the one who recovered the eschatological mood of the New Testament.

The great counterforce against Schweitzer's thoroughgoing, consistent eschatology has been the work of C. H. Dodd.[14] Dodd began with the climactic dictum of the early ministry of Jesus: "The time is fulfilled, the Kingdom of God is at hand,"[15] which Schweitzer took in the apocalyptic sense. Dodd showed that the perfect tense of the verb forms, "has been fulfilled," and "has come nigh," indicated that the eschaton so central in Jesus' message and that of the whole New Testament was not a future but a present reality. It was a final time being realized in the ministry of Jesus. The special benefit of Dodd and his subsequent correctors with their "inaugurated" eschatology was to repair to some extent the christological breach left by Schweitzer's other-worldly, apocalyptic Jesus.

The eschatological interpretation of the New Testament has now entered upon a new phase. The development of this has been primarily in the hands of the post-Bultmann students of the New Testament from the biblical standpoint. The other important factor on the scene is the resurgence of Christian ethics and the urge to root this in biblical and christological ground.

The new quest for the historical Jesus[16] embraces in considerable measure the historical scepticism of Bultmann, namely, that the Gospel narratives are so heavily overlaid with the theology of the early church that it is very difficult if not impossible to distill from the records a biography of Jesus which would commend itself to the empirical historian. This does not mean that the work of historical criticism has been abandoned. It does not mean that Chalcedon has conquered the confusion of biblical theology. It does mean that the Gospels exhibit with distinctiveness the personal involvement of the witnessing community in the history of Jesus. This development is saturated with ethical importance.

There was seen in the results of all the work of historical and literary criticism a certain twoness. This was the unmistakable interchange in the Bible between the person of Jesus and the men who stood under his lordship. Jesus faces the cross, but so do Peter and the church. Peter's facing of the cross and his understanding of it from the Easter perspective most adequately explains the complexities of the Caesarea Philippi confession.

Now there is seen a certain threeness in the comprehension of christology. It is seen that beyond the twofold character of gospel christology (Jesus and the church's response to him then) there is the third element in the continuing hearing and believing of men now.

It is clear that the communal and social aspect of the disciple's cross is consciously set forth in Mark 8:34a where Jesus is described as calling to him "the crowd and also his disciples" for the sermon on cross-bearing. So no distinction between the individual's cross-bearing and that of the communal (crowd-disciple) one is possible. The distinctly ethical character of the disciples' cross is evidenced, furthermore, in the whole problem of the popular pre-Christian view of messiahship, political and military in nature, as over against that messiahship to which the church is called in Jesus' experience of crucifixion. Despite the notable contributions of Christian existentialists to the theology of the New Testament, it must be affirmed against some of them that "authentic selfhood" can never be reduced to a private and individual matter, nor can it be seen in some way as removed from economic, political, racial and all other human relationships.

The contributions which have come to the aid of theology from the work of the psychologists are able to help us at this point. A good example is Lewis Sherrill's book on *The Struggle of the Soul.*[17] Sherrill draws on the rich vocabulary of the Epistle to the Hebrews to show how the self is required by the unfolding demands of life to draw near to God in the emerging maturity of Christian manhood. Faced with these demands, the self may see in them the divine possibilities into which life may enter, or he may freeze himself in his present posture of development, or even revert to the security of previous patterns of response which belonged to lesser levels of his maturity. This view of Christian personality has decisive implications for both christology and ethics in that all the struggles defined by Sherrill (such as marriage and parenthood) have a social dimension, and it is by no means accidental that his point of biblical reference, the Epistle to the Hebrews, is one of the most christological books in the New Testament.

Matthew 5:48 raises all the perplexities of the radical nature of the Christian ethic: "Be, therefore, perfect, as your father in heaven is perfect." The Greek adjective for "perfect" (*teleios*) which is used in this text may be taken as referring to moral maturity. While it would be hazardous at best to read into the Sermon on the Mount the vocabulary of modern Christian psychology, a number of writers have justifiably explored the Sermon from the psychological angle. Judging from the general character of the Sermon and its setting in a Gospel which has strong Judaistic characteristics, Schweitzer's conception of the Sermon as a heightened moral demand meaningful only for those living in the brief tension before the final parousia of the Son of Man (*Interimsethik*) has much to commend it. It may be wiser to acknowledge with Schweitzer the presence of an apocalpytic ethic in the New Testament—who could refute this in I Corinthians 7:25-35?—and then to give this for modern men a psychological and moral significance. Thus the Sermon on the Mount becomes the ethic of the new man in Christ.

In the story of the rich young man in Matthew 19:21 the adjective "perfect" (*teleios*) also occurs. In the struggle of this man's soul the demand of Christ is a cataclysmic one. He recoils from it. This experience has for him a decisive, eschatological character, but again the ministry to the poor carries the matter beyond a question of personal existence into the domain of social and moral life.

In summary of what we have considered up to this point, we may turn to a famous christological text, II Corinthians 5:16-17: "So we know no man henceforth according to the flesh; and if we have known Christ according to the flesh, no longer do we so know him. If then anyone is in Christ he is a new creation. Old things have passed away; behold, all things have become new." It is of crucial importance to remember that "according to the flesh" does not modify "Christ," as some historical critics have suggested, but it modifies the verb "have known." Paul sees that it is the knower that has undergone the ultimate transformation. Paul is not discussing the change which has occurred in the Jesus of history as the object seen, but the change which has occurred in the perspective of the seer. This perspective is no longer "according to the flesh" but "according to the spirit." In Paul's view the point of eschatological transition is found at the confession of faith. If one questions whether this eschatological transition can be regarded as more "personal" than "ethical," he needs only to read Romans 6 to see that such a distinction is quite remote to Paul.

Now to bring this whole subject into a contemporary ethical setting, let us follow out the implications of what has been said with an illustration.

A FINAL ILLUSTRATION

There is no ethical issue which presses itself upon the attention of Christendom at this time with greater urgency than the relations between Christians and the state. Corollary problems are the moral implications of nationalism, international relations, nuclear power, and the extension of politics into war. Christians of all persuasions feel the crucial implications of all these matters, yet no clear response to them has been in evidence in the church.

The question "how shall modern war be conducted justly?" employed in a recent restatement of the "just war" belief by Paul Ramsey[18] fails to put the problem eschatologically. The ultimacy of our situation is better expressed by Taylor and Bilheimer in *Christians and the Prevention of War in an Atomic Age* when they write that "There is now set before us as a stark matter of life and death the choice to end war or be ended by it."[19]

One may further affirm that when the "just war" belief emerged in Christianity after the third century the erosion of the eschatological ethic rooted in the disciples' cross had already taken place. The narrative of the third temptation of Jesus in Matthew 4:8-10 reflects the church's rejection of the Jewish demand for a political-military messiah and her refusal to meet the injustices of Roman imperialism with the expected pattern of violence. This conviction rooted in the experience of the historical Jesus.

The loss of the eschatological dimension in church-state relationships occurred in the period of Constantine.[20] The process was crystallized through Augustine's acceptance of state coercion on the church's behalf in the matter of the Donatists[21] and his tendency to identify the church with the Kingdom of God.[22]

John Yoder has described the loss of eschatology in the following manner:

> The classic expression of this attitude in the Christian epoch is known as constantinianism; the term refers to the conception of Christianity which took shape in the century between the Edict of Milan and the *City of God*. The central nature of this change, which Constantine himself did not invent nor force upon the church, is not a matter of doctrine nor of polity; it is the identification of church and world in the mutual approval and support exchanged by Constantine and the bishops. The church is no longer the obedient suffering line of true prophets; she has a vested interest in the present order of things and uses the cultic means at her disposal to legitimize that order. She does not preach ethics, judgment, repentance, separation from the world; she dispenses sacraments and holds society together. Christian ethics no longer means the study of what God wants of man; since all of society is Christian (by definition, i.e., by baptism), Christian ethics must be workable for all of society. Instead of seeking sanctification, ethics be-

comes concerned with the persistent power of sin and the calculation of the lesser evil; at the best it produces puritanism, at the worst simple opportunism.[23]

Since Puritanism has passed from the scene of modern Christianity, opportunism is the result with which we are left although it is not very "simple" when one reads the toilsome discussions of modern Christian moralists. Charlemagne had his Augustine; Roosevelt had his Niebuhr; Kennedy has his Ramsey.

Even if we take Sherrill's idea as a more naturalistic, developmental view of the Christian man with a series of eschatons in which the mature self emerges after each new crisis upon new levels of maturity in the imitation of Christ, we could be no less pessimistic about politics and international affairs. The context of our decision here is that war has entered upon a distinctly new phase with the advent of nuclear bombs coupled with missile delivery systems. But the pattern of response at this time is that with which we met the issues of 1914, 1939, and 1950. There is the general feeling that occasions and circumstances of 1962 are not after all different, that gunboat diplomacy and military deterrency still "fit" our new predicament. Thus our continuance in the constantinian pattern threatens to invert the biblical eschaton of the new man in Christ into the apocalyptic Armageddon of humanity's death.

FOOTNOTES

[1] An illustrious development of this is found in T. W. Manson, *The Teaching of Jesus* (Cambridge: University Press, 1951), pp. 3-44.

[2] Mark 8:34-37 = Matthew 16:24-26 = Luke 9:23-25.

[3] B. H. Streeter, *The Four Gospels* (London: Macmillan and Co., 1930), pp. 137-38, 162, 174, 188, 303, 423, etc.

[4] *The Confession of Faith of the Presbyterian Church in the United States* (Richmond, Va.: John Knox Press, 1948), p. i.

[5] Rudolph Bultmann, *Theology of the New Testament* (New York: Charles Scribner's Sons, 1951), Vol. I, pp. 26-32.

[6] "For I tell you that these words of Scripture must find their fulfillment in me: 'And he was reckoned among the lawless' (Isa. liii. 12); for indeed that saying about me now has its accomplishment." (Weymouth).

[7] Alan Richardson, *Introduction to the Theology of the New Testament* (New York: Harper and Brothers, 1958), pp. 134-35.

[8] *Ibid.*

[9] *Ibid.*, p. 133.

[10] *Ibid.*

[11] Vincent Taylor, *The Gospel According to St. Mark* (London: Macmillan & Co., 1953), pp. 377-79 backs up Richardson's view with a few more exegetical details.

[12] Richardson, *op. cit.*, pp. 63, 89, 99, 107, 311.

[13] Bultmann, *op. cit.*, p. 26.

[14] Notably in C. H. Dodd, *Parables of the Kingdom* (London: Nisbet and Co., 1935).

[15] Mark 1:15.

[16] See James M. Robinson, *The New Quest of the Historical Jesus* (Naperville, Ill.: A. R. Richardson, 1959).

[17] Lewis Sherrill, *The Struggle of the Soul* (New York: Macmillan and Co., 1951).

[18] Paul Ramsey, *War and the Christian Conscience: How Shall Modern War be Conducted Justly?* (Durham, N. C.: Duke University Press, 1961).

[19] Thomas M. Taylor and Robert S. Bilheimer, *Christians and the Prevention of War in an Atomic Age* (London: SCM Press, 1961), pp. 80-81.

[20] A good statement of this on which I have depended in this section is found in John H. Yoder, "Peace without Eschatology," a *Concern* Reprint (Scottdale, Pa.: Mennonite Publishing House, 1961).

[21] See Frederick W. Dillistone, "The Anti-Donatist Writings," in *A Companion to the Study of St. Augustine,* edited by Roy W. Battenhouse (New York: Oxford University Press, 1955), p. 193. Roland H. Bainton, *Christian Attitudes on War and Peace* (New York: Abingdon, 1960), p. 92 also discusses how Augustine's concept of the church tended to confuse the interests of church and world.

[22] *The City of God,* XX, 9.

[23] Yoder, *op. cit.*, p. 13.

6

THE MISSION OF THE CHURCH
IN RELATION TO CIVIL GOVERNMENT

Clinton Morrison

••

HE CRITICAL CIRCUMSTANCES prompting our study are at once
so immediate and immense that biblical exegesis appears irrelevant and theologizing impotent; the situation requires that we
turn stones into bread. We are in the classic situation: weakness
and foolishness offer themselves in a time that cries for miracles.
By this we may be both heartened and warned, for it has been
the historical peculiarity of divine redemption that God has
chosen the foolish and the weak as means of his power and
wisdom. Yet there is for his servants no more pernicious temptation than that to act in the wisdom and power that is expected
and desirable in momentous circumstances (1 Cor. 3:18 f.,
2:1-5, cf. 1:18 ff., Matt. 11:25 f.). If this discussion lies within the
vocation of Christians, it may be pursued in confidence as it
must be pursued in faithfulness.

This introductory point should be sharpened and emphasized, ,
for it touches upon a common presupposition that severely limits
the contribution to be made by biblical exegesis to the Church's
concern with contemporary affairs. The presupposition underlies and exercises its influence through the idea of "relevance."
The most formidable barrier facing this paper, or any other
biblical study in this series, is the test of its "relevance."

The question of "Christ's relevance today" is a common rhe-
torical proposition for prophetic discourse. It is crucial to understand, however, that the very idea of Christ's "relevance" assumes some norm by which he is to be judged. Likewise, the

common effort to "make Christ relevant" in particular circumstances postulates an end for which he might be used. It is pertinent to observe that the temptations of Jesus (Matt. 4:1-11, par., cf. Mk. 8:11 f., 32 f., Jn. 6:15) are precisely a testing of his "relevance." His refusal to be used for the commonly desired goal was his own decision to be *ir*relevant (cf. Jn. 6:66). By proclaiming the Kingdom of God and pursuing his calling with divine authority, Jesus passed from irrelevance, not to relevance, but to commination; he called his judges into judgment (cf. Mk. 2:1–3:6, 12:12, Matt. 23. The tradition is biblical: cf. 1 Kings 18:17, Acts 17:6 f.). It is the service of exegesis to set forth the meaning of scripture, not its relevance. It is the function of theology, not to judge Christ, but to subject our thought, even our most holy aspirations, to his judgment and direction. The cause of peace is no exception.[1]

Also by way of introduction we note, with most exegetes, the Bible's acknowledgement that civil rules are fully capable of carrying out their divinely appointed responsibilities apart from special revelation.[2] Social justice and international peace are not directly dependent upon world-wide evangelization or the personal faith of governmental officials. Any proposition that the Church, or the knowledge of the gospel, or acceptance of Christ's lordship has an essential role in political government must be demonstrated. That such has not been demonstrated has not hindered the popular assumption among churchmen that the scope of civil responsibility is larger than secular competence,[3] i.e., that specifically Christian guidance is essential to responsible government. But this position remains an assumption unsubstantiated biblically.

In other words, although a matter of grave political concern calls for urgent solution, it is not at all clear that the proper or best contribution of the Church is to deal with the question of peace politically. In any case, this is a matter for careful study, not postulation, a subject to be illuminated by exegesis, not a principle to judge its relevance.

The second, more specific assumption, that Christian guidance is essential to civil government, together with the first, that the

Church, Scripture, even Christ himself may be judged by external norms of relevance, derive from scriptural "principles." The biblical view that Christ and the Church have been sent to "serve men" (cf. Mk. 10:22-45) or "minister to their needs" has served repeatedly as the bed for the Church's tragic prostitution to the highest aspirations of its culture. The emergence of "the service of men" as the guiding principle of the Church goes hand in hand with its abandonment or loss of any distinctive calling of its own and its addiction to self-justification in the light of secular norms of relevance. The Bible's sturdy prophetic tradition, especially the ministry of Jesus, stands squarely against the prevailing concept of "ministering to the needs of men" as the norm of the Church's obedience and faithfulness.

In sum, the intent of this introduction is to urge the reader, who is aware of the enormous crisis confronting civilization, to be aware likewise of assumptions that prejudice a patient study of the Bible and limit its benefit to the Church and its members. Although subjection to the rule of scripture is a common doctrine, it is not a common practice. Hence, we must be cautious lest scripture be subject to our will rather than the reverse. Biblically, the prior question is not peace or war, but the will of God.

I

This paper will proceed from the New Testament faith in the victory and lordship of Christ, for the victory and lordship are increasingly recognized to be central and basic to the early Christian understanding of God's redemptive work and the nature and mission of the Church, as well as the relationship of Christians to the world. It is well to begin with something agreed upon.

Our purpose cannot be advanced, however seriously we may take the early Christian faith, unless we from the first take it seriously in the same way that it was originally held. This is where our troubles begin, for few articles of the primitive faith are so inextricably interwoven with an alien (mythological) cosmology as the very ones we find to be central and propose to take seriously as our point of departure. The victory and lordship of Chirst are consistently set forth in the New Testament in relation to spiritual powers. We have no time to reflect upon the so-called "demythologization" controversy. For our purposes, ancient cosmologies need not be "proved," they need only be read. The task is to participate in a communication, to listen to an ancient mind, not to remake it into the likeness of our own.

What did the victory and lordship of Christ mean to the biblical writers? On the basis of historical study, it appears mandatory to distinguish between the realm of Christ's lordship and the locus of his victory, for the same reason that we must distinguish between his authority from creation and what was accomplished by his special work.[4]

(a) *The nature of Christ's victory* is a crucial question. Whether it affected objectively the "order of things" is decisive for understanding the mission of the Church and its relation to the civil order. This paper holds that, according to the New Testament, the locus of this victory was not the cosmos in general, nor was the defeat of the powers, sin, and death objective *per se*. But the locus of the victory is the Church, and the powers, sin, and death are defeated in relation to those who believe in what was manifest by God's act in Christ. That is, it is not the principalities who are acted upon, but the Christian, who is freed from their power.

It must be noted, however, what this statement does *not* imply. To find the locus of Christ's work in the Church, among those who believe, does not in one degree limit the range of his lordship, which has been over all things from the beginning [cf. (b) below]. Neither do we in any way deny or limit the once-for-all completeness of God's act of love and sacrifice for all men in Christ. Rather, we hold that in the New Testament Christianity has to do with the reconciliation of men to God, not with a cosmic system (2 Cor. 5:17-20). It is precisely the failure of modern students to take the earliest creeds seriously in the same way as the early Church did that they present us a cosmological gospel so vulnerable to the demythologizers. Properly understood, the kerygma is not, was not, an assertion about what has happened to the cosmos, but because the Word was made flesh and was first proclaimed in the Graeco-Roman period, it was only natural that the divine reconciliation of men should find a cosmological expression.

(b) *The realm of Chirst's lordship* is quite another thing. According to the New Testament, Christ has been lord over all things from the beginning. (Jn. 1:3, 1 Cor. 8:6, Col. 1:15 ff., Heb. 1:2, 10 ff., 1 Pet. 1:20). It is altogether unbiblical to suppose that the victory in Christ gained for God some freedom he did not have before or the supremacy over some evil which had confined or threatened him (cf. Jn. 10:18, 19:11, 1 Cor. 2:8). The Bible has no place for a dualism of this kind. He has had the whole world in his hands from the beginning. Neither the Father nor the Son needed or gained anything; the mission and victory of Christ was for us, realized in the Church, the community of those who believe, to whom the Spirit has been given and among whom the new age has dawned. The evidence of his *victory* cannot be found elsewhere, but his *lordship* extends everywhere, and it is executed by whomever he may appoint, whether they know him or not, believe him or not, love him or not.

If "nothing happened" to the principalities, and if Christ has always been lord, what was the event, and why the emphasis upon the creed "Christ is Lord"? The event at the heart of the kerygma is God's act in Christ *for us,* once for all: an act of love, forgiveness, assurance, and vocation. But from the very nature of that act, its effectiveness is impossible apart from faith. It is, however, precisely the character of Christ's victory and the fact that it comes to pass in those who believe that renders the confession "Christ is Lord" more than a statement of general, eternal truth. For that victory in the believer is *Christ's* victory and it removes the believer from the dominion of principalities to a free and faithful obedience to Christ (Col. 2:10, 3:3, Eph. 2:1-7, Gal. 5:1). The Christians' relationship to Christ as lord differs from the subjection of all other things to him, for it is founded not only in knowledge and loyal obedience, but in reconciliation. The Christian confession of Christ's lordship does not arise from an observation of Christ's rule, i.e., from nature or creation, but from the experience of Christ's victory. The creed is always the Church's creed. But this does not imply that Christ is lord because of Christian faith or experience, for he was lord from the beginning. Nevertheless, it is well to observe that the rule of Christ is complex: "For God has put all things in subjection under (Christ's) feet" (teleologically) until "all things shall be subjected to him" (eschatologically) (1 Cor. 15:24-28, cf. Heb. 2:8). He rules now over all to the end that his victory may be realized in all. But this does not imply that his victory proceeds from his lordship, for the victory follows from the work that he performed as a servant rather than as a lord. The confession that all things were created in and for Christ follows his victory in the believer. Again, the lordship and victory are distinct, neither causing the other, but are both directed to the occasion when the spheres of Christ's lordship and victory shall be identical. At present this coincidence may be found (and there imperfectly) only in the Church, for whom he is thus Lord in a special sense, for the Church alone confesses him lord, and the Church alone enjoys the benefits of his redemptive work, and the Church alone proclaims his reconciling word in conflict with the powers of this age.

II

We have observed that the direct benefits of Christ's victory are to be found nowhere else than among believers. This is a corollary to our introductory observation, that rulers are capable of just rule apart from revelation or faith. It appears now that in Christ God did not revise the structure of the cosmic order or the nature of the State, which in the Graeco-Roman world was widely considered one aspect of that order. Affairs of State have been in God's hands from the first and his redemptive work did not alter or replace his government of "this age."

On the contrary, far from being a "physical" act, God's work in Christ has been called a Word, and thus its effectiveness depends upon hearing and believing (Rom. 10:13-17). As it is by Word and Spirit that the work of Christ is communicated, so it is only by abiding in that Word and Spirit that the Christian life and the Church itself are sustained (Gal. 4:8-11, 19).

The next step is to understand the nature and mission of the Church in light of Christ's victory and lordship. If what has here been asserted to be the New Testament view is sound, it will affect some prevailing views of the role of the Church in society.

The current view that God's work in Christ radically altered the created order and reoriented the whole structure of things encourages the conclusion that the State, as a significant aspect of that order, is not properly constituted or legitimate unless it acknowledges the change, or submits to Christian guidance one way or another. Further, since the work of Christ is widely assumed to have had universal effectiveness (whether known or believed), the task of the Church appears to have no direct continuity with Jesus' lowly and suffering ministry, for the circumstances of that ministry no longer pertain. Inasmuch as his humiliation has been vindicated by his resurrection and triumph over the world rulers, the Church's ministry now appears to be the publication of what is an accomplished fact, and gaining submission to it. In relation to the State, that can mean any number of things from lobbying for the Sunday closing of business to demanding official recognition of the Church and its doctrine or the establishment of a Church political party. If Christ is Lord over a reconstituted world order, the Church acquires a peculiar significance for the exercise of his sovereignty. It is fully in keeping with this line of thought that the Church serve as the conscience of the State and the State as the arm of the Church whereby that for which Christ died may be enacted for a just and peaceful society, the Kingdom of God in our time.

But such a view cannot be supported by the New Testament. Because the work of Christ was quite otherwise, the task of the Church is quite different. Because the created order has not been reoriented, *our task is to serve as Christ served, not to reign as he reigns* (Mk. 10:35-45, Jn. 20:21, 1 Cor. 4:1, 8, Col. 1:24). The point is twofold: (a) Civil government does not require special revelation, and the work of Christ did not modify the nature or duty of the State so that the Church should be essential to its proper function. (b) The Church has a special calling in God's Heilsgeschichte as surely as did Jesus, and it is called to an undeviating obedience no less than he. In a world under the domination of principalities and powers—yet created in and for him, and always subject to him—he did not undertake the needed "political task," but proclaimed the love of God that would bring all who believe to freedom from sin and the possibility of obedience.

All authority in heaven and earth has been given to the Son, not to the Church. The authority of the Church does not extend beyond its calling; it is the authority of the servant, not of the Lord, the authority to preach, not to rule.[5] Its service offers the possibility of faith, which characterizes the new life of reconciliation to God and man, the possibility for a new obedience. In the light of its mission, the ethical task ought not to be oversimplified. The question is not merely whether a "Christian ethic" applies universally, or whether an "eschatological ethic," is valid today. It is crucial, rather, to observe that the Christian ethic is one of *possibility*. The eschatological ethic is not characterized merely by futurity, but by the new possibility of obedience which is founded upon a restored integrity, a new covenant in which the law is upon one's heart and he knows the Lord as one forgiven and reconciled (Jer. 31:31-34, 32:38-40, Ezek. 11:19 f., 2 Cor. 5:17). Christian ethics begins, not with the imperative, but with the indicative. From a hearing of the gospel arises the possibility of obedience (1 Jn. 4:10 f., 19).

The mission of the Church is not the publication of a "higher ethic." For all his controversy with the law, Paul steers clear of derogating its holiness and righteousness. He does, however, observe that it is impotent to accomplish what it was given to do. What promised life soon became an instrument of death and sin (cf. Rom. 7:7-25). There is nothing whatever to prevent a "Christian ethic," in any form, from becoming like the Law of Moses, if it is regarded and "applied" without careful consideration of the Church's eschatological mission. *The Christian ethic is founded upon possibility.* When applied by pressure, legislation, or any other external means, it becomes an instrument of wrath.[6]

No less important is the fact that a Church intent upon legislating the Kingdom of God, or a reasonably accurate facsimile, denies its mission. (a) It assumes that the obedience desired can come about another way than from the freedom which characterizes the new possibility in reconciliation by faith. (b) The Church thus becomes a pressure group among pressure groups and the end it seeks, however noble, is essentially its *own* will in a society of diverse wills.

The eschatological mission of the Church is necessarily worldly. The Church, like its Lord, is sent to sinners, and every departure from the world's arena is a retreat from its calling. It was not the early Church's social pronouncements or political action which "turned the world upside down"—the absence of such activity is the embarrassment of many social reformers—but its faithfulness to its eschatological mission at the crossroads and market places of the world. The early Church met with opposition and violence in the execution of its calling because the gospel, which liberates men from the domination of principalities, at the same time places the Christian outside the domination of forces whose balance guarantees social order. By liberation from the "wrath of God" (Jn. 3:26, Rom. 1:18 ff.), the Christian departs from the symphonic laissez-faire interplay of ambitions, fears, superstitions, and the like, which not only tempt men to evil but also inspire them to government and agreement upon social rules and standards. The gospel inevitably, quite against the best intentions of the early Church, appeared to threaten the State, and Christians were charged with atheism and sedition (Acts 17:7, 19:23 ff.) because the execution of the eschatological mission in faithfulness to the Church's vocation struck at the very roots of human behavior.

A specific ethical problem for the early Church was the task of making clear to converts that Christ's victory in them meant not only freedom from the principalities of this world, but subjection to Christ as Lord (cf. 1 Cor. 8:9, Gal. 5:13, Col. 3:1 ff.). The gospel was not to be mistaken as an opportunity for self-indulgence, but was rather the basis for the new possibility of

new obedience (1 Pet. 2:16). A particular instance of this confusion is the supposition that freedom from the principalities and
subjection to Christ as Lord meant freedom from the authority
of Rome and Caesar. The consistent early Christian exhortation
to civil obedience (Rom. 13:1-7, 1 Pet. 2:13-17, Titus 3:1) re-
lates to several matters we have mentioned. (a) The order in
which civil government shares is divinely established and instru-
mental in God's rule of all things, quite apart from the faith or
knowledge of its officials. (b) God's work in Christ did nothing
to revise his rule in this world. It remains the same as before and
is God's approved means of rule in the sphere of wrath (Rom.
1:8 ff., 12:19, 13:4). (c) Because the principalities were not
the objects of Christ's work, not only was the State unaffected,
but the rule of spiritual powers, sin, and death were uninter-
rupted in the world as a whole. (d) This circumstance underlies at once both the mission of the Church and the authority of
the State, for to dissolve the State in the period of wrath could
lead only to chaos, and for the Church to fail to proclaim the
word of the gospel in the world would render the work of Christ
of no effect, for the established means whereby his victory comes
to pass would be lacking.

Thus far we have seen that the work of Christ not only did not
have its object or purpose in the cosmic order, to which the State
belongs, but the mission of the Church does not lie in that order.
Further, the Church's eschatological mission is worldly, both in
the sphere of its service and the scope of its effectiveness. In
other words, by dealing politically, the Church not only forfeits
its calling, but can have no more effect upon the political structure of its time than another pressure group. *But by adhering
faithfully to its calling, the Church's role in bringing to pass the
victory of Christ in men may have immediate and far-reaching
consequences for every aspect of human experience, especially
in the social-political sphere.*

III

The distinction in the New Testament between the realm of
Christ's lordship and the locus of his victory has a parallel dis-

tinction in the authority of the State and the mission of the Church. This distinction, however, must not be identified with the classic "two realms" theory. Despite certain similarities, the early Church was free from the weakness which was exposed in Nazi Germany, and this was largely due to its consciousness of eschatological mission as defined by Christ's work.[7] The early Church knew that it did not live in a benign universe, and it proclaimed the gospel as the power of God in a spiritual warfare against the principalities of this world. The victory of Christ is no generally realized condition, but is so related to preaching, hearing, and believing the Word of God's love that it is definitive of the Church's mission as well as of its nature.

But please note carefully that the alternative to the Church's assuming active political responsibility is neither total renunciation of the world and its affairs nor "individual" Christian action. The former alternative is alien to the New Testament, the latter is too narrow. The Church is neither the only social institution nor the only one worthy of Christian membership. Mature and dedicated Christians will find opportunity to participate effectively in a variety of social and political groups; in fact, to renounce such participation is tantamount to withdrawing from the world.

The paragraph above must be emphasized, for there is a common malignant assumption that there are only two possible forms of Christian political concern and activity, through the Church as an institutional pressure group, or "individually." Consequently, any suggestion that the Church should not assume a direct political role is countered by the indignant assertion that "individual" Christian witness is ineffective in the modern world. My point is twofold: (a) The Church is not the only group in the world. Non-Christians belong to groups! There are thousands of groups, and many are large and exert tremendous influence. It is positively perverse to maintain that if a Christian does not support a Church lobby he prefers to act as an "individual" and alone. There are as many possibilities for the Christian to assert political influence in groups apart from the Church as for anyone else. The charge of individualism attacks a straw man.

(b) On the other hand, there is something suspect in a churchman's preference to act always under the name of the Church. Must one's witness be broadcast from behind the walls of the institution in order to be "Christian"? Isn't there something to be said for Christians going *out* of their monastic confines and participating actively in society? Should they not join other groups and encourage them to think about the common crisis? A package of yeast will permeate nothing until the package is open. If Christians are to create a ferment in society, let them move beyond the Church walls and speak and act boldly according to their convictions. The Church must prepare its members to assume this responsibility intelligently and effectively; it is not the Church's duty to relieve them of this responsibility by doing it for them. Not only can Christianity be more effective in its impact upon society where its members assume active roles in community groups, but until the Church has equipped its members to do this, it has failed in its responsibility.

While evangelization takes many forms and it would be inaccurate to say that nothing in that way is accomplished by Christians in their worldly associations, that is another story and not our concern at present. *We are concerned with the role of the Christian citizen (participating in society and its groups) as the means of Christian influence within the realm of the State's authority as distinct from the Church itself assuming a political role.*

The first alternative is surely older than the second and has been of tremendous influence. It is, however, very difficult to trace or measure although it is going on wherever mature Christians have the opportunity or responsibility of commenting upon civil policy. This conscious political activity by Christians is to be distinguished from activity of the Church in that they are acting in freedom and integrity on the basis of personal responsibility to God; they are not acting as agents of a Church, carrying out a program enacted by it. Presumably the Church has played a significant part in the revelation of God's will to its members and has encouraged them to faithful obedience, but while the Church does not shrink from discussing the social and political issues of the day in light of Christian doctrine, the responsibility and decision is always the individual's in his relation to God. The role of the Church is only that of servant, never that of Lord.

What must be unambiguously clear and emphatic is this: At the same time that the Church itself refrains from political activity, it makes unmistakably clear to its members that *politics is not an optional concern for Christians*. The man in Christ as a whole, renewed man is a concerned and active man. He is responsible to his Lord for the integrity of his way of life in the world; he can neither avoid politics nor be careless or unscrupulous in its practice. The Church has an important role to play in the nourishment and maturing of its members that the full victory of Christ may be realized and that they may serve him in wisdom and courage in the world. This eschatological mission belongs to no one but the Church. The work of the servant is crucial in the redemptive work of God's; *it is enough for the Church to be found faithful in its calling. And where it is faithful there will be found Christians acting with courage and integrity in the affairs of the world.*[8]

The needs and concerns of the day have tempted the American church increasingly to act politically as a Church. This must be distinguished from addressing its Church membership on political subjects. The point of distinction may be found in the role of the speaker and in the indirect object, not in the object or content of the speaking. The Church's speaking to its members ministerially is to be distinguished from its addressing a branch or officer of the government on behalf of a constituency. The former is in keeping with its eschatological purpose; the latter is not merely a deviation, but it yields to the classic temptation to bring about a desired social condition without disturbing the hearts and minds of the people, i.e., the Church thus works "redemptively" in precisely the opposite manner from its lord, whose victory did not consist in the external establishment of peace but came to pass in those who believe.

From the viewpoint of this paper, the direction in which the Church should be encouraged to labor today, is utter faithfulness to its calling. This means (1) the continuing evangelization with which it was charged, to the end that all men know and believe the love of God and be gotten into the freedom and possibility of a new obedience, and (2) the patient and diligent teaching of its members, discussing all matters which pertain to the Christian life in the contemporary world in the light of God's revelation and purpose, to the end that they may grow into a mature manhood in Christ, exercising with courage their full responsibility in society.

As to the fearful circumstances which beset us, which make men anxious for their lives, we may be confident that God is lord over us all and that he rules in the era of Kennedy and Khrushchev as he did in the days of Pharaoh, Cyrus, Herod, and Nero. It is a terrible thing to live in a world held in balance by terror, our only apparent protection from annihilation being our ability to annihilate. This is one of the grimmer ways in which a world in wrath forestalls utter chaos. Realization that this is not a new arrangement does not make it less terrible, but it may make us more cautious in assuming that the Church is faced with an unprecedented crisis. The States involved have not ceased to be States and there is surely no indication that the Church's calling has been either accomplished or rendered unnecessary.

It is to be hoped the Church will carry out its mission with vigor and faithfulness to the end that its members, nourished by the Word of God, may walk through this valley as men not anxious for their lives but rejoicing in hope, patient in tribulation, fulfilling with courage their social responsibility in the world.

FOOTNOTES

[1] A study of *shalom* in the Old Testament will indicate that peace is far more a human value than commonly supposed. The divine promise of peace is like the promise of health and prosperity. It is therefore not inconceivable, biblically, that one should have to choose between obedience to God's will and the pursuit of peace (Lk. 12:51).

[2] This is integral to the biblical doctrine of providence (e.g., Isa. 40:15, 23) and *Heilsgeschichte* (cf. *The Powers That Be*, pp. 35-39, 107-109; Isa. 45:1 ff.; Rom. 9:17, 13:1-7. Note 1 Pet. 2:13: government is a "human institution.").

[3] As will appear below, this assumption derives not so much from the seri-

ous study of the nature and duty of civil government as from the historic zeal of ecclesiastics to achieve "evangelical" goals by means of civil authority.

4 On this point and (a) and (b) below, cf, *The Powers That Be,* esp. pp. 114 ff. for a more detailed treatment of the New Testament than can be undertaken here.

5 The Church's authority is founded upon its divine commission, not upon its constituency. Although it gets more notable results when it says "Thus say 20 million Baptists, and 12 million Methodists, and 8 million Lutherans . . ." than when it says "thus saith the Lord," such exercise of power does not appear consonant with its calling and the character of its authority as servant rather than Lord.

6 This is one of the periodic and classic follies of the Church. The desire of churchmen to legislate the Kingdom has repeatedly resulted in inhuman and unjust societies as well as perverse and diabolical churches. This zeal for righteousness undertakes precisely what Jesus rejected. On the other hand, it omits what appears central in the ministry of both Jesus and Paul, the proclamation of a word that transforms those who believe it and opens to them the possibility of obedience.

7 Contemporary confusion of the American Church as to its mission makes it especially vulnerable to the fate of the German Church in the Nazi era. The common identification of Americanism and Christianity appeared clearly in ecclesiastical and political reaction against the Supreme Court's disapproval of civil prayers for public schools. Few seemed to recall that our fathers preferred to die rather than recite harmless civil prayers to a non-partisan deity.

8 The New Testament never envisioned the possibility of Christ incarnate becoming "Christ Incorporated." Rather, his body on earth must at all times be flesh and blood. There is no consensus of a committee or pronouncement of an assembly that can replace men and women of understanding and courageous faith at large in the world.

7

CONFLICT AND RECONCILIATION

Otto A. Piper

Kingdom of God and Social Order

For the ethical approach to social and international problems, it has becomes customary in modern times to resort to abstract concepts such as Love, Justice, or Humaneness. Yet as should be expected, the choice of such an abstract starting point results inevitably in abstract solutions. In order to find answers that are commensurate with the demands of a given situation, it is necessary to supplement the abstract principle with a view to the pattern of that situation. American politicians, e.g., are prone to think in terms of utilitarianism. They realize that people in general, and American people in particular, want to enjoy life and to be happy. They are therefore apt to react violently to any international development that seems to threaten their quest for happiness. Hence they hate war and are anxious to emphasize their country's love of peace. Nevertheless, at the same time, they are in favor of the most extensive military preparations, because they are able thereby to express their determination to defend their country's happiness as an inalienable right. In other words, Justice, as they understand it, demands a kind of politics by which this right is asserted and defended.

Pacifist circles in the USA, including the "Peace Churches," have widely adopted the same utilitarian position, except that they insist upon the fact that life and the pursuit of happiness, far from being a special privilege of the American people, are inalienable rights of the whole of mankind. Hence the supreme principle by which politicians should be guided, is Love. In those circles, Justice is not considered an independent principle but rather the manner in which Love expresses itself in social, political and international relations. It does not take too much sagacity, however, to discover that both modern American "realpolitik" and American humanitarianism have espoused views of reality which are both superficial and leave uncovered wide areas of life. Not only is the gravity of evil slighted both in nature and in human life, but history is considered quite naively a process over which man is in absolute control.

In order to embrace the human situation in its totality and depth, it is necessary to heed Jesus' announcement that God is about to establish his reign here on earth. This message implies a directionality of history which is God's work, a manifestation of powers of evil here on earth which is so terrible that man is unable successfully to cope with them, and the divine promise that through faith in Christ man will be enabled to become God's agent in the complete transformation of this world. The message of the Kingdom cannot be truly understood, however, when it is severed from God's work as Creator. The apocalyptic view, while underscoring the sovereign will of God who on his own and independent of any outside pressure has started to transform this world by making his might felt in it, may easily be misinterpreted. It might look as though prior to the Kingdom period the conditions of this world had been brought about by factors inside this world only, while God had nothing to do with its development. It is therefore most important to learn from Matthew and Luke that Jesus himself buttressed his proclamation of the Gospel by pointing to the care which God had taken of this world ever since he created it.

In this perspective the social order, in its actual condition, is not to be interpreted as a purely human achievement but rather as man's methodical way of satisfying the needs which God has implanted in him when he created him for communion with his maker. What was wrong with the Social Gospel was not the direction in which man's faith moved but rather the definition of the goal. Christian social ethics in the past eighty years or so had adopted the modern eudaemonistic view of life. The Church and its members were urged to cater to the greatest possible happiness of the greatest possible number. The inevitable result was a separation of ethics from religion. The social goals for which Christians were urged to work were derived from the idea of a satisfactory human life rather than from the will of the Creator. Hence it made no difference whether those who espoused these goals were Christians or not, and frequently Christians were urged to collaborate for a common goal with non-Christians and even with people who were opposed to Christianity.

As a result, those who overlooked the role of conflict in the making of the social order, hoped for a final stage in international relations, in which people by a simple vote or treaty could abolish war. Political authority would then be reduced to legislative functions. Others, conversely considered conflict so deeply rooted in human nature that even periods of peace were interpreted as mere times of preparation for new wars. There is nothing wrong in our making efforts to improve social or international conditions. But it should be kept in mind that what we practice in these areas never does make that specific contribution to the destinies of mankind which Christians owe to it, and consequently it does not bring about that radical transformation of human conditions, for which Christ appeared here on earth. Characteristic of the conditions of this world is the fact that things do not steadily and constantly move toward a higher goal. Rather this is a world full of conflicts; yet within its conflicts Christ manifests his power by bringing about peace.

Conflict and Political Order

As all social institutions, the body politic is the result of two divergent tendencies. The very association of people is a source of power, and as such acts coercively both upon the members of the group and upon other groups. At the same time, however, the body politic is a community of human beings who are destined for communion with God, and as such it displays a powerful aspiration for order. No matter how often this longing for order is thwarted or disturbed in historical life, order is the *raison d'être* of the state. This means that the rule of law and stable institutions form the basis of domestic life and render possible the conclusion of treaties which are the foundation of peace and neighborliness in international relations. The body politic can therefore be defined as a manifestation of power used for the realization of the common good. But disruptive forces are also at work everywhere and at all times, and thus it is only with difficulty and after heavy efforts that the two requirements for the well-being of the state can be maintained. Except for very small entities, political power cannot be wielded directly by all the members of the commonwealth. The body politic is held together normally by the power of the government, and thus the whole power of the body is concentrated in the will of rulers, e.g., the three branches of government in this country. Through government the collective power is rendered articulate, and thus can be manipulated with relative ease through the directive activity of the government. Hence the specific nature of the common good pursued by a given state will depend on the will of the government.

But the very notion of a common good is related to interests; not only to those of the various members of the body politic, but also to those of the state as a whole both in its dealing with its citizens and in its relation to other countries or states. Interests have their origin in needs, desires and plans, and since the goods of this world are not evenly distributed, interests are the point at which the disturbing influence of the power of evil makes itself felt. The very fact that not everybody has as much as the other members of the body politic, and that people think they would be happier if they had a larger share of the goods available than they possess, becomes a source of conflict. This law applies not only to economic goods but also to political power, social influence and status, reputation, physiological and cultural enjoyments. The social order, and the political order in particular, is therefore a way in which conflicting interests are brought to compatibility under a general principle. This does not happen incidentally. It is the collective pressure which causes the common consent. Our income tax system, for instance, does not express what each citizen is prepared to sacrifice for the benefit of his government; on the contrary, most everybody feels robbed by the tax collector. Nevertheless, realizing the power of enforcement, of which the government disposes, the ordinary citizen prefers paying his taxes to being jailed for refusal to do so.

No other way has yet been devised to serve the common good except the use of coercive power by the government. When Marx and the Communists hope that some day the state will be replaced by society, and that coercive power will give way to voluntary consent, they overlook the fact that there is no generally valid and commonly recognized criterion by which conflicting interests can be measured and contained, and since interests rest upon plans, desires and wishes no less than on needs, even an economy in which all vital needs have been satisfied, will still harbor conflicting interests.

International life offers very much the same picture. Territorial problems are here of paramount importance. The primitive techniques and living conditions of prehistoric man must have led to quarrels over places which for climatic reasons, food supply and raw materials seemed to be particularly desirable. The development of technological know-how has enabled an increasing number of people to live in constantly shrinking territories. Nevertheless, the scramble for territory has inevitably resulted in blatant inequalities as to the quality of soil, supply of natural resources and climatic conditions. There are no "natural" areas in which nations live. One has only to open an historical atlas to see how tribes and nations and races have moved to and fro over wide areas. The "historical rights" by which a national group claims a certain territory as its homeland seldom date more than a few centuries back.

The inequality of natural conditions, under which the various nations and ethnic groups live, explains the role that expansive urges and aggressive men play in international life. In this sphere, too, no generally valid principles are known through which the right of a nation to the territory settled by it can be supported. This absence of "natural" principles seems to justify the envy of the have-not nations. Why should the neighboring nation enjoy a higher standard of life or have a larger supply of raw material than one's own country? The fact that the well-to-do nation may have toiled more than its poor neighbors or that it has used its resources in a more intelligent and economic way, seldom comes to an envious nation's mind once it is obsessed by greed. It will fain go to war because it sees the booty that could be the victor's share. The same greed is found underlying the colonial system and the wars of conquest by which it was established. The availability of raw materials and cheap labor was deemed a sufficient justification for establishing one's rule over the "less developed" countries.

The Inevitability of War

The co-existence of aspirations for order, on the one hand, and of disturbing cosmic forces, on the other, forms the basis of all historical life. This fact explains the instability of political regimes and the constant occurrence of wars. They form the warp and woof of the social texture. The conflict of interests is at the bottom of upsetting events, yet it would be absurd, as communism does, to hope for an abolition of conflict by divesting the individual of his particular interests. For it is the stake that the individual has in social life that moves him to participate in it and to promote its order and peace. Social unrest, rebellion and revolution, far from being the normal phases of social life, are exceptional enterprises. The same holds true of international life. Notwithstanding the surmise of certain anthropologists, according to whom primitive man was in a constant state of warfare, the opposite must have been the case. The natural difficulty and the time consuming character of food gathering and preparing shelter and raiment must have made it imperative for our ancestors to refrain from conflict and warfare as much as possible. In turn, the amazing spread of primitive civilization and the parallel succession of the use of various metals point to the intense and peaceful interchange that must normally have gone on not only between neighboring groups, but probably also over vast distances.

In these circumstances, the fact of warfare could not be explained unless an historical group had seen a definite advantage in fighting its neighbor. The lust of adventurers will seek satisfaction in any area and will turn to soldiery only when a government or a nation needs soldiers for a war to be waged. That there are many evils concomitant with war, man must have realized after the first skirmish. But since the awareness of war's evils has not prevented nations and states from engaging in new conflicts, the reason can only be that war was considered a means toward ends which otherwise could not be attained at all, or not as satisfactorily. The economic motive, which since the days of Marx has been frequently mentioned as being at the bottom of all wars, plays actually but a subordinate role. For wars are not waged by individuals against individuals but rather by nations against nations. While the economic advantages accruing to the victor nation will give satisfaction to individual members of that nation, war against a rich nation or a rich territory is deemed advisable primarily because it increases the political power of the aggressor nation.

In the Middle Ages, the will for power manifested itself on a dynastic or feudal basis; in modern times it has become a national aspiration. That is the reason why it is relatively easy for a government to win a nation's support for a war or a warlike enterprise, as long as there seems to be a reasonable chance to emerge victoriously from it and thus to increase the nation's political power. The evils of war are well-known and they have grown larger in substance and more painful in method in proportion with the numerical increase of both total population and armed forces, and with the technological development, as it is used for military purposes. But since the social order is established against the background of the disturbing forces of evil, the organization and maintenance of its institutions demands not only effort but also sacrifices of life, property, health and comfort for the benefit of the whole community. Apart from such will to sacrifice no one e.g., would join the police force, work in the mines, or face the hazards to health and life in industry or transportation. It is generally recognized that such sacrifices are unavoidable and necessary for the common good. Public life requires the recognition of the fact that some members of the social group are expendable for the well-being of the whole. The problem confronting those in charge of the social institutions is only, how to keep these sacrifices in a reasonable ratio to the goods thereby to be engendered. It would seem that war is but the application of the principle of sacrifice to more comprehensive goods than those earned in the economic and social field, especially to the power and public recognition of the body politic.

Since wars have their roots in historical reality, namely conflicting claims and interests, it seems difficult to apply moral standards to the waging of war. As a matter of fact those who turn in this matter to the Bible for advice will be rather disappointed. Just as the Old Testament commandment, "Thou shalt not kill," did not refer to warfare, so the New Testament injunction, "Love your enemy," was not understood by the primitive Church as forbidding military service and warfare. It was obviously taken for granted that the social order in this world requires the sword not only for the maintenance of domestic peace (Rom. 13:4) but also as an instrument of national policy. The apocalyptic literature of the New Testament (e.g., Mark 13:7-8 par., Rev. 14:14-19) interprets warfare as a characteristic of this world.

The medieval Church attempted to subject war itself to moral standards by differentiating between just and unjust war. But is it possible at all to apply the concept of justice to international life? Obviously the concept of justice can be applied only to relations within an institution or organization that is established upon a legal principle. This is the case, e.g., when two nations have concluded a treaty, because by doing so they place themselves under a legal obligation which is to be respected regardless of the interests and wishes of either party. A party that breaks a treaty is legally wrong, and the wronged party has the right to seek indemnities or restoration of the treaty relationship. But nations do not by nature form international institutions based upon law. The United Nations, for instance, is an organization based upon a treaty made first by the charter members and then adhered to through solemn pledge by other nations. Within that organization it is possible to brand a nation as an aggressor. But since one of the aims of the U.N. is to stop war among its members, it is not in a position to give any of its members the green light for a just war. The U.N. is not sold on the moral idea that war is by itself wrong, however, but rather its members hold that war is not a desirable means of solving international conflicts. Far from being a moral issue, war is even in the U.N. a tool of international diplomacy. It is obvious, of course, that the enormous material and moral evils, which war, particularly in modern times, carries with it, require great restraint and wisdom on the part of the governments.

Christianity in a World of Conflict

By stating that war is not a moral issue but rather a natural means of political life we do not hold that moral standards should not be applied to social life and in particular to life in the body politic or international relations. But just as the state's function of legislation is not a moral issue but rather the manifestation of the sovereign life of the body politic so also is the recourse to war. There are numerous ethical issues implied in such activities e.g., when a legislator has been bribed, or a faction in parliament has passed a law that is positively harmful to a section of the nation. Similarly actual warfare provides all kinds of temptations to those concerned, beginning with the general who betrays his country and the business leader who uses war as a means of making profits and up to the enlisted man whose uniform serves him as a cloak for theft or rape. But these are not specifically Christian problems. They concern the general moral order which a body politic has established for its citizens. Yet this fact does not doom the Christian to complete inactivity. Living in the existing social order, the Christian considers it a means by which he is enabled to give expression to his longing for fellowship with God. But that goal itself is not realized by man's efforts but rather by God as he establishes his Kingdom through Christ. As his disciples, we are called upon through our whole conduct to manifest our belief that God's eschatological work is under way, and that God has power enough, despite all obstacles and opposition eventually to reach his goal.

In view of the conative character of the social order the goods engendered therein cannot be regarded as supreme values. Of course, there is no harm, for instance, in satisfying our physical needs by means of economic activities; but when our business becomes the supreme goal and determines our outlook in life, it is wrong, because it keeps us from aspiring for the realization of the Kingdom (Matt. 6:25-30). The same consideration applies to political life. One cannot live in the body politic without identifying oneself with its striving for political power and influence. Jesus himself was not opposed to the Jewish longing for freedom from the Roman yoke. One of his disciples, Simon the Zealot, was a member of the Jewish Secret Army Organization (Acts 1:13). But Jesus realized that the Kingdom which he helped to usher in, far from being a part of the social order (John 18:36), was rather to transform it into a higher way of life.

Hence the follower of Jesus leads a seemingly ambiguous existence. He does not fully identify himself with the existing social order, yet he participates so thoroughly in it that he is thereby able to transform it. This attitude explains, e.g., Jesus' strange saying about paying taxes (Matt. 22:15-22). He does not say that a believer ought not to pay taxes; but it is not a moral issue to him, either. Inasmuch as we are living in a state and under a government and inasmuch as every government is in need of taxes in order to function, it is evident that these have to be paid. It was only because the Jews dreamed of a kind of glorified Israel outside of the rest of the world, that they were in doubt as to whether they should pay taxes to Rome. But Jesus' additional commandment to give to God what is God's, is no less important. He might have treated the issue as a merely social one because in that context the necessity of taxes was evident. But Jesus wanted also to emphasize that the state is not the supreme good. Its existence is necessary only because it transcends itself and derives its meaning from God's Kingdom.

The injunction, "but give to God what is God's," indicates that by refusing to ascribe ultimate value to the goods of social life we are set free to that "better righteousness" (Matt. 5:20) of which those are unaware who stress the absolute necessity of the social order. It is by living in the Kingdom sphere and seeing the things of the social order in that perspective that the commandment, "love your enemy" (Matt. 5:44), makes sense. It starts realistically from the fact that social life implies the possibility of conflict. Nevertheless we ought also to be aware of the opportunity to deal with the political enemy in a personal way, e.g., as a prisoner of war or as a citizen in an occupied country. The political relationship is to be subordinated to the human one. Likewise, what Paul says in Rom. 12:14-21 applies not only to enmity in social and economic relations, but with equal force to political life. Like his master, the Apostle realizes the great danger inherent in enmity. While it is a prerequisite of political life to make a clear distinction between friend and foe, that is to say between those who foster our commonwealth and those who want to harm it, there is danger nevertheless that hating the enemy should gradually engender a general attitude of negativism. People who give free rein to their anti-communism, e.g., thereby may become a danger for their own country, because they get so obsessed with their suspicions that they fail to work for the common good.

Similarly, by admonishing Christians to give food and drink to their enemy whenever he needs it (Rom. 13:20), Paul gives priceless political advice. The Christian, ready as he is to defend the interests of his country, is reminded by the wants of his country's enemies, that they too, are human beings. Even apart from any international convention through which the enemy would acquire a right to be taken care of in his needs, he and his nation are God's work no less than is our country. To bring home this fact to their respective nations by advocating foreign aid, e.g., is one of the primordial political tasks of Christians all over the world.

Above all, however, there is Paul's great admonition to hold peace. The apostle enjoins the Romans, "If possible and as far as lies with you, live at peace with all men" (Rom. 12:18). Some critics have scolded Paul for destroying a glorious principle by a weakening conditional clause. Others will feel, however that the admonition grows more powerful through the addition of the clause. It gives evidence of Paul's realism. Taken as a general and unconditional principle and a commandment, it may sound wonderful, but is as impracticable as any of Khrushchev's high sounding absolutes. Did any of Paul's critics ever try to live by this principle without restriction? "If possible" means according to the spiritual strength that is granted to you. To live at peace with people who are congenial with us is no problem. But there are those who irritate us, e.g., by their stubborn determintation to remain what they are, although they realize that we do not like their outlook or principles. If it is not their racial characteristics which exasperate us, it is perhaps their political views or their religious convictions. The saying applies to international life no less than to domestic relations.

Moreover, Paul adds, do so "as far as lies with you." Peaceful relations cannot be brought about by unilateral action. People may have good reasons for not responding to our peace overtures. They may suspect that our show of sympathy might be but a trap; that we want to humiliate them by our condescension, or that we try to cheat them by exhibiting kindness. Or they may belong to the emotional type whose longing for friendship and love has been so consistently frustrated that they have finally become embittered and are now unwilling to receive kindness. But again, Paul's formulation of the prerequisite shows his profound wisdom and knowledge of the human soul for the conditional clause implies that I may not give up without having seriously tried to live according to the principle. Before I conclude that it is the other person's fault when I do not get along with him, I have to scrutinize myself. The fault may lie in my own attitude, or in the way in which I attempt to perpetuate a situation, in which from the other person's viewpoint no peace and friendship can be cultivated.

The Church's Protest

What opportunities are there open for the Christian when he wants to work for a political order that shows respect for the goal set to it by God? First of all, Christians are in a position to influence public opinion in all countries, though in some less than in others. In doing so, it will be wisdom, however, to address oneself less to the evils than to their causes. People overlook the fact e.g., that in our days the greatest danger for the preservation of international peace does not come from the politicians and the people whose business they may do, but rather from the scientists and the engineers. With a breathtaking speed these people are building around us an artificial world of machines and mechanical devices, which threaten completely to engulf social life. By letting the computer think for him and the robot work for him, man is reduced to the role of consumer of food, pleasure, and information. Technocracy is not interested in human values and is therefore indifferent to the mass destruction of life. If this trend is allowed to continue, war will break out because the computer in Washington or Moscow has indicated that taking all things together this is the moment when the U.S. or the U.S.S.R. have their best chance. But obviously such danger cannot be met merely by writing books on it. We have to change our whole pattern of life instead of complacently conforming with the mechanization of human life.

One important thing Christians can do in the present situation is to propagate the biblical view of social life over against the naturalism and secularism of the sociologists, economists and psychologists. Unfortunately, what we notice is a growing tendency on the part of Protestant theologians to adopt those secular views and to advocate them as though they pursued Christian goals. Take one instance. When they discern in the international situation the disturbing consequences of the cosmic powers of evil, friends of peace will often take a moralizing position and tell us that in a political conflict the other side is not absolutely evil and that there is a good deal of injustice and wrong on our side too. That is true, of course. But unfortunately such an attitude will lead to moral relativism; the problem confronting us is thereby transformed from an ultimate issue into a matter of expediency. Consequently, the Christian fight is no longer directed against war as a disturbance of the international order but rather against the evils which a modern war will bring with it. People, who, e.g., accepted World War I and II as the inevitable outcome of international tensions, get almost hysterical, when the prospect of atomic warfare appears on the horizon. Yet from the biblical viewpoint, this is a fatal error, for in God's eyes it makes no difference, whether people wage a "limited" war with conventional weapons or kill each other in a "total" nuclear war. Yet there is no point in urging statesmen and politicians to engage in politics of peace, unless one has first succeeded in persuading the majority of the nation that that is what they need. For while politicians are fully aware of the evils which a war brings over a country, they will and must also ask themselves, whether or not the consequences of not going to war will be worse than war itself. There can be no doubt but that some of the modern pacifists are motivated by a sentimental utilitarianism. Many politicians and statesmen will oppose such an outlook, since in their eyes national independence, freedom and justice are values to be appraised more highly than life and material possessions. Likewise, while one may regret the inactivity and lack of imaginative characteristic of the international politics of the U.S., it is doubtful as to whether the readiness to negotiate is so advisable in all circumstances. Some of those who advocate negotiation, e.g., seem to be disposed thereby to look for a solution by which the U.S. would advance its own interests upon the back of her friends or allies. That is hardly a road that will forever and effectively banish the threat of war.

There is no sense in criticizing statesmen and politicians for acting according to political wisdom. The axiom that you cannot apply the Sermon on the Mount to public life, ambiguous as it is, implies nevertheless more than a kernel of truth. We contribute only to a growing confusion in political life, when we advise the political leaders to pursue Christian utopias becoming to a sinless world only. One is more than surprised e.g., that an agency of the World Council of Churches should appeal to the world to abrogate war, possibly by creating a U. N. army. In such instance, political idealism becomes blasphemous, because it trusts that man has the power to accomplish what the Son of God only is capable of doing, namely the defeat Satan so completely that he will no longer be able to harass this world.

The Christian faith, as has been shown, is warfare against the forces of evil. But in order to do so effectively we have to adopt the right strategy. Since in the final analysis the conflict is one in which God's Spirit is engaged with the powers of confusion, the Christian's task consists above all in making the Spirit articulate in this world. The nefarious influence that the powers of evil have upon social life would not be possible but for the skillful way in which those powers conceal their purpose. Seemingly they serve to intensify and improve social life. So subtle is their deception that some philosophers hold that evil is the most effective stimulus of progress. It is of utmost importance to unmask that fallacy and to bring to light the true purpose of social life.

To do so is the function of the Church. The Church has an unique opportunity of influencing social life, because it is a social institution notwithstanding the fact that it differs essentially from all other social institutions and occupies a place of its own. The significance that the Church has for social life lies in the fact that through its very existence God upholds his claim to be the Lord of the world and thereby he discloses the wickedness of the forces of disturbance. In its message of redemption the Church proclaims to mankind that it is God's will to deliver man from the tyranny of the forces of evil and that God is capable of bringing about a reality in which man depends exclusively on his Creator. By so manifesting that God's redemptive work is going on in this world the very presence of the Church is a challenge to the whole social life inasmuch as it is influenced or disturbed by the forces of evil.

The effectiveness of the Church in social life depends on the degree to which it is anxious and willing to be different from the rest of mankind and to act differently. The fact that sociologically the Church is a social institution is apt to conceal seriously its nature and specific character. It is therefore necessary that its differences should become articulate by way of a protest against the sinful nature of the existing social order. The more specific the protest the more influential it will be, whereas a general condemnation of social injustice will not be given much attention. This protest can be directed against any area of social life, e.g., against absolute government as in the case of the Anabaptists, against luxury and love of pleasure as in the case of the Puritans, against the love of money and self-righteousness as in the case of the Lutherans, and so on.

The international situation will not be changed, however, as long as the Church contents itself with adopting new political or social ideologies, for by them the power of the disruptive social forces will not be broken. Rather the Church must emphasize the absolute lordship of God over this world in contrast with a belief in cosmic or social fatalism, on the one hand, and an extolling of man's self-sufficiency and autonomy, on the other. Yet a change of outlook in preaching and teaching will have little influence upon social life, if it is not implemented by a protesting attitude on the part of the membership of the churches. Here lies the significance of the sit-ins and sit-downs, the picketing and the protesting ads in the newspapers. Although they have symbolical significance only and do not really change the structure of political life, they are nevertheless a challenge which cannot simply be ignored. The excessive severity, with which some states of the South have reacted against such actions, when performed for the purpose of improving the conditions of the Negroes, e.g., is an indirect witness to the effectiveness of such actions. On the whole, however, such acts of protest will be of little immediate consequence, because they are mere abstentions from what others consider their right or their legitimate privilege or pleasure. The true significance of such actions lies in their conditioning the will power of church members. It is by means of such relatively insignificant protests and abstentions that a person's will is strengthened so that he will be prepared to participate in a radical protest, when the time arrives.

Reconciliation and Peace Making

Although the heavenly origin of the Church necessitates its protest against the structure of the social order in which it lives, the very genius of the faith cannot be manifested in a negative act. Christianity's real contribution to political and international life must be made in a positive way. Our analysis has shown that the social life of mankind receives its structure from the clash of God's redemptive purpose, on the one hand, with the disturbing influence of the cosmic forces, on other. But rebellions, wars and other disruptions of social life would not happen but for the fact that people yielded to the prompting of these disrupting forces. Apart from man's consent, they would be mere possibilities in social life. It is man's consent, that is to say, his sinful disregard of God's purpose, that actualizes them. In turn, by faith man recognizes God's redemptive plan as his supreme law and thus becomes willing to act accordingly. Hence war cannot be considered a sociological necessity which arises irresistibly out of the existence of nations. If people did not want to go to war, no battle would ever be fought. People go to war, because they have so often yielded to feelings of hatred, enmity and destructiveness in their dealings with other individuals. The numerous passages in the New Testament, in which believers are enjoined to practice reconciliation and love of their enemies are directed primarily toward the sphere of personal relations. What we think of the value of human life, will manifest itself with the greatest clarity in areas where most intimate personal contacts are the rule. Every harsh word, every unkind act committed against the brother (Matt. 5:22) is an indication of our lack of esteem. We would not treat him in that way, if we thought him to possess the same dignity as we do. It is the disturbance of personal relations that brings about trouble in social life.

The disruption of social life is not caused by a "fighting instinct" in man but rather by this sinful habit to ascribe to the fellowman lesser value than to ourselves. Accordingly any act on the other person's part, in which he does not give us what we consider our due, provides an opportunity for showing him how little we think of him. Similarly, whenever he seems to obstruct our way or to impede our plans we take it for granted that we have a right to insult him, to stop him violently, or to harm him. As a result of this attitude we form social habits and attitudes which serve to intensify the tensions between classes, races and vocational groups. They are particularly harmful, because the restrictive influence that makes itself felt in family relations is absent from the patterns of social relationships. Rebellions, civil wars, and revolutions can easily originate on that basis. Once conditioned in this direction people will feel little restraint to resort to warfare when their nation has unsuccessfully disputed the claims of other nations.

In these circumstances there is little hope of affecting warfare directly by Christian action. It is only as people learn again fully to respect the personal dignity of their fellowmen and to help them to satisfy their needs that the problem of war can be dealt with effectively. In this connection, the Christian family can play an important role. It is no exaggeration to say that it is in the family circle that the warlike spirit is nurtured, because in that environment we feel less inhibited than in public life; but since there is no permanent escape from its fellowship it is there also where the spirit of peace-making and reconciliation is developed. Yet this latter goal can be reached only when faith permeates the home. For then alone parents can combat the children's tendency to quarrel with each other and to assist them in the difficult period of adolescence to learn to assert themselves without getting into conflict with others. A prerequisite of such an education is the parents' determination to live in peace with each other notwithstanding different viewpoints and plans. Where human reason fails to discern solutions in which either partner receives his due, the eyes of faith discover opportunites of mutual service and mutual enrichment.

Beyond the blissful experience of living together in peace and holding peace (Rom. 12:18) there is for the Christian the opportunity to work for peace (Matt. 5:9). We are not obliged to treat the conflicts which arise around us as inevitable. By following Jesus we are enabled to show people that their divergencies can be composed to mutual satisfaction, and often it is the very presence of such "comforter" that suffices to effect reconciliation. Likewise, when we are attacked or harmed by another person, faith does not demand a passive acquiescence in his wrongdoing. We would completely misinterpret the mind of Jesus, if we understood his admonition, not to resist the evildoer (Matt 5:39), as meaning that his followers should condone all wrong. The best commentary of Jesus' saying is Paul's exhortation to overcome evil by good (Rom. 12:21). We should attempt to show the person whose enmity we encounter that we do not therefore hate him. The illustrations given by Jesus disclose the fact that conflicts arise frequently because people set a premium on their material belongings. Thus their dealings with others remain determined by considerations of property and this perspective will confirm the same attitude in others. Often our relations to others could improve considerably if we took the trouble to enter into their personal problems.

The discouragements and difficulties of Christian peacemaking will prevent the disciple of Jesus from indulging in unwarranted optimism, as though world peace were just around the corner. But there is no reason for despondency and apathy, either. The meek have Christ's promise that they will become the owners of this earth (Matt. 5:5). It is by the humility of our faith that Christ will be enabled to overcome the forces of disruption in social life. The peacemakers shall be called "sons of God" (Matt. 5:9), that is to say, the ones through whom the purpose of God is executed here on earth. Thus Christians are not people whose interest lies altogether in an imaginary world. But they live their life on two levels. Firstly, as they participate in the social life of their environment they work for short term goals. In politics, business or education one cannot plan for the next century or millenium; one has to content oneself with the compass of the next two or five years, or at the best with the duration of one's generation.

Over and beyond the short term activities, however, in which we participate with the rest of mankind, there is the long term or eschatological perspective of the mature believer. Undoubtedly the world in which we are living abounds with error, confusion and falsehood. Nevertheless the truth cannot be suppressed forever. False ideologies, once they have been unmasked, are unable to recover and to start a comeback. The neo-Nazis or neo-Fascists, for instance, are no real danger any longer. Their judgment has been pronounced not only on the part of the populace but also of God.

The results of Christian peacemaking and reconciliation may appear insignificant and infinitesimal, but they are lasting results, or, to use the biblical language, God's people receives its divine reward. Much of Christian defeatism and despondency is due to a wrong perspective. God's purpose implies the progress of his cause, and in the advance of God's work, the believer is privileged to share. Too frequently, however, we are like those disciples who were more interested in the seats of honor they were to occupy in God's Kingdom than in the triumph of God himself (Mark 10:35-37 and // Matt. 20:20-21; Luke 22:24). Yet what we are promised is not wide recognition and public honor here on earth but rather the satisfaction of experiencing the triumphant power of Christ as its manifests itself through the sinfulness of our activities and insights and in spite of them.

part 4

SOME PROPOSED SOLUTIONS

8

MESSIANIC LICENSE

Krister Stendahl

▪▪▪

I N HIS RECENT STUDY of the Sermon on the Mount, Harvey K.
McArthur[1] has rendered good service by giving us a clear
classification of the different approaches toward the Sermon on
the Mount through the ages; he has also furnished us with a
fresh and rich collection of quotations, which actually amounts
to a rather precise history of the interpretation of these bewilder-
ingly significant chapters of Matthew's gospel. He identifies not
less than twelve main lines of interpretation of the Sermon as it
applies to ethics. Hence anyone would hesitate, or even feel
arrogant, if he were to add a thirteenth alternative. Yet I am
encouraged to do so since I find McArthur's approach somewhat
unsatisfactory on methodological grounds, when he in his last
chapters attempts an eclectic solution.

When we thus begin with a critique of McArthur, we do so
since his study at the same time registers the pulse of much contemporary Christian life and thought in these matters.[2] He
divides the twelve approaches into two groups: Six Views of
Secondary Value and Six Views of Primary Value. While this
method may make immediate sense to our feelings and predilec-
tions as twentieth-century Westerners, it is worth noting that the
views of "secondary value" are by and large the ones which are
closest to rigorous descriptive and historical attempts to understand Jesus is his first century setting. The views of "primary
value," on the other hand, are mainly those which are less
conscious of the distance between Jesus' situation and ours,

but which consciously or unconsciously treat scriptural material as timeless truth, unconditioned by changes or developments within history or within the history of salvation.

This becomes especially clear when McArthur without much ado relegates "the modern dispensationalist view"—as e.g., in the Scofield Reference Bible—to the lowest place in the "secondary value" group: "I cannot regard [it] as shedding any light on the interpretation of the Sermon" (p. 139). This view makes a distinction between the Kingdom dispensation, to which the Sermon on the Mount has primary application, and the dispensation of Grace (in which Christians now live), to which the Sermon has only secondary application. I would agree that in Scofield's form this is a misleading interpertation, but this should not eclipse the fact that this interpretation is the one which makes use of the most significant elements of the messianic and eschatological fabric of the New Testament.

The other "secondary value" views include Schweitzer's "interim ethic," which was a conscious approach to break through later Western developments in order to recapture the strange and shocking eschatological setting of Jesus' teaching. The "modification" approach may be evidenced already in the first century by Matthew's exception clause, not found in Mark's command about divorce (Matt. 5:32, 19:9; cf. Mark 10:11-12). The "double standard" approach with its distinction between "precepts," which are binding upon all, and "evangelical counsels," which are meant only for some, can be easily criticized when those "some" became identified with the clergy and the monasteries; but even McArthur has to admit that the distinction as such is well substantiated in the New Testament (e.g., 1 Cor. 7; cf. also Didache 6:2f.). Luther's interpretations of the "two realms" is more attractive to McArthur. "With great reluctance I must place [it] in the list of interpretations of 'secondary value'" (p. 133). His reluctance may be due to the fact that this view seems to be more removed from the first century issues, as are all of his "primary value" views. But the "distinction between the two realms" is only a systematic and a-historical theological translation or transposition of the original New Testament awareness of dispensations and personal differences, which also underlies dispensationalism, interim ethic and precepts/counsels. Finally the use of analogy from Scripture in order to tone down the "difficult" passages in the Sermon on the Mount is the oldest and most obvious method in the history of religious interpretation. While it has—and should have—little attraction to modern interpreters with a sense for historical criticism, it is an approach that belongs to the very age in which the Sermon was written down.

Hence we find that McArthur—unconsciously, I am sure—has given secondary significance to those approaches that unearth or express the issues of the first century. Conversely he has listed as of primary significance those views that presuppose a more philosophical or theological or social or literary awareness: The Absolutist View (à la Tolstoy)—Hyperbole—General Principles—Attitudes/Not Acts—Repentance—Unconditioned Divine Will. In this group the last alternative is that of Dibelius, and is the one closest to the temper of contemporary theology with its dialectic stress of the unconditioned divine will on the one hand, and the stress that this will should not and cannot be fulfilled as a law, since the "Christian Law does not demand of us that we *do something* but that we *be something*."[3] When exposed to such an interpretation it is worth remembering that the dialectic mood may well be a useful contemporary technique to hold biblical teaching in balance, but that such a dialectic has its root not in Jesus' teaching but in the tension between statements which in the actual ministry of Jesus were given in specific situations and to individuals, and the problems that face the Christian consciousness of Western twentieth-century man.

The fact that Schweitzer's insistence on an eschatological understanding of the Sermon on the Mount took the positive form of an "interim ethic" has had a somewhat unfortunate impact on the later discussion. The issue became "interim" *or* universal and timeless validity. This alternative, coupled with the constant Christian concern for proving the superiority of Jesus over against Judaism, has made it difficult to discuss the Sermon in the light of the Jewish question: What is to happen to the Law—the Torah—when the Messiah comes? In more recent times this question has received much attention. In 1952 W. D. Davies devoted a monograph to this subject[4] and H. J. Schoeps has furthered Pauline studies by making this issue central to the understanding of Paul.[5] In this he followed up the intimations of Albert Schweitzer.[6] The Qumran texts have given us access to a new angle from which to view the Sermon, and H. Braun has made a thorough comparison between the "Sharpening of the Law" [Toraverschärfung] in the Qumran texts then available (the Manual of Discipline, the Habakkuk Commentary—and the Damascus Document) and the New Testament.[7] Hence there is a fair amount of material available for a discussion of the Sermon on the Mount in the light of a question that is authentic to the Jewish community in which Jesus lived and taught. We are not limited to arbitrary and atomistic quotations of isolated ethical statements of Judaism. We may be able to recapture the framework in which this kind of ethical issue had to be discussed in first-century Judaism.

It is a common view in Christian thought that the Pharisees constitute the epitome of strict legalism. Their attitude is often described in accordance with the principle *fiat justitia, pereat mundus,* let justice have its way, even if the world is destroyed in the process. But if one interprets the Pharisees along such lines, he overlooks the fact that one of the principles which guided the Pharisees in their interpretation of the Torah was actually driving them in the opposite direction. They were in fact the ones who argued, against, e.g., the Sadducees, for the right of innovation and adaptation. They could justify such procedures by quoting Ps. 119:126—with a different twist from the Masoretic text—as saying "It is time to do something for the Lord."[8] Such new interpretations grew out of the conviction that the Torah was "livable," and hence it could not require anything which proved to be obviously impossible or detrimental to the life of the people. The classical example of such adaptations was the so called *prosbul,* a legal fiction devised and argued by Hillel, by which the law of Deut. 15:1-3 [all loans should be cancelled at the beginning of every seventh year] was bypassed. As it read in the Torah it had become a serious threat to economic development.[9] In the Talmud this principle reaches the point where it is laid down by rabbinical authority that a decree is not to be imposed on the public unless the majority are able to abide by it.[10]

In the Qumran material, including the Damascus Document, we find the designation "seekers [or: interpreters] of smooth things" presumably with reference to the Pharisees (CD i, 18; 1 Q) ii, 15, 32; 4 QpNah. 2; cf. Isa. 30:10). It is quite possible to relate this term to the tendency of which we have just spoken, since the Qumran texts give precise examples of a more strict interpretation than that of the Pharisees, e.g., in the matter of rescuing animals on the Sabbath (CD xi, 14) and in marriage laws (no sexual intercourse in Jerusalem, CD xii, 1-2; no marriage with a niece, v. 8).

Such criticism of the Pharisees for an interpretation which tampers with the strict words of the Torah is not lacking in the clashes between Jesus and his opponents in the gospels. The best known example is the discussion about divorce (Mark 10:2-9.). Here a "Sharpening of the Law" is carried out in an even more drastic fashion by applying the principle of the supremacy of earlier decrees in the Torah as superior to later ones. The divorce decree in Deut. 24:1 is secondary and motivated by the hardness of men's hearts: it was a concession given through Moses; but the pure will of God which is from the beginning demands a union between man and wife, which cannot be dissolved.[11] It is significant to note that Paul uses the same type of argument when he establishes the unchangable priority of the promise to Abraham over against the Law given later through the mediator Moses on Sinai, a Law which is conditioned by the sins of Israel ("it was added because of transgressions"), and which hence cannot claim to be the ultimate and unconditioned expression of God's true plan and nature (Gal. 3:15-20).

Thus even the Law decreed through Moses can be seen as a concession, a step in the direction of pragmatic awareness of the possible and the livable. This is, however, unusual and we are more familiar with the distinction between the Torah and the injunctions prescribed by the Pharisees. Such a distinction appears self-evident to us, but we should remember that the Written Torah and the Oral Torah were one entity in the minds of the

Pharisees, and both had their roots in Moses' revelation. Nevertheless, Jesus seems to have criticized the latter as "human tradition" (Mark 7:8), and his critique is striking since it is not motivated by saying: "you make it too hard for people," but by pointing out how such tradition leads to a cancellation of the actual commandments of the Law: The giving toward *Korban* overrules the commandment to honor father and mother (Mark 7:9-13).

In Matt. 23—the discourse against the Pharisees—there is a more advanced and systematic handling of these issues. While the tone and the composition are peculiar to Matthew, it agrees at many points with the picture we can draw on the basis of the Markan material. Again the shortcoming of the Pharisees is not in their demands, which are accepted on principle—"whatever they teach you, you should do and keep" (v. 3)—but the hypocritical element as, e.g., in the matter of oaths. "The smooth interpreters" had recognized that there had to be some room for oaths. Hence they made distinctions which kept the most holy things out of the area of oaths (the Temple and the Altar) while allowing oaths by matters related to these (the gold of the Temple and the gift on the Altar). In language of irony the words of Jesus claim that such distinctions are ridiculous in the eyes of God and/or in the light of common sense (23:16-22).

Some of the above examples, but especially this last one, bring us close to material contained in the Sermon on the Mount. In Matt. 5:33-37, in one of the five antitheses, all swearing is dispensed with while Lev. 19:12 speaks only against *false* oaths. Apparently contemporary Judaism had moved in the same direction, in its ever growing awe toward using God's name. Judging from this passage one had settled for "Heaven" or "Earth" or "Jerusalem," or "one's head," but again Jesus' words argue for these as tantamount to God himself. No clever, softening interpretations are allowed.

In the light of our observations the much debated saying in Matt. 5:20 becomes as clear and as natural as one could desire: "If your righteousness does not exceed beyond that of the Scribes and the Pharisees, you shall not enter into the kingdom of heaven." Most difficulties in the interpretation of this programmatic sentence emanate from the presupposition that the "Scribes and the Pharisees" were already the champions of an extreme rigor in the obedience of the Law. But we have seen that their obedience, including "the fence around the Law" (Aboth i, 1), was built on a principle of accommodation. It is against such "smooth interpretations" that Jesus is reported to speak, and the five antitheses in Matt. 5, give ample support to such an understanding.

It is, however, too easy for many Christian interpreters to glorify Jesus' searching consistency over against the Pharisees at this point. The more one takes for granted that Jesus' ethic is superior *qua ethic*, the more he finds himself entangled in the discussions whether the Sermon on the Mount is "possible" or not, or whether it is meant to be "possible," or whether it has as its point the promulgation of the will of God as being by definition beyond man's capacity, etc., etc. The often hopeless confusion of such discussions should open our eyes to the deep and serious level on which the Pharisaic ethic was elaborated. Once in a discussion about these matters with a rabbi who knew a good deal about the New Testament and the history of Christianity, I was much helped when he stated his views somewhat like this: The trouble and the glory of Christianity is that the Church and the Christians for some reason think that the principles of the Age to Come can be applied already in This Age. The Jews also know of a time in which the prophecy in Jer. 31:31ff. shall come true, when the Law shall be within us, written upon our hearts, a time which will be characterized by that messianic fulfilment to which Jesus witnessed in the Sermon on the Mount. But that time has not come yet. Just as we find it wise and necessary to accept the Law of Gravity in our earthly existence, so we find it wise and necessary to live by Torah as long as we find ourselves in this world and This Age.

While there can be different Jewish interpretations of how the Age to Come and/or the Messianic Age will affect the Torah, or affect man's relation to the Torah, there can be little doubt that this distinction between Judaism and Christianity is one of the most adequate, and most illuminating. The difference goes back to a question of eschatology. It all hinges on whether the New

Age, the Age to Come has arrived for a full or partial manifestation here and now. The Christian would—and should—say yes, while the Jew would—and should—say no.

There can also be little doubt that the Jew would have the obvious facts of life on his side. This should help us to see that Society as we know it, a society kept in order by law and justice, is built on principles identical with or similar to the concerns and practices which are criticized and invalidated in the Sermon on the Mount. The principle of retaliation is and remains an absòlute necessity for any just society. The specific wording "an eye for an eye and a tooth for a tooth" was in its own time not a harsh decree but a step toward just limitation of oversized retaliation in the uncontrolled wrath of the vendetta: an eye— not a life! In New Testament times it was of course not applied literally, but as a principle of equitable justice. And a society without some machinery for divorce is an impossiblity, as can be seen from the complicated legal fictions of annulment etc. devised by churches that do not allow divorce.

Hence, the thrust of the Sermon on the Mount undercuts the order of society. It was this insight that forced Schweitzer to speak about the Interim Ethic of the Sermon on the Mount. But his interpretation was bound up with *his* interpretation of the New Testament eschatology, and it grows out of his despair as a theologian to relate the stark words of the Sermon to the world in which the Church finds itself. And yet, exactly this despair set him free from domesticating the Sermon, and hence his interpretation of the actual text is more valid than most other attempts. But I wonder if there is not another possibility. That possibility could be called "Messianic License." The key to this interpretation may be found in Matt. 19:10-12.[12]

Here it is obvious that Jesus' interpretation of marriage and divorce appears to the disciples—just as we have said it should— totally impossible. At that point Matthew gives a logion in which —again—one of the commandments of the Law is cancelled, and this time one found even in the Creation. On the basis of Gen. 1:28 every Jew was under obligation to marry and procreate. Not even the most ardent Rabbi could say that he forsook marriage for the study of the Torah. When one of them is quoted as saying so, he is repudiated.[13] Only two types of excuse from marriage were recognized: those who were born "eunuchs," and those who had been made "eunuchs." To these the logion in the Gospel adds a third category: Those who make themselves eunuchs for the sake of the Kingdom of Heaven. This is a truly Messianic License, promulgated by Jesus, and running counter to the Law. By his arrangement Matthew interestingly enough gives this "ruling" as an ancillary to the impossibility of Jesus' "ruling" on divorce. We should note that also at that point the issue was that a marirage *had* to go to divorce under certain circumstances; the more modern question "Is divorce permissible?" turns the problem upside down.[14]

We know that the issue about "celibacy" was a genuine one in the Primitive Church, since Paul argues in favor of it in 1 Cor. 7; yet, we note that Paul has no knowledge of a "command from the Lord" in this matter (v. 25). While his argumentation is similar to that of Jesus, the issue is whether it is permissible to forego marriage, also in the case where a man already has promised to marry a woman (v. 36ff.); Paul holds that even in such a case it is better and more blessed to refrain from marriage. His motivation is eschatological: the form *(schema)* of this world is about to pass away (v. 31), and the birth pangs of the New Age are upon the Church (v. 26). Hence he also argues from the point of view of the coming of the Kingdom, and he does it on his apostolic authority, as one who has the Spirit of God (v. 40). The fact that he does not refer to a Word of the Lord (as in v. 10), indicates that the *logion* in Matt. 19:10-12 may well be a later development, or at least one known only in some quarters as, e.g., in the Matthean church.[15] Since Matthew and Paul are the best examples of early Christian teachers with more advanced Jewish education, we can feel confident that such an argumentation is well in accordance with the Jewish setting of the teachings of the Early Church and of Jesus himself. And we note that also the Sermon on the Mount has to be understood primarily on exactly this Matthean level, not by uncontrolled attempts to reach directly back to Jesus himself. Especially in the five antitheses of Matthew 5, which constitute the key passages of the Sermon for our purposes, the material is to a large extent peculiar to Matthew and the arrangement is totally his.

The Messianic License would then mean that Jesus gives his disciples the permission, the license to act in a way which undercuts the very structure on which society is built; his sharpening of the Law reaches an intensity where the Law is fulfilled at the expense of its function as the Law of this Age, or as the Law of Moses given to men in order to counteract sin, i.e., at the expense of that Law which was tainted by its accommodation to the hardness of men's hearts.

The authority for such teaching can be found in Jesus' consciousness of being a messianic figure. Or one can equally well stress the high eschatological intensity in his teaching. The Messianic License is possible since the power of the New Kingdom is at hand. Since God is about to judge the world, man can be allowed to refrain from meting out His judgments. By complete trust in God's impending judgment man is *allowed* to turn the other cheek and leave the ultimate judgment to God (cf. Rom. 12:17-20 and 1 QS x, 17-20). Man can even afford to love his *(and God's)* enemies, just as God in his knowledge of the final judgment can afford to treat the good and the evil equal in this world (Matt. 5:43-48). Whether we like it or not, there can be little doubt that the ethical teachings of the Sermon on the Mount, and vast areas of the New Testament, have their ground in the strong conviction of God's impending judgment of the world.[16] While much of its beautiful specifics cannot be deduced from this ground—many other, and less attractive alternatives were possible, alternatives which would breathe hatred and arrogance—it is nevertheless true that they could not exist without such a firm ground. The specifics are to a large extent peculiar to Jesus, but the structure of thought is part and parcel of Jewish eschatology, and the Qumran texts have corroborated this state of affairs.[17]

Against such a background Jesus tells his disciples that they are allowed to turn the other cheek, thereby disregarding the dangers which such behavior would constitute to a society built on justice. Such an understanding of the Sermon on the Mount comes strikingly close to what seems to be at the heart of the discussion about pacifism. For many a Christian—and for many who arrive at pacifist leanings without conscious reference to Christianity—the problem is this: Is it right to enjoy the clean thinking and feeling of pacifism in a world and in a country where chances are that the pacifists will remain a minority and where they hence "profit" from the protection of the Armed Forces? Or one could ask in a more general way: Do I have the right to decide for others in this matter? Granted that I would be willing to take the consequences of my convictions as a disciple of Christ, what about those who do not share my faith? (Such a discussion of pacifism is of course not suited for the cases where passive resistance, etc., is thought of as a superior means to political or social goals, but it is highly relevant to pacifism as a non-pragmatic, religious conviction).

The understanding of the Sermon on the Mount as Messianic License speaks directly to this type of qualm and question. It does so precisely since the answer given has the form "you are allowed to," not "you must" or "you can." The Sermon on the Mount is actually a rebellious manifesto which gives to disciples of Christ the right to break the Law in the name of Christ. But it is important to remember that it *is* subversive, and that the disciple must be prepared to pay the price for such action. So it was then and so it may be now. The license cannot be easily translated into a higher ethic. It can only be appropriated in faith, and will always threaten the equilibrium of God's created world, which after all is God's world under Law, sometimes even under God's Law.

One question remains, and that question throws us back into the very confusion of the many ways in which Christians have tried to come to grips with this powerful piece of biblical legacy. How do I know when or if I have the right to claim such Messianic License for my actions? Many of the interpretations through the ages show awareness of this momentous question. But if this license is, as the Jewish rabbi pointed out, related to the bold and strange claim that the Kingdom has come, although it does not look that way, then our next question must be: In what sense does the Church claim that the Kingdom has come? To me the answer is—theoretically—simple. The Kingdom manifests itself in the Holy Spirit, which is the down payment and the first fruits of our inheritance (2 Cor. 1:22; 5:5; Eph. 1:14; and Rom. 8:23). And I would argue that this answer is relevant to our inquiry. As far as man is driven by the Holy Spirit he can claim the Messianic License when he finds himself faced by the question—be it from the inside or from the outside—whether he has the right to act as a partaker of the New Age.

Much can be said against such a view and I would like to distinguish between validity of the interpretation of the Sermon on the Mount as Messianic License—which I would like to defend as a possible historical interpretation—and this attempt to answer the question of actual application to our present-day situation—which I would offer in a more tentative mood. Such an application hinges upon most complex hermeneutical considerations and requires scrutiny by both systematic theologians and ethicists.

There is much power in the Sermon on the Mount. The Church is responsible for the right handling of it. It is responsible for the right use of this divine atomic energy; it is also responsible for avoiding undesirable fallout. Paul shows himself to be aware of both, e.g., in his letters to the Thessalonians concerning work. By and large, the Church has at this point been more successful in this latter, protective function. Perhaps the time has come when we dare to speak more openly about the Messianic License.

Many would say, that if what matters is the Holy Spirit, then this license should be for everyone, since every Christian has the right to know himself as sharing in the Spirit. Yet it should be noted that the gifts and the promptings of the Spirit differ. There is much wisdom in the Roman Catholic distinction between the commandments for the majority and the counsels for those in Orders, since the Messianic License should not be transformed into a command for everyone. It may well be that such a distinction in itself is a valid one, and that without it the Sermon on the Mount and many other words of the New Testament lose their serious specificity and become hopelessly watered down to general principles or maxims, which are seldom taken seriously. We may fall into a dishonest romanticism, in which we read and sing about the costly discipleship, but little happens, and the structures of the world quench the Spirit. It may well be that what was wrong with the distinction between "commandments" and "counsels"—the latter understood as Messianic License —was not the distinction itself, but the way in which it became institutionalized and identified with the ecclesiastical structures of the Roman tradition. In any case, it should not be forgotten that there is the diversity of the gifts of the one Holy Spirit, and that Jesus told some people to go home (Mark 5:18-19) while others were ordered to leave their homes and follow him (Mark 10:29-31).

Many questions remain, and new questions are raised by an awareness of the Messianic License. Such a reading of the Sermon on the Mount—or the parts thereof immediately relevant to our discussion[18]—seems to have little direct significance outside the Church. From the point of view of historical exegesis, this fact could be used to defend our interpretation as being well in keeping with the original setting and intention of the Gospels.[19]

We are also faced more acutely with the "testing of the spirits." The tension between the individual and communal reality of the Spirit can hardly be resolved by any formula. But without the Church's recognition of diversity in the promptings of the Spirit it would be hard to set the Sermon on the Mount free to work creatively and productively in the Church in ways which could be more in accordance with its intention.

FOOTNOTES

[1] Understanding the Sermon on the Mount (1960).

[2] Cf. I. W. Batdorf, "How Shall We Interpret the Sermon the Mount?", Journal of Bible and Religion 27 (1959), pp. 211-17.

[3] M. Dibelius, The Sermon on the Mount (1940), p. 136; McArthur, op. cit., p. 127.

[4] Torah in the Messianic Age and/or the Age to Come (Journal of Biblical Literature, Monograph Series 8; 1952); see also H. J. Schoeps, *"Restitutio principii* as the Basis for the *nova lex Jesu,"* Journal of Biblical Literature 66 (1947), pp. 453-64.—For the development in the Early Church, see now P. G. Verweijs, Evangelium und neues Gesetz in der ältesten Christenheit bis auf Marcion (Studia Theologica Rheno-Traiectina 5; 1960).

[5] Paul: The Theology of the Apostle in the Light of Jewish Religious History (1959; Eng. Tr. 1961), pp. 168-218.

[6] A. Schweitzer, The Mysticism of Paul the Apostle (1930; Eng. Tr. 1931), pp. 176-204.

[7] Spätjüdisch-häretischer und frühchristlicher Radikalismus. Jesus von

Nazareth und die essenische Qumransekte, I-II (Beiträge zur historischen Theologie 24:1-2; 1957).

[8] See G. F. Moore, Judaism I, p. 259.

[9] For further discussion and examples, see Moore, op. cit. I, pp. 260 ff.

[10] Ibm., p. 262, note 4.—Cf. also D. Daube, "Concessions to Sinfulness in Jewish Law," Journal of Jewish Studies 10 (1959), pp. 1 ff.

[11] Cf. D. Daube, The New Testament and Rabbinic Judaism (1956), pp. 71 ff.

[12] For the exegesis of this passage about the "eunuchs," see now J. Blinzler, Zeitschrift f. d. neutestamentliche Wissenschaft 48 (1957), pp. 254-70.—B. does not accept "eunuch" as a term for celibacy; cf. however W. Bauer, in Festschrift für G. Heinrici (1914), pp. 235-44.

[13] He diminishes the image of God, which is man (Tosephta Yebamoth 8:4); see Strack-Billerbeck, Kommentar zum N. T. aus Talmud und Midrasch, vol. I, p. 807.—See pp. 805-807 for other rabbinic material relevant to the discussion of Matt. 19:10-12.

[14] Cf. Joseph's attitude when aware of Mary's pregnancy (Matt. 1:19): on the one hand, he was *dikaios,* righteous, and hence he *had* to divorce her, on the other hand he was kind, and hence he wanted to do it without unnecessary publicity. For this interpretation, see A. Descamps, Les Justes et la Justice dans les évangiles et al christianisme primitif hormis la doctrine proprement paulinienne (Universitas Catholica Lovaniensis, Diss. Theol. II:43; 1950), pp. 34-37.

[15] It is of course possible that the pre-Mathean setting of this logion referred to the fact that Jesus himself was unmarried.

[16] See K. Stendahl, "Hate, Non-retaliation, and Love," Harvard Theological Review 55 (1962), pp. 343-355. On the basis of Qumran and intertestamental material it appears that non-retaliation is not to be too easily identified with love; it is often, but not in Matt. 5:43-48, more closely related to the eschatological "hatred" toward evil and toward the enemies of God, of his Messiah and of the messianic community.

[17] Cf. K. Stendahl, The Scrolls and the New Testament (1957), pp. 16 f.

[18] It is important to remember that what we have come to call "The Sermon on the Mount" is not more of a unit than any of the other four "discourses" in Matthew (10:1—11:1; 13:1-53; 18:1—19:1; 24:1—26:1), although the Lucan "Sermon on the Plain" (6:20-49; cf. 6:12) may indicate that there was a similar composition prior to our Gospels. Many difficulties in the over-all interpretation of the Sermon on the Mount would be avoided if the interpretation of the parts and the interpretation of the total "Sermon" were clearly kept apart.

[19] Cf, however, A. N. Wilder, Eschatology and Ethics in the Teaching of Jesus (1950[2]), especially pp. 133-141, for a penetrating and balanced analysis of the Wisdom element in Jesus' teaching in its relation to the eschatological sanction.

9

LOVE YOUR ENEMY:
A STUDY OF NEW TESTAMENT
TEACHING ON COPING WITH AN ENEMY

William Klassen

THROUGHOUT THE HISTORY of mankind various approaches to the question of dealing with one's enemies have been proposed. In biblical literature this is a recurrent theme and biblical scholars have searched for a correct understanding of it with as much energy as they have any other. It is apparent, however, that in times of international tension, with war threatening or actually in progress, biblical specialists have spoken on the issue with special urgency, even though with perhaps less objectivity. Such discussion has not been limited to obscure men.

In the field of Old Testament studies, to cite only one illustration, Hermann Gunkel used Old Testament literature to demonstrate that the Israelites had war heroes and a definite war piety which had specific relevance for Germany during the first World War. There is no difference between religious and national heroes in Israel he maintained, and Israel fought both aggressive and defensive wars. The history of Israel is seen by Gunkel as a result of her heroic ability to fight bloody battles. Her wars were more bloody, more wild, and filled with more hatred than those of the present. Without the heroes of Phinehas and the Maccabees the religion of Israel could not have endured. He explains the attitude of Jesus through the loss of the strength of the Jewish religion in which one cultural layer, a more pacifist one took the upper hand. "To us, for whom war has become the solution for the problems of today, this book (the Old Testament) can become a source of strength. Our people also will remain invincible if we know both: the heroism of the sword and the heroism of faith."

The reason the New Testament does not follow this line says Gunkel, is that the Jews had become exhausted through defeat. He asserts that the New Testament was born among oppressed provincials, people who neither could nor would fight. Because of this preachers must during war years refrain from using New Testament texts and rather turn to the Old Testament. For on almost every page the war cry resounds in the Old Testament and there we find an intimate union between religion and war. The reader is urged to extract from the Old Testament not those elements that speak of meekness but rather those that have eternal validity. Israel was warlike until she was knocked down brutally by stronger nations. The book of Judges clearly teaches that a nation which is at peace will follow after Baal, and this should be a warning to us. What war can do to the religious piety of a nation, says Gunkel confidently, has been experienced in World War. I.[1]

American and British scholars likewise have felt that the Bible speaks to human conflict.[2] There should be no doubt that in spite of the fact that these studies strongly reflect the nationalism of the scholars we can only commend them for their desire to allow the Scriptures to speak to the specific situation in which the Church found itself. It is not the nation to whom the Biblical theologian speaks, first and foremost, but the Church. Certainly the recent stress on the covenant and the Lordship of Christ in biblical studies has taught us this. The Church is the context in which our studies are made and we expect the response from its members whether that be correction, rebuttal, or commitment.

With this in mind it is the purpose of the present study to look anew at the question: Does the good news brought by Christ give us direction on the way that Christians are to deal with enemies? Is the power of the gospel available to deal with this most vexing human problem? Who, indeed, are these enemies? What aspects of this approach does Christianity share with contemporary Judaism or with Greek thinkers prior to and contemporary with the emergence of the Church? The precise application of this question to the modern scene must be made only after the subject has been looked at from the various angles presented in this discussion.

Since the beginning of modern critical scholarship a number of comprehensive studies have been published, beginning with K. O. Fischer (1787) and Neeb (1791) in the eighteenth century. In the nineteenth century Doesburgh (1820-21) published an extensive study on the Christian teaching on this subject while L. P. Hüpeden (1817) published what is still referred to as the best comparative study of the Old Testament and Greek and Roman writers on this theme. The same topic is dealt with in a comparative way in an article in *Theologische Studien und Kritiken* by Schaubach who is the first to save himself a good deal of labor by simply using Hüpeden's Latin work and publishing its results in German.

The work of Michael Waldmann (1902)[3] represents a thorough study of the same topic by a Roman Catholic scholar. While the earlier studies seem to be motivated primarily by the point of view known as "comparative religions," Waldmann writes from the standpoint of ethics and morality and makes a lasting contribution, refusing both to glorify the uniqueness of Christianity and to denigrate the specific contribution Christ has made to this issue. Stephan Randlinger (1906)[4] worked on the same theme using a similar method and reaching the same conclusions as Waldmann, even though he worked quite independently, having completed his study in 1901. The work by Eugen Bach (1913)[5] is rich with comparative material from other cultures and from the Greek writers, but is most outstanding in its dealing with enemy love in its moral and psychological dimensions. While the author is like Waldmann and Randlinger, a Roman Catholic, his conclusions are not determined by ecclesiastical positions. These three studies deserve more attention than they have received.

As is to be expected, the coming of the first World War did

much to stimulate discussion on this subject. Significant was F. Kattenbusch's thorough article on the Christian meaning of "love your enemy" in 1916.[6] He made an exhaustive exegetical study of the sayings of Jesus and Paul, applying the results to the situation in Germany at that time. The exegesis is masterful, yet in its application we may question whether the principles that he draws from the material for the world conflict really emerge from the material he has studied. Nor is it clear today that the commandment to love our enemies rules out only revenge, and thus permits all kinds of disciplinary action including killing to demonstrate that love.

Two years later Paul Fiebig studied the rabbinic parallels in his thorough study of the words of Jesus on the subject of loving one's enemy. Again the exegesis is thorough and we will seldom find objection to that. Nevertheless our fuller understanding of Judaism and the alternatives open to Jesus as well as our own experience during the last forty years may make it more difficult to accept his conclusion: "In the midst of war and the shedding of blood we can still see ourselves as instruments of God's judgment, a judgment which God seeks to carry out because of his love."[7] Possibly his reference to Hindenburg's claim that he was God's instrument will remind us more of Phinehas, the Maccabees, and the Zealots than of the words of Christ.

That parallels exist in other religions besides Judaism is demonstrated in an excellent study assiduously collecting sayings on this topic from other religions, and questioning at the outset the frequent claim that the teaching "love your enemy," is the most original ethical teaching of Christianity. This study by Hans Haas (1927) gives such a plethora of evidence in refutation of that claim, that the focus of any comparative study must now be on the motivation, the scope, and the grounding of this commandment, rather than any supposition that the imperative "love your enemy" is unique to Christianity. Even if Tertullian were correct in his assertion that Christians alone love their enemies, Walter Bauer (1917) has demonstrated beyond dispute that already the early Christian martyrs did not display this love consistently.[8]

Among more recent publications, Henry Fast's *Jesus and Human Conflict* deals with this topic as a part of his comprehensive study of the use and place of force in the teaching of Jesus. Many of his exegetical insights are keen and his discussion of the problems is judicious and circumspect. There is a disturbing attempt, however, to separate religious and ethical issues from political and personal advice and to minimize the evidence of the clearly significant role played by the Jewish resistance movement in Jesus' life. It appears to be an overall statement of the issues as they were seen by the Church thirty years ago. Nevertheless his critique of the expression "nonresistance" is justified and consistently carried through, and the beginning that he makes towards anchoring this teaching in Christology rather than in a new code of conduct is admirable.

Many excellent discussions of this topic are to be found in commentaries and in treatments of Christian ethics. It is impossible here adequately to trace that development and no attempt will be made to do so. In the exegesis it will become more or less clear where the parting of ways occurs.

THE NEW TESTAMENT TEACHING: LOVE YOUR ENEMY

There is agreement that self giving love *(agape)* is at the center of the Gospel. The Gospel is the good news that God loved men to the extent that he gave his own Son (John 3:16) and this love makes it possible for the Christian also to love his fellow men (I John 3:16). The Christian belongs to the brotherhood of Christ, not of Cain who hated and murdered his brother (I John 3:11 f.). Love is recognized most fully in Christ, most specifically in his act of laying down his life on our behalf (I John 3:16) This act of Christ took place while we were "weak" and "ungodly" (Romans 5:6). The ultimate evidence of God's love for us is that while we were still sinners, in fact enemies, this act of love was demonstrated to us. This unique act of reconciliation (Romans 5:10 f) is the only basis on which Christians at any time can carry on their own life of peace making which is the stamp of their actual sonship (Matt. 5:9).

When the Christian life is seen as a continuous ministry of reconciliation flowing out of Christ's initial reconciling act (II Cor. 5:19) we are in a better position to understand the admonition to "love your enemy."

Who are the enemies that are to be loved or reconciled? Of the three related words, hatred (*misos*), enmity (*echthra*) and war (*polemos*), available in Greek, the first represents the inner attitude out of which opposition springs; the second the opposition itself without considering whether this opposition takes on a visible form or remains merely an inner attitude; whereas the third word designates the form that opposition between nations and their leaders takes.[9]

In the Old Testament *'ôyēb* designates the personal as well as the national enemy, while *echthros* seems to refer more to the personal antipathy. The Septuagint refers to the following as *echthroi:* 1) The warring foes among the heathen nations (I Sam. 29:8; Nahum 3:11, 13), and the personal enemies met in daily life (Ex. 23:4; Num. 35:23); 2) the nations that surround Israel, the Gentiles who oppose God and his people; 3) the enemies of the just; 4) the enemies of God. Foerster remarks that "the roots for this usage lie in the fact that the relationship between Israel and the nations was not purely a political one, which at one time could be one of friendship, at another time one of enmity; that the Gentiles cannot be enemies in war time and friends during peace time; but that the relationship is one of continuing opposition, which can only express itself in war and other animosities!"[10] Where such a position exists it is understandable that those who follow God would hate what God hates.

In the New Testament *echthros* may designate the personal enemy who encounters us in daily life (Gal. 4:16), but it also occurs in the Old Testament sense of those who are enemies of Israel (Luke 1:71, 74; 9 1:43). The Apocalypse refers to the foes of the two witnesses (11:4, 12), and Matthew alone records the saying where Jesus quotes Micah 7:6 that his ministry will tend to make enemies of members in the same household (10:36).

In a special sense however the term *echthros* designates that which is abhorrent to God and his Messiah. The parable of the nobleman refers to his political enemies (Luke 19:27) who did not want him to rule over them. Paul refers to the enemies of the cross of Christ who avoid martyrdom by denying Christ, "setting their mind on earthly things" (Phil. 3:19). The political loyalty of the Christian is not on earth but in heaven (*politeuma*) (Phil. 3:20). Elymas the magician is called an enemy of all righteousness (Acts 13:10) because he sought to use the Gospel for his own purposes. It is in the same sense that the many occurrences of Psalm 110 appear (Mark 12:36, Acts 2:34-35; I Corinthians 15:25; Hebrews 1:15), and which Paul thus applies to all the powers that are at enmity with God.

The use of the term enemy as an opponent of God and his people occurs also in Matthew 5:43 f. Here the enemy is the one who is actively persecuting the Church and is the opposite of the *plēsion* or neighbor. Likewise in II Thes. 3:15 the one who refuses to obey Paul's letter is not to be treated as an opponent of the Church but dealt with as a brother still within it.

It should be clear that the New Testament does not idealize the enemy. The Christian way of dealing with an enemy is not to imagine that he does not exist or to demythologize or spiritualize him. Behind the manifestations of evil and enmity in this world stands the enemy who continues to sow pernicious weeds in the world. The Christian as servant of the householder, however, although tempted to root them out, must allow them to grow together until the end time. (Matt. 13:30). He cannot use violence to rid this world of evil in any of its manifest forms. This is the error of all enthusiasts who seek by political action, pressure on governments, etc., to impose a Gospel ethic on the state. In taking this position, however, the Church is not saying that brute power of one state can best be met with the greater brute power of another state. Rather the Church affirms that in Jesus Christ Satan has fallen like lightning from heaven, and that from Jesus Christ his followers have received power (*exousia*) "over all the power of the enemy" (Luke 10:19). Hate can be conquered only with love, not by more intense hate. The enemy can only be conquered as he is overwhelmed with love—a love which can lay down its life if necessary to demonstrate its own nature. An examination of the New Testament teaching con firms this.

Christ's Teaching on the Enemy: Its Background

Of the four Gospels, Luke (6:27-36) and Matthew (5:38-48) record the teaching of loving one's enemy. In Matthew it comes as a climax to a series of antitheses in which Jesus takes up some points from the Old Testament and tradition and shows how he fulfills them or sets them aside. Much energy has been expended in trying to discover where the words "and hate your enemy" (Matthew 5:43) of the last antithesis come from. It has been correctly observed that the Old Testament nowhere explicitly commands that one is to hate his enemy. Nor does Matthew necessarily imply that the last part is a direct quotation. Just as the Rabbis did not always clearly indicate where a quotation left off, so it may be the case also with Jesus. In adding the words "and hate your enemy," Jesus is referring to an attitude common enough among people throughout the whole world. Tacitus described the Jews of his day with the words: "Among themselves they are inflexibly honest and ever ready to show compassion, but they regard the rest of mankind with all the hatred of enemies."[11]

While there is no explicit command in the legal codes of the Old Testament to "hate one's enemy" the admonition certainly does exist. When the Hebrew was commanded to totally destroy his enemy it is doubtful that he displayed the brilliance of modern man by drawing the conclusion that this does not necessarily imply hatred. Further, such passages as Psalm 31:6, "I hate those who pay regard to vain idols" (certain manuscripts), and Psalm 139:21 f, "Do I not hate them that hate thee, O Lord? And do I not loathe them that rise against thee? I hate them with perfect hatred; I count them my enemies," should caution us to refrain from the assertion that hating one's enemy does not find expression in the Old Testament.

In the apocryphal literature it is not difficult to find allusions to what Jesus is here saying, e.g., Tobit, 13:12, "Cursed are all who hate you; blessed for ever will be all who love you." Nor did the writers always distinguish between hating the sin and the sinner, for the Wisdom of Solomon explicitly says: "For equally hateful to God are the ungodly man and his ungodliness" (14:9). Jesus ben Sirach warns the philanthropist to pick his recipients carefully, to give to the godly man, but not to the sinner; to do good to the humble, but not to the ungodly:

> Hold back his bread, and do not give it to him,
> lest by means of it he subdue you;
> for you will receive twice as much evil
> for all the good which you do to him.
> For the Most High also hates sinners
> and will inflict punishment on the ungodly.
> Give to the good man, but do not help the sinner.
>
> (*Sirach 12:5-7*)

Here man's hatred of his enemies is based upon God's hatred of them. One could not, however, imitate God in everything. The Rabbis taught that men should not imitate God in jealousy, revenge, exultation, and acting in devious ways.

There are those who see the commandment to hate one's enemy in the Qumran material. E. J. Sutcliffe has carefully studied this aspect and concludes that "this teaching is not found at Qumran."[12] However in arriving at this conclusion it appears that he differentiates too sharply between the hatred that was preached there against wicked men and hatred toward external enemies, instigators of persecution, which he maintains were to be repaid with good and not evil. It is highly doubtful that either the Old Testament or the Qumran material differentiates as sharply as Sutcliffe does between the hatred of sin and sinners and entertaining personal hatred or rancor especially when the Israelite and the Qumran Sectarian are called upon to act as instruments of vengeance.

When the Sons of Light, the members of the Congregation, are "to hate all the Sons of Darkness each according to his guilt with the vengeance of God" (1 QS I, 10f.), is it really so plain that this hate has "for its object only the sinfulness of the wicked"? And must the unqualified hatred in 1 QS IX, 21 f, where we read of "eternal hatred towards the men of corruption," be understood in the same way? When the degree of hatred becomes a criterion by which the worth of a member is ascertained then it certainly has considerable importance as seen in 1 *QS* IX, 15 f: "It is according to his spirit that each one must be judged, and according to the innocence of his hands that each is to be admitted and according to his understanding that he is to be promoted, and similarly with his love and hatred."

On the Sons of Darkness God will eventually take vengeance, a destruction without a remnant (1 *QS* IV, 14; cf. V, 12f). Emblazoned on their battle standard are the words: "The anger of God with fury against Belial and all the men of his party to leave no remnant" (*Rule of the War* (10 *QM*) IV, 1f). The agents of vengeance while unspecified at some points clearly include the members of the community (1 *QS* II, 6f). Part of the responsibility of the members of the community is "to pay the wicked their deserts" and to "decree judgment on wickedness" (1 *QS* VIII, 6f, 10). The army of the Sons of Light would be God's agents when "the time appointed for vengeance" would come in the eschatological war (1 *QM* XV, 6). Inscribed on one of the trumpets were the words: "Memorial of vengeance at God's appointed time" (1 *QM* IV, 12). Perhaps the same belief that they were God's agents for retributive justice is expressed in the *Habakuk commentary* (1 *Q peser Habakuk* V, 4) when the author says: "Into the hands of His elect will God give judgment on all nations."

In the above, citations have been given from Sutcliffe's own essay in order to note the different interpretation one can arrive at while using the same material. Sutcliffe argues that this hatred and vengeance is deferred until the future eschatological hour. The conviction that they were appointed for a time of vengeance existed alongside a conviction that it would be wrong to harm even the Sons of Darkness prior to that time. In support of this Sutcliffe cites: "I will not requite any man with evil. With good will I follow men, for thou art God to whom it belongs to judge every living being and He it is who will requite each his deserts. . . . And strife with men of perdition I will not take in hand till the day of vengeance, but mine anger I will not withdraw from men of iniquity and I will not be content till justice is established" (1 QS X, 16-20). So also 1 QS, IX, 16: "there will be no strife with men of perdition." Sutcliffe deduces from these words that "as regards external enemies, instigators of persecution, they are not to be repaid with evil, but on the contrary with good." Do they not rather say that until the Day of Vengeance he will stoke the fires of anger, or at most bank them, but that by no means will he allow them to die? Is it more likely that the fellow members of the community will be repaid with good when they do evil? Victor Hasler in commenting on 1 QS X, 17 notes: "To be sure other sayings from the Qumran community indicate that such good will is confined to the community. Matthew does not confine it to that."[13]

In any event the crucial junctures at which the New Testament and Qumran separate are: 1) Hatred for evil or evil men is never encouraged in the New Testament.[14] The closest we come to it is in Romans 12:9 where the word used is *apostogeo* or in Revelation 2:6 where hatred is explicitly described as directed against "the works" of the Nicolaitans. Jude 23 should perhaps best be translated as "loathing." 2) A second significant difference is as Sutcliffe has correctly observed, "it is not for Christians to act as agents of divine vengeance,"[15] whereas the Qumranites saw themselves as such agents.

It is possible that Kurt Schubert is right in seeing a distinction between an attitude of personal enmity and eschatological enmity and in maintaining that Jesus rejected both. The Qumranites refused to retaliate only for one reason: God's judgment was coming. However, the fact that they considered themselves as instruments of God's judgment made it impossible for them to come forth with a consistent position. When the Romans came it is quite likely that they were convinced that the holy war had begun, and they defended their retreat to the end, adding one more evidence to the history of the Jewish people that those who take the sword perish with the sword.[16]

Here we would see the cleanest and most significant break between all that the Old Testament and Judaism have to say on the subject of the enemy. For the conviction that one could best serve the Lord by becoming, as it were, His dagger of vengeance, having only the motive that his people be pure, goes back at least to the Phinehas narrative (Number 25:6-13).[17] In a vicarious way men are filled with the zeal of God and become instruments of his. The Maccabees clearly saw themselves as followers of Phinehas for Mattathias is described as "burning with zeal for the law, as Phinehas did" (1 Macc. 2:26) and he began the Maccabean uprising with the cry: "Let everyone who is zealous for the law and supports the covenant come out with me!" (1 Macc. 2:27). Finally at his death he urges his sons to "show zeal for the law, and give your lives for the covenant of our fathers" (1 Macc. 2:50). Again Phinehas is held up to his sons as an example, "because he was deeply zealous" (1 Macc. 2:54). In his praise of famous men, Jesus ben Sirach lists Phinehas third, "for he was zealous in the fear of the Lord" (45:23). In this line of zealots for the Lord belongs Elijah (1 Macc. 2:58) and Jehu (II Kings 10:16). In the latter case zeal is expressed through complete extermination of God's enemies.

It may be argued that we are dealing here primarily with passionate zeal for the cause of God which may not necessarily express itself as brutally as in the case of Phinehas, Jehu and Mattathias. This is true to some extent of Elijah (yet compare II Kings 1:9-16)[18] and possibly of the book of Judith. In the latter, however, one should not overlook the reference to Uzziah's words of farewell: "Go in peace, and may the Lord God go before you, to take revenge upon our enemies" (Judith 8:35). Throughout the charming narrative runs the motif: God will accomplish his purpose through the murder of Holofernes at the hand of a humble widow. Judith distinctly sees herself in a historical line of those who were "zealous for thee" (9:4), praying that with her as his instrument God will: "crush their arrogance by the hand of a woman" (9:10). The desecration of the sanctuary is to be avenged (9:13). Whatever may be the germ of historical truth in this folk tale, if any, such a tale would have great impact upon people with the religious convictions of the Jews.

The carriers of this tradition at the time of Christ were the

Zealots. There have been attempts in scholarship to show that Jesus was himself a Zealot, and in reaction to this it became the fashion to play down his contact with the Zealots and the place this option played in his life. As a result of the work of W. R. Farmer,[19] and more recently the definitive work of Martin Hengel on the nationalistic movement and the Zealots, it is evident that any attempt to interpret the New Testament without taking into account this movement leaves out an essential element. Precisely at the time when Jesus was deciding on the nature of his ministry the issues raised by the Zealots were intensely debated. As Hengel puts it: "In the Zealots we are dealing with a relatively well defined movement with individual religious points of view, which influenced the development of Judaism considerably in the decisive years A. D. 6-70."[20]

For "the Zealot the active zeal for God's law is the determining drive of his total outlook on life; with pride he calls himself a Zealot" (Josephus, *Bell.* 4, 161).[21] If Josephus can be trusted at this point the Zealots were patriots whose fanaticism could lead them to give up all scruples, and to pursue their aims without any regard for either their own lives or lives of their enemies. Originally their motivation was purely religious; but as the Maccabean movement changed from a religious revolt to a political rebellion and the various sects and parties came into being the Zealots emerged, possibly from the matrix of the Pharisaic party. At least the Pharisees were on their side on a not insignificant point when they permitted a speedy punishment for someone who had been caught in a marital union with a non-Jew. Furthermore there is additional evidence that Phinehas was held in high regard in some of the writings of the Pharisees. Later, after the destruction of Jerusalem when the outcome of such zeal was all too clear, the Pharisees made a clean break with the remnants of the Zealot party and disclaimed any connection with it.

Jesus' Teaching on the Enemy: Its Formulation

Our interest lies in the relation of Jesus to this position. Surely he knew of it; and, if we accept Cullmann's conclusions, then

Jesus certainly had one disciple from that party, with several others who had leanings in that direction.[22] This can only mean that Jesus constantly confronted this alternative, and a reading of the Gospel supports this impression. Jesus repeatedly faced the temptation of allowing popular demands to mold his conception of what the Messiah should be, for they saw him as breadwinner, political leader, perhaps even as revolutionary king.

Having formed the outlines along which his Messiahship would express itself Jesus was prepared for the rejection of the multitudes and concentrated increasingly on teaching the disciples in smaller, more intimate groups. It is here that the teaching on loving one's enemy first emerges, and in both Luke and Matthew it is a teaching which is born out of Jesus' own experience with people who were at enmity with him. While Luke stresses this more than does Matthew, this motif is not missing in the latter. Luke describes his rejection in Nazareth (chapter 4), the anger of the lawyers and the Pharisees (Luke 6:11), and the beginning of their plot to do away with Jesus as the turning point. After that the smaller group of disciples became the focus of his teaching.

Thus it must be clear that the teaching of Jesus to love the enemy was understood first of all as applying to his disciples. Matt. 5:2 clearly indicates this while in Luke 6:27 the phrase *humin . . . tois akouousin* (you that hear) also restricts it because the word *akouo* has here as elsewhere in the Gospels a restricted meaning—that is, "hear" in a special sense. The earlier statements were addressed to a wider audience. The teaching on love is not left in the realm of sentiments or feelings nor is love to been seen as a principle. The way in which love expresses itself is defined by both Matthew and Luke as follows:

MATTHEW

General Statement:	Love your enemies
Description: How?	Pray for your persecutors

Love Your Enemy

Motivation: Why?	So that you may become sons of your father in heaven Who lets his sun shine and rain fall upon all
	Reciprocal or mutual love brings no reward—even the worst in society (tax-collectors do that)
	Greeting only our brothers is not exceptional (*perisson*)—even the Gentiles do that
	Our goal is to become mature as is our Father in Heaven

LUKE

General Statement:	Love your enemies
Description: How?	Do good to those who hate you
	Bless those who curse you
	Pray for those who treat you spitefully
Examples:	Being hit on the cheek—turn the other
	Your coat is taken—give him your shirt
	Beggar requests alms—give them
	Someone ·steals—do not demand it back
Motivation: Why?	Golden rule
	Superior behavior as compared with sinners
General Statement:	Love your enemies and do good

Motivation: Why?	Great reward
	Sonship
	Your Father is compassionate

We note here a number of variant traditions. Yet we may agree with Walter Bauer that those who would challenge the genuineness of the basic teaching, "love your enemies," and question whether Jesus ever spoke these words, bear the burden of proof.[23] Matthew's account appears to be more original while it appears that Luke has been condensing a source common to Matthew and himself. Matthew gives some of the same examples as does Luke but he places them under his discussion of the talion principle (5:32-42). In this paragraph, often referred to as the nonresistance passage, his line of thought seems to be:

General Statement	Do not resist the evil one
Examples	If someone insults you with a slap on the right cheek—turn the left one towards him
	If someone sues you for your shirt—let him have your coat also
	If a government official forces you to go a mile—go two
	Give to a beggar who asks, and don't refuse the borrower

Paul's Teaching on the Enemy

When we look at the Pauline writings which were, as far as we know, written prior to the Gospels, and constitute the first written commentary on these words of Jesus, we find here a consistent picture. "See that no one pays back wrong for wrong, but always aim at doing the best you can for each other and for all men" (I Thess. 5:15). In a similar vein in Romans 12:17 he writes: "Never pay back evil for evil, aiming at that which is good for all men." Thus the general statement is found also in Paul. Furthermore some of the specific examples are found in

Paul as well, e.g., in the last part of Romans 12 where he deals with the application of love to community life, and especially the way in which the boundless love of Christ expresses itself to those outside the community. It participates in the alleviation of the needs of the saints, pursues hospitality (13), but most radically *agape* love expresses itself towards the enemy thus:

> Bless those who persecute
> Bless and do not curse
> Instead of pursuing vengeance
> Feed the hungry enemy
> Give your thirsty enemy a drink

In the last example Paul is following a Proverb (25:21) of the Old Testament and goes beyond the mere admonition of Christ to share money or clothing. Paul seems to say that the enemy is to be invited to share the dwelling and be given the substance of one's life. When Jesus refers to "greeting" the meaning is much more profound than the shallow greetings modern man tosses over his shoulder; and so also for Paul to share bread and drink indicated a communion on a deeper level than for the modern man. The Negro who works for his right to share a lunch counter with the white man, however, has some appreciation for the deeper meaning of eating with someone.

Likewise the meaning of "blessing" goes beyond the prayer for one's enemy. In intercessory prayer one can recognize the need for repentance and pray for it. In blessing one intercedes on behalf of someone to God that God will bring good into his life. The curse on the other hand is a prayer that God will damn the enemy to perdition and generally commits the speaker to do what he can to bring it about. In antiquity the result of an effectual curse was generally seen immediately or at least soon after it was spoken (e.g., the fig tree, Mark 11:12f).

Paul does not content himself with generalities in Rom. 12. His line of thought moves on to a warning that we are not to continue thinking of our own ingenuity (16); that we are never (*medeni* cf. Rom. 13:8) to pay back evil for evil (17); but to do everything in our power to live at peace with all men (18). When wrongs are done to us we are not to seek revenge but move over and give place to God's vengeance. In the interim we are not to nurse our wounds with the anticipation of the eventual vengeance that will be inflicted upon the enemy, but to extend our love to him through concrete deeds.

The vexatious sentence giving the motivation, "for in so doing you will heap coals of fire upon his head," is a quote from Proverbs. The original expression would appear to go back to an Egyptian repentance ritual in which the tokens demonstrating that a change of mind has taken place were a two-pronged staff and a platter of burning coals upon the head. As the enemy saw these two tokens he realized that reconciliation might now be possible. Paul is not aware of this ritual, although the Proverb certainly has Egyptian origin and thus may reflect a knowledge of this ritual. In Paul's case we must reject any attempt to see a "burning sense of shame" in this image and allow the context to define the meaning of this term allowing for the possibility that the original meaning does not conflict with that of Paul.[24] Paul offers us a way by which we will not allow evil to conquer us, but will conquer it by using means that are good (12:21).

There is certainly some significance to the fact that Paul now turns his attention to the higher powers. Resistance to evil cannot be simply equated with resistance to the higher powers (13:2). The authorities are God's agents working for our good (Rom. 13:4). This does not mean however that they also now define the good for the Christian, for Paul does not grant them supreme authority to define what is good. The Christian remains subject to only one law, and "he who loves his neighbor has satisfied every claim of the law" (13:8). Christians thus are to throw off the deeds of darkness and put on their armor as soldiers of the light (13:12; cf. I John 2:9-11), and that armor is Jesus Christ himself (13:14).

In Colossians Paul has also described the great endowment of the Christian as *agape* (3:14) and it would seem that in Rom. 12 and 13 the themes of "the good" and "love" are intimately interwoven. Basing his exhortation on the mercies of God (Christian behavior is always a response to God's mercies), Paul appeals for a commitment on the part of Christians which will be clearly differentiated from the world, and this commitment will result in their ability to test what is the will of God, namely what is *to agathon* (Rom. 12:1-2). The climax of the appeal comes in the clause, *"eis to dokimadsein . . . "* The ensuing material is Paul's attempt, based on the grace God has given him (3), to spell out what that good is. *Agape* love is transparent in its rejection of the evil, and its alignment with *to agathon* (9). It seeks good for all men, those within the brotherhood, those traveling and in need of hospitality, those weeping, those rejoicing, and those persecuting the Church. To the end of the thirteenth chapter Paul continues this theme (*agathos* or *kalos* occurs in Rom. 12:2, 9, 17, 21; 13:3 (*bis*), 4). The contrast between those working good and evil is sharply drawn toward the end of chapter thirteen.

Knowing that Paul was writing to a church at the heart of the Roman Empire, an empire obtained and sustained by force, it is difficult to miss the point he is making. Perhaps the church has paid too little heed to contextual considerations in interpreting Rom. 13:1-6.[25] The time is certainly ripe for the church to recognize that Paul is not displacing the Lordship of Christ with the demands of Caesar; and that even Paul with his more optimistic view of the state did not grant it as much claim to the Christian's allegiance as modern man does.

If the secular prophets are right it is not a question of whether we will suffer in the future or not. The question is whether we will suffer rather for "well doing, if such should be the will of God, than for doing wrong. For Christ also died for our sins, once and for all. He, the just, died for the unjust, to bring us to God" (I Pet. 3:17-18).

The Relevance of Christ's Life

The pattern for this kind of behavior is stressed especially in Peter as being the behavior of Jesus himself, and in his summary he urges his readers: "Do not repay wrong with wrong, or abuse with abuse; on the contrary retaliate with blessing, for a blessing is the inheritance to which you yourselves are called" (I Peter 3:9).

What is striking about Peter's portrayal of Christian behavior is the extent to which it uses the motif of following Christ (I Pet. 2:21). While we find in Romans 12 many apparent allusions to the teachings of Jesus, Peter abounds with indications of an eyewitness who observed the behavior of Jesus during his own capture, arrest and trial. This becomes for Peter the pattern that Christians are to follow. It has been abundantly illustrated that we are in the presence here of an early Christian catechetical core and the "common catechetical substratum, known to their readers as well as to themselves" no longer needs proof.[26]

This raises the question whether Jesus treated his enemies as he himself urged his followers to treat theirs. In John's description of the cleansing of the temple much discussion has revolved around his use of the whip in an attempt to show that Jesus did not use violence of any kind. To some extent this is motivated by the desire to retain the portrait of "the gentle Jesus, meek and mild," a motive which needs to be rejected. G. H. C. MacGregor's careful study of this passage, and especially his observation that the Greek allows for the possibility that the whip was applied to the animals and not to the people, can be noted even when we see in this action an exercise of Christ's prophetic role against those who desecrate God's house. It is significant that John alone of all the Gospel writers quotes the verse from Psalm 69:10: "The zeal of thy house consumes me" (John 2:17). This verse apparently had no prominence among the Zealots, and the Early Church saw in this Psalm an announcement of Christ's work and suffering (John 15:25; John 19:29).

It is thus not denied that Christian love calls for drastic action by way of prophetic symbolism or sharp words of judgment, such as we find in Matthew 23.[27] Such action may offend our stoic sensitivity and certainly is disagreeable to a modern age steeped in non-directiveness, but it does not change the consistency of the New Testament picture of dealing with an enemy. It certainly does extreme violence to all sound canons of hermeneutics to use such passages to support Christian participation in retaliation and war.

The incident with the Samaritans reported in Luke 9:51-56 shows a contrast between the approach Jesus took toward acts of inhospitality and those taken by the prophets Elijah (II Kings 1) and Elisha (II Kings 2:23f). Since Luke reports the conversation which took place with Moses and Elijah on the Mount of Transfiguration and the exuberance of the disciples with this experience, their rebuff led James and John to consider following Elijah's example to call down fire from heaven to destroy the rude Samaritans. The fact that Samaritans were more friendly toward the Romans only added to the racial and religious factors which caused the Jews to consider them with contempt. But Jesus will have nothing to do with the truculent proposal of the disciples. Marcion and some of the other manuscripts have additions here. What is clear is that Jesus rebuked the disciples for their proposal. The word Luke uses to describe the action of Jesus (*epitimao*) is clear and forceful. It is used of demons (Mark 9:25) and in other instances where the disciples need to be rebuked (Mark 8:33). In his rebuking of the demons, of the elements of nature (Mark 4:39), and of his disciples the unconditional lordship of Christ is mightily revealed. The differences between Christ and his method of dealing with enemies is here clearly differentiated from that of Elijah.

In the passion narrative the author of Peter saw the best illustration of the way in which Christians are to relate themselves to their enemies. When we examine the accounts of the passion it is striking that no Gospel writer indicates that Jesus literally fulfilled his own advice. John indeed informs us that when Jesus was struck in the face by one of the officers, Jesus did not turn the other cheek but replied: "If I have spoken wrongly, bear witness to the wrong; but if I have spoken rightly, why do you strike me?" (John 18:23). We would see in this some evidence that the illustrations Jesus gives in the Sermon on the Mount are to be taken seriously but not in a legalistic, slavishly literal sense. There may be occasions when turning the other cheek may infuriate the enemy and thus worsen the relationship. In the presence of such an insult it is not wrong to ask the reason for it; Jesus recommends that instead of an impetuous response to slug back, one cultivate the ability to endure punishment. Turning the other cheek is doing something about the insult, it is not simply ignoring it.

Before one too hastily rules out the redemptive value of such an approach one should look at the evidence in modern psychotherapy which has shown some amazing results in inviting the patient to "hit the other cheek." The Christian Gospel affirms that one can only do this when we are motivated by Christ's love and that his power makes it possible for us to be the therapeutic agents who absorb the hostility rather than inflict it upon others. The redemptive value of personally absorbing evil thus has direct relevance for the way in which Christians are urged to deal with their enemies. Where there is sin and transgression it can only be overcome if someone takes the beating for it; perhaps only if the innocent suffer for the guilty.

Paul, according to Acts 23:1-5, also did not literally follow this admonition. It would seem in fact that Paul lost his temper in this instance, and while his appeal is to the law and to justice he actually reviles the high priest. The bystanders point this out to him when they ask, "Would you revile God's high priest?" (Acts 23:4), whereupon Paul claims that he has acted in ignorance and admits a transgression of the law. It is apparent that his norm for this discussion is the law which is recognized by the Sanhedrin which he is addressing.

Both of these examples are drawn from encounters that Jesus and Paul had with governing authorities; but both deal with Jewish religious leaders not with pagan governors. Is it farfetched to assume that we have evidence here that both Jesus and Paul experienced the greatest difficulty in their expressions in the presence of the religious leaders of the people who were betraying their responsibility? Whatever we may conclude we note that the illustrations used in the Sermon on the Mount were not applied in a legalistic manner.

This does not mean that the basic teaching, "love your enemy," is denied. It only warns us that there may be a variety of ways in which love expresses itself. On the cross Jesus prayed for his enemies: "Father forgive them for they know not what they do" (Luke 23:34). While the saying has only scattered manuscript support it is in keeping with the word of forgiveness God spoke in Jesus Christ. Stephen likewise, the first martyr, prayed that God would not punish his murderers (Acts 7:60). Jesus absorbed the insults of the thieves who were crucified with him (Matt. 24:44; Mark 15:32), and according to Luke this resulted in the conversion of what we might call the first member of the church (Luke 23:39-43).

Later in the book of Acts we find the description of the conversion of the Ethiopian eunuch. A man schooled in power politics who was baffled by the account of the suffering servant who would "not open his mouth" but allow himself to be led to the slaughter like a lamb (Acts 8:26f). Thus this scandalous aspect of the Gospel became the cutting edge of the church's mission. And in the corporate life of the church the standard of forgiveness was "just as (*kathōs*) the Lord has forgiven you, so also you must forgive—over all of these, endue yourselves with love, which is the bond of perfectness" (Col. 3:13). "Let all bitterness and wrath and anger and clamor and slander be put away from you, with all malice and be kind to one another, tenderhearted, forgiving one another, as God in Christ forgave you" (Eph. 4:31-32).

WHO IS MY ENEMY?

The history of exegesis reveals many attempts to split hairs on the issue of loving one's enemy. Whereas the teaching of Jesus on this subject seems to have been provoked by the tendency of some Jews to teach that killing was forbidden while hating to the point of killing was not, modern casuistry reverses this by saying that Jesus forbids us to hate whereas murdering one's enemy is necessary for survival.[28] General David Shoup recently testified: "I don't think you have to hate to be a good fighter. We fight any enemy the President designates. . . . We don't teach our men to hate. Hate I consider an internal sin." American Christians certainly have not been a particularly noble example in the degree to which they have taken Christ's teaching seriously on this point. That the Cross represents God's way of dealing with human enmities as well as human enmity against God may be admitted creedally, but this has little bearing on the position the Church has taken. American Christians consequently would think of Communists when the word "enemy" is used and have joined themselves with frightening alacrity to campaigns with the goal "Know Your Enemy." Nor have Christians been particularly outstanding in the things they have said about such issues as "instant massive retaliation," "obliteration bombing," "preemptive war," etc. Small wonder then that J. K. Jessup concludes in a national magazine: "Christianity as a whole has nothing of commanding uniqueness to say to the world on (the subject of atomic warfare)."[29] Even the recent assembly of the World Council of Churches at New Delhi, when it attempted to address itself to this issue, came forth with an eviscerated statement reflecting much more political considerations than any light the Gospel might conceivably throw on this subject.[30]

Our major ethical treatises evade almost entirely the question of enemy-love and instead concentrate on justice and the present responsibility in human order.[31] Observing in this context the ambitious and courageous actions taken by atheists like Bertrand Russell and the psychologists and psychiatrists in this nation who profess no particular creed one is tempted to despair.[32] Is the Church really so inextricably bound up with the state that the state's enemy is likewise the enemy of the Church? Must our attitude merely be a carbon copy of the attitude found in the Pentagon? Is it perhaps a tragic watering down of the Gospel through stoicism that we glorify the virtues of the soldier and his "courage" in laying down his life for freedom[33] while we gloss over the courage Jesus displayed in his refusal to call armies to his defense (Matt. 26:53f), calling his disciples instead to a regal loyalty "not of this world" (John 18:36)?

We have been repeatedly reminded in past decades that the New Testament church lived in the breathless exuberance of victory over the powers (cf. Eph. 6:10-18) and in basic allegiance to Christ whom it recognized as Lord. Few however have drawn the consequences of this allegiance for political loyalties in the modern world. Whatever will be done in the future on this question will call for courage and moral strength. If the Church does not believe firmly in Christ's relevance for this age it will not be able to make that witness. Who can doubt that at this hour in history a radical solution to the problem of human conflict is crying for an audience?

In former times those who studied the Bible were told that the radical solutions to human conflict proposed there could apply only to a few select people, perhaps those in monasteries. By applying Biblical teachings to social problems one might destroy society itself. Thus the so-called Christian realists saw it as their responsibility to jettison Biblical ethics and allow prudential maxims (masked under noble words like justice) to guide them. In this day, however, there is serious doubt whether anything is more irresponsible than the faith that is invested in the philosophy that enemies can be conquered only by weapons of warfare. The Church, sometimes reluctantly, sometimes all too eagerly, used to align itself with the state in the fight for "freedom and justice." In the twentieth century such an alignment becomes impossible for we are told that after the next war there will be no freedom, probably no democracy, and certainly no just and lasting peace.

What then are the values that cause the Church to reject the teaching of the New Testament and align itself with the state in this "religious crusade"? The Church's ethical teaching has remained in the sixteenth century while the world has changed so drastically that the solutions proposed then are lame solutions to our problems if not blatant denials of the Lordship of Christ today. It is not proposed here that changes in modern weaponry are the decisive factors in our reading of the New Testament. Christians are not interested primarily in survival; but for this very reason we ought to be able to read the message of the Gospel with clearer insight today. At least we should not begin with the assumption that Jesus did not take into consideration the hard realities of life. It is we who are influenced by idealism—

not He; it is we who have introduced a clash between justice and love—not He. Above all He was primarily interested in *the will of God* and demonstrated in his own life that it can be found above the din of propagandists, militarists, religious zealots, and the orthodox who have aligned themselves with Caesar.

It is here also that pacifism and nonresistance need to be corrected. Their misinterpretation of the words of Jesus, "do not resist evil", is after all corrected to some extent by both James and Peter when they warn the Christians to resist the devil (James 4:7; I Peter 5:9). The Gospel does not call us to close our eyes to evil, but it offers us a new way to overcome it. It does not try to impress us with the extent to which evil permeates all that we do and drive us merely to seek the mercy of God's face. Rather it seeks to impress us with the magnitude of Christ's victory over the power of evil and invites us to follow in the radical solution he proposed to the problem of evil.

The theme of victory is predominant in early Christian literature. The early Christians were confident that in Christ this victory had been accomplished and that in the Church it would continue to be accomplished. If the Church believes that this conviction was vitiated either by a false understanding of the complexity of the problem of human life, or by an overzealous affirmation of what Jesus Christ really accomplished; or if it believes that the way of life Jesus proposed was determined by his naive conception that men would not long live together on the earth before the final conflagration, then we could honestly say so. We should not claim his Lordship if we are not willing to do what he said, or what the early Church believed he said.

Given this conception of the enemy and the victory available to us, we may however be forced radically and repeatedly to redefine what this means in modern culture. Having now admitted the Russian church into the World Council of Churches we are, however, in a position to do just that. We are in a position joyfully to declare that the Church penetrates behind every curtain and consists of believers everywhere; that the people of God stands as a "third race" above East and West, and that the Christian's primary group loyalty is not to nation, family, or

race, but to the body of Christ. Repeatedly Jesus declared that
to place family ties or responsibilities above him was to dis-
qualify one as a disciple (Lk. 9:57-62; 14:26). We might commit ourselves to the simple pledge that at no price would we
ever compromise our basic loyalty to Jesus Christ by adding to
the hatred and enmities existing in this world. The Church
might devote itself to the task of one great peace effort in an
attempt to transcend the narrow nationalism which has for so
long plagued all of man's attempts to live peacefully on the
earth.

Further we would admit the possibility that seen in Biblical
light the enemy whom we are empowered and authorized
through Christ to love and forgive may dwell in our home town,
in our state, in the Pentagon, just as well as he may dwell in
Peking or the Kremlin. The enemy is after all anyone who allows himself to be used of Satan to destroy the Church.

In the literature surveyed there exists something of a consensus in asserting that the concept of "the enemy" cannot be
narrowed down; but that it includes personal, national and religious enemies.[34] Love for the neighbor definitely includes the
enemy if indeed in Christ's teaching it does not yield to love for
the enemy (parable of the Good Samaritan). Is not by definition
anyone who attempts to set aside, implicitly or explicitly, the
teaching, "love your enemy," an "enemy of the Cross"? Is it not
on the Cross that we see most clearly that enemies cannot be
changed by hatred but only by nonviolent action driven by love,
and that the demonic circle of hatred cannot be broken by anything but loving sacrifice?[35] Thus we may never be content with
"knowing the enemy." We must allow ourselves to be instruments of God's love toward him.

To address ourselves to these problems is an urgent and chal-
lenging task. What we will find hardest perhaps is to divest ourselves of the encrustations of past centuries. If anything is clear,
however, it is surely that St. Augustine, St. Thomas, Martin
Luther, the Anabaptists, John Calvin or John Wesley have not
given us a solution to the problem of living with an enemy which
applies to us today. The question is whether Jesus Christ has.

Some Proposed Solutions

Is the testimony we have to Christ's answer in the New Testament adequate for us today? To this question we must address

FOOTNOTES

[1] Hermann Gunkel, *Israelitisches Heldentum und Kriegsfrömmigkeit im Alten Testament* (Göttingen: Vandenhoeck und Rupprecht, 1916), 2, 3, 23, 25.

[2] G. H. C. MacGregor, *The New Testament Basis of Pacifism* (London, 1936); C. H. Dodd, "The Theology of Christian Pacifism" in *The Basis of Christian Pacifism* (1938). In F. Kattenbusch, the last few pages deal with some of the earlier statements by German and English scholars on this issue. More recent treatments are those of Jean Lassere, *War and the Gospel* (Herald Press, 1962); Walter Besinert, *Krieg, Kriegsdienst und Kriegsdienstverweigerung nach der Botschaft des Neuen Testaments* (Stuttgart, 1952); and Walter Dignath, *Kirche, Krieg, Kriegsdienst,* (Hamburg, 1955).

[3] Michael Waldmann, *Die Feindesliebe in der antiken Welt und im Christenthum* (Vienna, 1902).

[4] Stephan Randlinger, *Die Feindesliebe nach dem natürlichen und positiven Sittengesetz* (Paderborn, 1906).

[5] Eugen Bach, *Die Feindesliebe nach dem natürlichen und dem übernatürlichen Sittengesetz* (Kempten, 1913).

[6] F. Kattenbsruch, "Uber die Feindesliebe im Sinne des Christentums," *Theologische Studien und Kritiken* 89 (1916) 1-70.

[7] Paul Fiebig, "Jesu Worte über die Feindesliebe in Zusammenhang mit den wichtigsten rabbinischen Parallelen erläutert," *Theologische Studien und Kritiken* (1918) 91:30-64, cited from 64.

[8] Tertullian wrote: "Our individual, extraordinary, and perfect goodness consists in loving our enemies. To love one's friends is common practice, to love one's enemies only among Christians" (*ad Scapulam* 1) cited in Hans Haas, *Idee und Ideal der Feindesliebe in der ausserchristlichen Welt . . .* (Leipzig, 1927) 3. In the variant reading Justin Martyr supplies for Mt. 5:46; Luke 6:32 the conviction is expressed that Christians are following a new way: "If you love the ones loving you, what new thing are you doing?" (*ti kainon poieite,* Apol. I 15, see Walter Bauer, "Das Gebot der Feindesliebe und die Alten Christen," *Zeitschrift für Theologie und Kirche* [1917] 27:51). Because of the popular idea that love for enemies is a uniquely Christian teaching, one does not expect to find it among non-Christians, but our integrity demands that we admit that we encounter it virtually nowhere in the Christian world. (Haas, *op. cit.,* 3).

[9] See the article *miseo* by Michel in *Theologisches Woerterbuch zum Neuen Testament,* ed. by Kittel and Friedrich (hereafter *TWNT*) 4:687-698.

[10] Article on "echthros," *TWNT,* 2:810-814.

[11] *Hist.* V. 5, "Apud ipsos fides obstinata, misericordia in promptu, sed adversus omnes alios hostile odium."

[12] E. J. Sutcliffe, "Hatred at Qumran," *Revue de Qumran* (1960) 2:355, p. 355.

[13] Victor Hasler, "Das Herzstück der Bergpredigt, Matth. 5:21-46," *Theologische Zeitschrift* (1959) 15:101. O. Betz, "Donnersöhne, Menschenfischer

und der Davidische Messias," *Revue de Qumran* (1961) 3:52 also takes this position.

14 Luke 14:26 deserves comment in this connection. It would seem that the word "hate" here means the same as it does in Deuteronomy 21:15-17 in which a man's attitude toward two wives, "the one loved the other hated" is described. Here it means merely preference, not hatred in the psychological sense. But such preference, as I John especially makes clear, is actually an expression of hatred. Perhaps this also applies to the argument so often heard that one can kill in war without hatred. Hating one's brother can mean merely to see his need, yet close one's heart against him (I John 3:17).

15 *Op. cit.*, 353. The attitude the Essenes took towards war is also of interest in this connection. Philo (*Quod Omnis Probus Liber sit*, 78) indicates that they would have nothing to do with the manufacture and sale of weapons of violence. Yet Josephus mentions at least one Essene who was a warrior and lauds the heroism of the Essenes in the war against the Romans. Millar Burrows thinks that the attitude of the Essenes and the Covenanters changed with the circumstances (*The Dead Sea Scrolls*, 292). Can Philo and Josephus be reconciled when we recall that Philo has something of a pacifist strain in his thought whereas the latter tends to exalt the heroism of battle? Hippolytus indicates that some people called the Essenes Zealots. As Millar Burrows notes some of the documents of Qumran "breathe a militant spirit that would have satisfied the Maccabees or the Zealots" and this is all we are trying to establish (*ibid.*).

16 Kurt Schubert, "Bergpredigt und Texte von en Fescha," *Theologische Quartalschrift* (1955) 135:320-337. See also Frank M. Cross, *The Ancient Library of Qumran and Modern Studies* (Garden City, 1958) 45, 47. G. Vermes, *Discovery in the Judaean Desert* (New York, 1956) concludes that "there is no question of their general participation in the Jewish Revolt of 68" (101), but leaves the extent to which they resorted to armed resistance an open question. His treatment of the historical relationship and roots of the Sect is excellent throwing much light on its relationship to the Zealots (see especially, 90). It is one of the oddities of history that the Maccabees were enrolled in the catalogue of Christian saints. When one exalts their heroism and is encouraged to "learn from them to die for the truth" (Augustine) the question of Jesus' new teaching is bypassed. Elias Bickermann (*Der Gott der Makkabäer*, Berlin, 1937) credits the Maccabees with the preservation of monotheism since he views the Maccabean conflict primarily as a civil war (137f). Many Christians would be sympathetic to such a view but it is debatable whether the real cause of Christ has ever been advanced by the sword.

17 Otto Betz (*op. cit.*) has carefully traced the history of Genesis 49:5f. and shown how Simon and heirs were idealized and their violence actually lauded.

18 The association of Elijah with Zealotism is difficult to date with precision. Jeremias (article on Elijah in *TWNT*, 2:935, 21f) places the association of Phinehas and Elijah into post New Testament times, although he notes that other rabbis saw him as a "kriegerischen Erlöser, der die Welt Mächte überwindet" (*TWNT*, 2:933, 19). Jeremias glides too lightly over 1 Macc. 2:58; Sirach 48:2. It is difficult to ascertain how early the Rabbis began to criticize Elijah for his zeal and interpret his removal from prophetic office as punishment for it. What seems certain is that the people were divided on this

matter during the first century (S. Schechter, *Some Aspects of Rabbinic Theology* (London, 1909) 204f). Is this perhaps the reason, in addition to his modesty, why John the Baptist denied being Elijah? Martin Hengel, *Die Zeloten* (1961) 160-172, deals with the Jewish sources that touch on this matter.

[19] *Maccabees, Zealots and Josephus* (New York, 1957).

[20] *Op. cit.,* 5.

[21] Stumpff, article on *zēloō* in TWNT, 2:886.

[22] *The State in the New Testament* (New York: Charles Scribner's Sons, 1956) chapter 1. The position of H. A. Fast *(op. cit.)* that the revolutionary movement played virtually no part in the answer Jesus gave to the question of how to deal with an enemy is no longer tenable. Anyone who sought to reform Judaism or had a high respect for it was confronted with the basic question: When will Roman might give way to God's kingship in Palestine? This is the reason that Palestine created such a headache for the otherwise ingenious Roman provincial system and the celebrated *pax Romana* was broken only by the Jews.

[23] *Op. cit.,* 37.

[24] For an attempt to deal more fully with this passage the reader is referred to an article, "Coals of Fire" appearing in *New Testament Studies* (July, 1963 pp. 337-350). Since this paper was written Krister Stendahl has also published a study entitled "Hate Non-Retaliation, and Love" in *Harvard Theological Review* (1962) 55:343-355, which came to my attention too late to draw into this discussion.

[25] See F. Keienburg, *Die Geschichte der Auslegung von Römer 13:1-7* (1952).

[26] E. G. Selwyn, *The First Epistle of St. Peter* (London, 1952) 406f. He notes (412) that "the verbal parallels are closest in the statement of the law of non-requital (I Pet. 3:9; Romans 12:17; I Thess. 5:15); and if I Peter is the borrower here (p. 413), dependence is more likely to be on I Thessalonians than on Romans, owing to Silvanus' association with I Peter and I Thessalonians." He prefers as "the more probable explanation" that "behind all three there lies common catechetical material" *(ibid.).* In I Peter's stress on *agathopoieo* the same theme Paul carries through in Romans 12 seems to shine through. The Christian life is "doing good" as this good has been defined and made possible by Christ.

[27] Those who take offense at Jesus' denunciation of the Pharisees as recorded in Matthew should note that an expression of woe is a far cry from a curse formula. The latter is missing almost entirely from primitive Christian literature (even in the Apocalypse) and reappears in the post-apostolic period. See L. Brun, *Segen und Fluch im Urchristentum* (Oslo, 1932) 34, 83, 90. Parallels to this abound in Jewish literature. See the Levitical curses in the Manual of Discipline (Vermes, *op. cit.,* 135). This may be maintained in spite of Montefiore's statement that Jesus' teaching would make sense if it were backed up with one kind deed to a Pharisee and Walter Kaufman's recent claim that "the new note struck in the New Testament is personal revenge and eternal damnation" (*Critique of Religion and Philosophy,* New York) 180.

[28] E. T. Thompson, *The Sermon on the Mount and its Meaning for Today,* (Richmond, 1956) 69, illustrates that one can kill without hatred, thus "Jesus does not command soldiers to abandon their trade" (64).

29 *Life,* 39:26:142.

30 *Christian Century,* January 10, 1962, p. 57f, reported by Howard Schomer, see especially p. 58.

31 E.g., Paul Ramsey, *Basic Christian Ethics* (New York, 1953).

32 See the article, "Breaking the Thought Barrier," by Jerome Frank in *Psychiatry* (1960) 23:245-266 who in another address asks why the church is not saying something to this problem.

33 See the interesting evidence of the influence of Epictetus' *Enchiridion* in the battles of the world given in the introduction of Higginson's edition (Liberal Arts Press, 1948). Max Pohlenz, *Die Stoa* (Göttingen, 1948), in a preface written in 1943 says: "In the fall of 1914 a dear young friend of mine who had previously read Epictetus with me and was then an officer in France wrote: 'When oppression and danger threaten, then I resort to Epictetus: I test them as to their content and if I come to the conclusion that this does not touch my inner being then I say: You are only a conception and do not concern me. Then it obtains no power over me.' It was his last letter. Soon thereafter he gave his life for his fatherland like a real German in stoic sense of duty."

34 Exegetically one can surely speak of a consensus on this point. In addition to the literature already cited we may cite: Hugh Montefiore, "Thou Shalt Love Thy Neighbour as Thyself," *Novum Testamentum* (July, 1962) 5:157-170, who confines it, however, to Jesus and thinks he detects a change in the early church on this point. Both Martin Rade, "Der Nächste," *Jülicher Festgabe* (Tübingen, 1927) 70-79 (see 74, 79) and Heinrich Weinel, "Die Nächstenliebe," in *Archiv für die gesamte Psychologie* (1932) 247-260 (see 260), agree that the term "neighbor" and "enemy" are all-inclusive and are in no way restricted either by Jesus or anyone in the early church. Rade suggests that the Greek term *plesion* should be translated "der Andere," in German (*op. cit.,* 74).

35 J. Goettman traces the theme of nonviolence in the Bible and concludes that the appeal to nonviolence pervades the Scriptures. The message of the Bible centers on the voluntary offering of the Lamb of God, who refrained from asking for twelve legions of angels and rebuked Peter's recourse to the sword. His essay, "Histoire de la non-violence dans la Bible," in *Bible et vie Chretienne* (1961) 41:58-73 is known to me only through *New Testament Abstracts* (1962) 6:214.

10

CHRIST'S MINISTRY
AND OUR DISCIPLESHIP

John J. Vincent

THE PROBLEM OF THEOLOGICAL ORIENTATION

THE theologians so far cannot be said to have made a very good showing in the nuclear debate. The challenge of a radically new situation has caught them at a time of uncomfortable transition. Consequently, many of the views of theologians have been all but entirely determined by the variables of strategic or political thinking. This has not been due to insincerity or obstinacy. It has been due to two facts. First, the theological categories available to us at present either do not help us in this situation, or else are themselves now open to question. Second, there has been little attempt so far to engage biblical-theological perspectives.

Some Categories Commonly Used

Here, the notion of the "Just War" is probably the most common. The revival of the "Just War" idea, however, has been almost entirely confined to the American Continent, and to one or two outstanding writers in it. The Roman Catholic discussion, when it has been concerned with nuclear weapons, has hardly mentioned the doctrine, or at least has admitted its inadequacy.[1] It is therefore all the more interesting to find the notion resurrected in Protestant thinking. My own Methodist Church has been discussing for five years whether or not its Statement on Peace and War, approved in 1957, and based mainly on the Just War idea, does or does not imply unilateralism. But in general the idea has only been considered to be rejected.[2]

The World Council of Churches in general has concluded that the Just War concept is no longer useful. The First Assembly at Amsterdam in 1948 stated that war was "contrary to the will of God" and that

> "Even though entering a war may be a Christian's duty in particular circumstances, modern warfare with its mass destruction can never be an act of justice."

This left us with the difficult possibility that, while war could never now be fought for a *just* cause, yet Christians might still find themselves engaged in it for other reasons. Wars could not be "just," but they might be "justifiable."

Paul Ramsey's great achievement[3] is to point out that in fact this type of reasoning leaves the politicians wholly free to do what they like, and engage in war for good reasons or bad. If there is to be war—and most ecumenical Christians, being Barthians or Niebuhrians, are not particularly optimistic about preventing war—then let us at least state on what grounds and in what circumstances and in what ways it must be fought. There is reason in this, if there are to be wars. But the whole weight of world opinion at present is that war itself is outmoded and must be avoided at all costs. Apart from this, a theory which has no obvious justification in the New Testament, and which arose out of necessities wholly unlike those either of New Testament times or of our own, can hardly be expected to answer today's needs.

Other theological "principles" have been brought into the nuclear debate with extraordinary results. The Commission of the World Council of Churches that eventually produced the two Study Documents on the problem evidently felt the need to find some kind of biblical foundation for current scientific, political and military writers who speak of the need for "discipline," "moderation" or "discrimination." Their conclusion, based on a Calvinism still unenlightened by John Wesley, is that God Himself is "discriminatory," and therefore prefers His followers to be the same. Thus, since God discriminates between men, the Christians should discriminate between the relative horrors of nuclear warfare, and plump for Limited Nuclear War (for which, two years ago, military apologists were still to be found).[4]

Meantime, a group of British theologians were constructing a theological edifice to justify the same military position on the basis of a completely opposite theological principle.[5] This was the idea that "God saves by many or by few"—that is, that He does not discriminate between halfhearted and wholehearted disciples (Constantinians and pacifists, they might have added), and somehow gets His Kingdom advanced by both groups making their mutually irreconcilable contributions to Christian social action. God sorts it all out in the end. But meantime, the Church is generally better advised for safety's sake to go with the Many, who do not take the commands of Jesus too seriously but are good and useful people to have around, rather than with the Few, who think that the Sermon on the Mount is to be taken literally and applied in life to the destruction of society in general.

One therefore approached a study seminar which began with two theological concepts as attractive and debatable as "*kerygma*" and "*ethos*" with some slight misgiving.[6] There is an obvious immediate relevance in such juxtaposition. Our policies seem to be determined by our commitment as nations and individuals to a sub- or post-Christian ethos, rather than by our allegiance to the *kerygma*, the Word which has been given us to proclaim.

Yet here, too, I would venture to think that we are in danger both of beginning with the wrong point and also of reaching the wrong conclusions.

Take the notion of the *kerygma*. I happen to be one of those who have greeted with joy the occasional borderline blasphemies which have appeared in recent years questioning the adequacy of the New Testament foundation of the *kerygma* concept. Dodd, like Barth, has no aspirations to divinity. Blasphemy pleases him more than adulation. And the *kerygma* idea has probably served its purpose and must be allowed quietly to retire from the theological battleground.

Even were the *kerygma* idea a wholly watertight theological position in terms of the New Testament evidence, however, it would, I think, still be true that its influence in the field of theology has not been entirely to the good. In the hands of the reactionary (I dare not say fundamentalist-inclined, much less "orthodox"), it has seemed to be the biblical rubberstamp on all forms of confessional revivalism, doctrinal obscurantism, and theological purism. It has confirmed our current predisposition to regard correct doctrine as more important than correct behavior. It has led us to believe again that, provided our "message" was right, all other things would be granted unto us. It has not led to political and social involvement. In the hands of the Bultmann followers, it has become the "essential element" in the New Testament, that which remains when the "myth" has been excluded. In the mouths of the existentialists, it has constituted that "truth" to which response was to be made. In a word, it has taken the place of Christ and of discipleship. It has become itself the new "myth" which needs to be demythologised.[7]

Again, if there are cautionary things to be said about *kerygma*, are there not, even in the company of enlightened American theologians, who know the "facts of today," some good things to be said about "ethos"? I wonder whether the pessimism of Reinhold Niebuhr has not led to an over-scepticism about the possibilities of redeeming the ethos, stemming out of a hypersensitiveness at attributing the good in American society to Christian influence. When one reads, for instance, Robert W. Tucker's study of the historical and contemporary American "doctrine" of the Justifiable War,[8] one cannot simply conclude that this whole "American way of life" and its attitudes to aggression and the rest is simply to be dismissed as a wilful perversion of Christianity. Indeed, it may well be that so long as the radical Christians continue to address the morass of "American ethos" from the ivory tower of their unassailable and untouchable "message," just so long will that message fall on deaf ears. Does Christ not come to redeem the ethos? And if so, *how*? If our thinking is determined by our "ethos" rather than our Gospel, then at least part of our persuasion must be addressed in terms acceptable by those living under the spell of the "ethos." And that implies an incarnation of the "message," if not an adulteration of the "doctrine," which will at least allow Christ to become "all things" to those in the morass. Such a "condescension" is an essential part of any evangelism or witness.

The Use of Biblical Categories

At any rate, the return to biblical theological categories indicated in the present volume is to be applauded. Biblical theology has contributed some of the most exciting elements in the present thinking of the Church. It has yet to make its full contribution to the actual life of the Church. However, biblical theological categories must only be employed when the place they occupy within the whole of New Testament theology is recognized. As James Barr insists so devastatingly, the mere study of word-occurrences or root-meaning does not entitle one to talk of this or that "concept," much less to assume that the idea can be taken over as a definitive one into theology.[9] Necessarily, theology and theologians seek dominant motifs or phenomena. Isolated elements must be seen as part of them. In this sense, the *kerygma* is legitimate and welcome—except that it reduces what the New Testament says to what the earliest Christians thought to be the most decisive elements.

Thus, it seems to me, we cannot receive an answer to our problem of war or society or violence or animosity *simply* by looking for these elements in the New Testament and finding out what it says about them. We must take the New Testament seriously both as an historical document and as a theological one. It seems to me that many of the pacifist statements I have seen make this mistake. To begin with the attitude of the Bible to war or violence or anything else is putting the cart before the horse. With the possible exception of the latter, the books on pacifism by MacGregor, Rutenber, and Ferguson all more or less assume that the New Testament attitude to violence and participation in war can be taken as a single issue, argued or arguable on the basis of six or seven individual texts, none of them dealing intentionally with the issue in question, and all of them being pressed into service within an area which was not the area of prime concern to the writers of the New Testament.[10]

The attitude of Jesus towards the zealots, or the attitude of the early Christians to a friendly or hostile Roman government, are all interesting enough matters. But they are features and aspects of something much wider, and they are present at all only because of the necessity to relate that something-much-wider to specific needs and situations that compelled comment and commitment in areas that were not the prime concern of discipleship. The New Testament basis of pacifism would have to be demonstrated in terms of the whole life, mission and ministry of Christ and His disciples, and would then only be one implication of that ministry within a specific area, and that, indeed, an area which is not dictated by discipleship itself but imposed upon it from outside.

Is there, then, an overall category within which we may listen to what the New Testament has to say to us on our present problems, which might avoid these difficulties?

I believe that we may find such a category in the New Testament conception of the ongoing work of Christ. Since Form Criticism, we have assumed that the Gospels were written not simply to describe the historical acts of Jesus, but also to describe the present faith of the Church as to the activity of Christ in the Spirit. The early Church believed that what was then true "in the days of his flesh" was now true in the days of the Church and the Spirit. Naturally, the Gospels do not tell us the whole of Christ's ongoing activity; but they contain the main lines of it. If we are to discover the activity of Christ in His world today, then we must discover the main lines of His activity in the Gospels and in the New Testament.

This is the starting point for my recent book, *Christ in a Nuclear World*.[11] For the sake of creating some kind of working rule, I there summarize five main aspects of Christ's ongoing work and activity:

1. Christ is wherever His deeds are done. Messiahship consists in the accomplishment of the "Deeds" the Father commands.
2. Christ is present in His ministry of healing, servanthood and redemption.

3. Christ is mysteriously present, being dealt with, ministered unto or spurned in the person of others.
4. Christ is on the cross, suffering in and with mankind, redemptively.
5. Christ is ruling His universe, both openly and secretly.

These five "main lines" may be characterized as Servanthood, Ministry, Mystery, Suffering and Rule.

It seems to me that many divergent elements in contemporary theological thought may be found to converge in some such guiding category as this. The elements of Righteous Man or Remnant, Prophetic Healer, Divine Wisdom, Suffering Servant, and Divine Word—all present in the Old Testament or in pre-New Testament Judaism—may be found to have their "fulfilment" more or less in each of the five "lines." They describe and delineate the areas in which God's grace is operative in Christ.

But what, we must ask here, does all this imply for the Church? The notion of Christ's activity in the world may be right or wrong. But we still have to make our decisions and determine our policies. How are we to do this?

At this stage, we must bring in the realm which corresponds on the human side to the ongoing activity of Christ on the Divine side. What shall it be labeled? Already, several studies of the New Testament conception of the Church and of the ministry have availed themselves of several of the leading "lines."[12] But to take "Servanthood," "Ministry" or even "The Church" as the overall category is already to limit what is to be said. I believe that the term "discipleship" is the best one. By it we shall try to bring the human, ethical activity and decisions of the Church into the realm of the ministry of Christ.

THE NATURE OF DISCIPLESHIP

The word discipleship has been called into service in a variety of senses. I understand by it that relationship which existed between the early disciples and Jesus Christ, which was continued in the early Church. Discipleship as such has had many detractors, particularly from modern theologians. It has had even more who regarded it as beneath consideration. Modern biblical theologians, especially Americans, have a "thing" about it, not unnaturally, for its influence has not been all for the good in American Church history.

I shall not take time now to attempt any rehabilitation of the Discipleship idea in terms of contemporary theology. This I have said something about elsewhere.[13] Nor yet shall I occupy time with detailed considerations concerning the value and authenticity of various sayings. This is not because I consider these matters unimportant, but because they could not possibly be covered in a brief paper, and because I have dealt with them in a forthcoming book.[14]

We may discern the same five characteristics in Discipleship as we found in summarizing Christ's ongoing ministry.

1. *Servanthood.* As Messiahship consists in Christ's "being with God," as His Servant, discipleship consists in "being wtih Christ" as His servant. Mark 3:14 gives the first part of its threefold description of discipleship as "He chose twelve, that they might be with Him," or "as His companions" (NEB). The whole Gospel story is the story of Jesus and of these men, of the destiny which the Lord first acted out and which, through their adherence to Him, became the disciples' destiny also. Discipleship is Christ-related existence. That is the first thing to say. The disciple is not the important person: Christ is, Christ and His "work." Therefore, the New Testament does not answer ethical or moral questions except by referring them to the Christ in whom alone the disciples or the Church have their existence. Again, the New Testament does not answer questions about Christology or soteriology or eschatology except by referring them away from the question altogether to the person, work and life of Christ. Discipleship is the key to these things, as discipleship simply means "being with" one who is alone the key to the new statement of all these things which becomes Christianity. There is, to be explicit, no answer to moral questions or dilemmas except by referring the questioner through discipleship to the Christ to whom all are to be discipled. Moreover, the Christ to whom the disciple is thus "discipled" is Christ not through "status" ("Are you the Christ?") but through activity, through

deeds. This is the significance of Caesarea Philippi—not that the disciples come to conclude something about Jesus' Messiahship, but that that Messiahship is revealed as a *Way*, a *Destiny*, a *Deed*, which is to be completed and which is then to become the Way, Destiny and Deed of the disciple (Mark 8:27-38).[15]

It is not a crude "Adoptionism" when writers of modern Christologies like Vincent Taylor and Oscar Cullmann draw attention to the facts that Christ "becomes" Messiah by doing the deeds which the Father wills Messiahship to consist in—and that the kind of Messiah Jesus is receives its shape from the things which Jesus actually does or suffers.[16] That is to say, there is no "propositional" or "substantive" concept called Messiahship which exists outside of Jesus as Messiah which He "fulfils." Nor are there a variety of pre-existing concepts which He "takes over." The fact that John the Baptist had to reckon with was the *deeds* of Jesus which put all notions of "Messiahship" "on the spot." God was present in the deeds.[17] That was what had to be "decided" about when one "believed." All this is urged by many modern theologians. What is now necessary is that this whole emphasis upon the activity of Christ shall be allowed to explain the nature of the Christian believer. If Christ is Messiah not by "nature" or "mystical union" but by deeds, then is the disciple not also "in Christ" by his deeds, his discipleship, and not by any of the more nebulous terms (such as "faith" has become, though it was not so originally) customarily used? This is not to urge "Pelagianism" any more than modern Christology urges "Adoptionism." But it is to insist that Christian existence shall not be a less material and concrete activity and commitment than Christ's own existence. For the disciple, too, by God's grace is what his Lord was and is—son to be obedient, servant to serve.[18]

2. *Ministry*. In practice, all this means that the disciple does the things which he sees his Master doing. He continues his Master's ministry of teaching, preaching, healing and "casting out devils" (Mark 3:15 etc.). Mark sees this as the continuation of Christ's own battle with the forces of evil and darkness— though the disciples themselves do not remain outside their powerful influence.[19] Luke insists in schematic style that the

disciples extend their Lord's ministry both in His lifetime (Luke 10:17) and after His Resurrection, (Acts 2:43 etc.).[20] Matthew envisages the twelve as constituted into a neo-rabbinical "school of preachers" who are to repeat the memorised traditions faithfully. John summarizes the whole matter plainly in the words of Jesus in 17:18: "As Thou didst send me into the world even so send I them." Mark 3:15 named the second function of the disciples as "to be sent out." Moreover, the early Church thought itself to stand in relation to Christ in the same position as the twelve and the rest had stood. They, too, in various "ministries," were to continue the function of Christ in the healing and redemption of those in need.

3. *Mystery.* As Christ's presence is hidden, so, too, is the issue of discipleship. It is not simply a matter of this or that person "chosing" to be a disciple. Discipleship is a veritable "Way," which many do not tread who claim to be followers or applauders. "Why call me, 'Lord, Lord,' but do not do what I tell you?" (Luke 6:46). Many will claim allegiance to Him and will be denied by Him (Matt. 7:21f), because they have not performed His deeds. At the same time, there will be some who have never claimed allegiance to Him who will find themselves accepted by Him because their deeds coincided with His deeds. This is the implication of the parable of the Judgement (Matt. 25:31-46). The thing to say about my neighbor is, "Well, I must be careful, for he might be serving Christ if He does His deeds" (Luke 9:49). The thing to say about myself is "My volitional or philosophical commitment to Christ does not mean that I am His disciple, and that He will own me" (Luke 11:23). Discipleship consists in fulfilling Christ's Way, and is acknowledged only and always when it does so. I never know when another's attitude *to me* makes him acceptable (Matt. 25:40). [21]

4. *Suffering.* Discipleship implies suffering and deprivation at the hands of the world. The mission of the Master had necessitated this, and so does that of the disciple. This disciple is to "take up his cross" (Mark 8:34), which seems to mean a conscious and willing parting with everything which ministers to his own egocentricity, such as family, livelihood, possessions and

status (Luke 14:26f, Matt. 10:37, etc.). It also means the willing acceptance of part in the Messianic sufferings of the Master at the hands of the world.[22] This is the "cup" of Christ, which the disciples suggest they might drink Mark 10:38ff), the "fire" with which they are to be salted (Mark 9:49), the "baptism" with which they are to be baptised (Mark 10:38). The contexts of the sayings about the disciples being "salt" likewise make it plain that the essential element, the salt, which is necessary, is complete Discipleship with its consequent self-renunciation;[23] and in these sayings also the aim of the "saltiness" becomes plain— notably, the usefulness of the disciples and of Discipleship to the world (Mark 9:47-50); Luke 14:26-35; Matt. 5:11-13). It should be noted that the suffering of the disciple in meeting the discipleship demands upon himself, and also the suffering which the world metes out to the disciple as he goes about his Master's will are both as it were prerequisites and consequences of discipleship, though they are not themselves discipleship. Discipleship is the continuing of the deeds and ministry of Jesus. The "cross" comes as the means to and the result of this Discipleship. The Christian vocation to suffering, to "fill up what lacks in the sufferings of Chirst" (Col. 1:24), is only part of the wider ministry of redemption, healing and reconciliation to which the disciple is called.

5. *Rule.* The disciple's task is to live in a world over which Christ is already the only Lord, and simply to bear witness to this by his deeds. The Lordship of Christ is both over the Church and also over the World. His exaltation to the right hand of God (Phil. 2:9) proclaims Him *kyrios* (Acts 2:35f). At present, this Lordship is visibly exercised only in the Church, but it shall be manifest to all the world in the end (Eph. 1:22), for He is heir of all things (Heb. 1:2). Within this situation of Christ's Lordship, the disciple must "proclaim His triumphs" (I Pet. 2:9), for "the grace of God has dawned upon the world with healing for all mankind" (Titus 2:11, NEB). Hence, the disciple follows his Lord into the heavens (Rev. 14:4), to judge both world and angels (I Cor. 6:3). Already, the Gospel picture of the twelve "sitting on thrones, judging" (Matt. 19:28), whatever

its original form, implies that the disciple stands in a decisive position between Christ the Lord and the world over which He is Lord. In fact, the parables of stewardship (Luke 12:13-21; 17:7-10; 19:11-27 etc.) may be taken to imply that the disciple's prime concern is not with his own self-preservation or purity but with the right management of God's affairs in His world. The disciple stands in a position of dual responsibility in the world. Before God, he stands praying (I Tim. 2), representing man (Intercession). Before man, he stands representing God (Rule). Thus, it is his task to try to ensure that, somehow or other, God gets done in His world what He requires to be done.

Such, then, are the main lines of Discipleship.

I believe that these characteristics of discipleship are present whenever Jesus Christ is rightly worshipped and served. They are determinative of the true Church. They are the basic insights and attitudes which must determine the Christian's economic and political involvement, because they are the human activities God can redeem and use. For they are, all of them, methods whereby we may co-operate with the work of Christ in His world.

WITNESS AND EXPEDIENCY

What, then, exactly, must the disciple do?

Obey His Lord and be "in on" the things His Lord is doing. That is the primary answer.

Only when this has been said can we come to the question of specific commands such as those in the Sermon on the Mount. The demands of the Sermon are the implications of discipleship within a hostile world. They do not themselves constitute Discipleship. The demands for nonresistance, universal benevolence, and the like describe the faithful disciple's reactions to the kind of response in others which the disciple may expect as he carries on his work as a disciple.

Let us make some general comments about this, and then attempt to carry the argument a few stages forward and meet some of the objections to our method.

First, we should note that the Sermon on the Mount is concerned normally with what the disciple must do in situations in which he has been put "on the spot" by the demands or ways of the world. And the latter are still "in the grip of evil." In this respect, the disciple is like his Lord. "As He is, so are we in this world" (I John 4:17). Peter tells us that "it is a fine thing if a man endure undeserved suffering because of his consciousness of God" (I Peter 2:19). God's praise is only given if one is punished wrongly, for doing one's task as a disciple; for this was the way in which Christ suffered (vv. 20-25). Again, we must say that nonresistance does not constitute Discipleship, but is the purely negative and passive way in which challenges to the positive outworkings of Discipleship are to be met.[24]

Second, I think that we must beware of too quickly or easily summarizing this in the word *Agape*, "love." Love does emphasize the positive outreach of Discipleship rather than its passive non-aggression. But we must not make a principle out of love. We must not talk of a "way of Agape." There is only one Way, and that is the Way of Christ. To take "love" as the principle, is already to move a step away from Christ and to make something other than Christ the determinative factor. Having recently been reading the debates of G. H. C. MacGregor and John H. Yoder against Reinhold Niebuhr,[25] I am inclined to say, "You are all wrong and none of you get prizes." Christ's complete passivity upon the Cross was not itself the most important element as Yoder suggests.[26] It was His *work* upon the Cross which was vital, His work of battling with and overcoming evil.

Third, the Christian disciple is not simply called to do nothing in the presence of evil. He is called to fulfill the ministry of Christ, which means a positive grappling with all that makes for unfulfillment, chaos or injustice. He must "let his light shine before men, that they may see his good works and give glory to his Father in heaven" (Matt. 5:16). The disciple is to be salt to enrich the world, a lamp to lighten the world, leaven to leaven the world. In each case, the enrichment, salvation, healing and reconciliation of the world is the aim, not the salvation merely of the disciple. That is to say, the disciple is only helpless at the hands of the world at points at which he has failed in his prime duty of working for the redemption and wholeness of the world.

The Cross is, indeed, not the only contribution the disciple has to make to the problem of an evil world. He also has the task of trying to make the world what its Creator intended it to be. Thus it seems to me that when Rutenber summarizes the ethic of the New Testament by saying that we are given "principles rather than rules,"[27] we are far away from the center. The New Testament does not give us either. It gives us Christ and His ongoing activity, in which we can either play our part faithfully or play the fool irresponsibly, reducing the whole thing to a private piety or morality. Precisely this reduction seems to be suggested by John H. Yoder, when he claims that pacifism is primarily a personal conviction, rather than a possible national policy.[28] If that is what pacifism is, then I cannot see that it has any foundation in the dominant theology of the New Testament.

Fourth, discipleship is not a private ethic which may be simply applied. Discipleship is somehow or other wrangling with myself and God's world so that, by fair means or foul, God gets His will done. This is the message of the stewardship parables. It is what Jesus meant when He told us to be "wise as serpents" ("cunning" says the AV) (Matt. 10:16). We cannot go blithely into the world and "apply the Sermon on the Mount" without considering its possible results. The light has to shine before men, not so that they will conclude that Christians are irresponsible crackpots who think that the world can go to hell so long as they can be kept pure and undefiled, but so that they will conclude that God is worthy to be glorified. Some of us, I sometimes feel, neither want nor expect discipleship to be a relevant solution to problems. We prefer to keep it as a private ethic, and to preserve ourselves from dangerous involvements which might compromise our ability to keep our hands clean. I believe that Jesus taught us quite explicitly to consider the expediency of our actions.[29] And this He did because He was more concerned with getting the world somehow or other put back on its feet than He was with securing His disciples' inviolability at the hands of the world. The disciple is not free to "do what he likes." He is, if we may use the attractive category of Krister Stendahl, only free to exercise "Messianic License" when doing so will assist the ongoing ministry of Christ.[30] The features of such "License" which have permanent validity are those which assist that ministry, rather than detract from it.

Fifth and last in these general considerations, discipleship is Witness. By this must be meant not simply the preaching of the facts of Christ, but their acting out. For this reason, Jesus employed symbolic, parabolic actions, and commanded His disciples to do the same. For this reason, the reduction of the Church's task to that of "faithfully proclaiming the kerygma" is a perversion of the New Testament. The Church must find strategic and crucial points at which radical discipleship will "speak Christ" to a generation which is largely impervious to the effect of words.

Do the demands of the last three paragraphs ever conflict? Does ministering to need and casting out devils ever conflict with the demands of expediency? And is the thing we have to do as witness always the expedient thing to do? Let us be honest. There is no infallible way out of these rival claims, short of a personal perfection and a cosmic perfection which are quite unlike the "it seemed good to the Spirit and to us," the "if the Lord wills," and the "I have no word from the Lord on this" of New Testament discipleship. Certainly, we must consider the possible *results* of our actions. The "results" God is interested in are the healing and the evangelisation of others. We, the Church, are of use to Him as His agents, to help carry these things forward. As William Temple said, the Church is the only organisation in history which exists solely for the benefit of non-members. This means that our deeds of "witness" will be such as will bring blessing to others, and will perhaps allow them to see the decisive issue of Christ in what we do, and thus glorify God. Only a deed which is at once *relevant* (that is, comprehensible and acceptable to "the world") and also *Christocentric* (that is, acceptable to Him as part of His manysided activity) can be a faithful witness. (Paul's comments on speaking with tongues suggest that Pentecost, for example, did not pass this test!).

How may we discern the times at which the Church and the disciple are called to act in this way?

George Edwards suggests that the time has come to develop a new phase in eschatology, in which the extremes of an irrelevant *Interimsethik* and the moralisms of conventional non- eschatological interpretations are both alike avoided. The *eschatological* issue of God's final and radical presence in Christ is seen in the immediate *existential* response of the man who is challenged by the presence of Jesus or by His teaching and who sees in both the decisive issue of his own selfhood. This is very close to the position of many of the German post-Bultmann scholars, such as Ernst Fuchs, Günther Bernkamm, and Hans Conzelmann, and it is probably already implicit in the writings of Bultmann.

What is now needed is on the one hand a realisation of the true nature of the "existential," and on the other hand a development of this in relation to community and cultural decisions. Regarding the first, it is already clear that there can be no Christology without ethics, no belief without discipleship, no "decision" without action. But what does this mean? Does it not mean that now, as in the days of Jesus' earthly life, the existential decisions which a man has to make when confronted by Christ do not relate to his opinions, attitudes, *Weltanschauung*, or beliefs, but relate quite concretely to what he is going to do with his life, his money, his relatives, his occupation, now that there stands One before him who by His very presence calls every one of them into question, and makes one's decision on such matters identical with one's "decision" about Him? The ethical question presents us not with a problem in which we may "work out" a faith otherwise established by taking up this or that attitude of belief, but rather with the opportunity in which we may for the first time recognise, receive and become discipled to Christ. This is what the whole discipleship tradition leads us to. Existential eschatology is ethical eschatology and ethical existentialism.

May we go a further step? Is there any sense in which ethical existential decisions may be said to partake of the eschatological when they are community, group or cultural decisions? Some words of Robert McFadden seem to point in this direction. Writing of a "teleological suspension of the ethical" in Kierkegaard, he says:[31]

> There is a leap of faith and a primary duty toward God in crucial choices; these are most evident when the struggle for decision is most intense. . . . In the nuclear dilemma has appeared the *kairos* for our epoch; there is only faith or unfaith in response.

Martin Buber speaks of "ever new spheres becoming regions of a theophany," of "revelations" appearing, which produce "a form that is a new form of God in the world," so that "in the course of history, in the transforming of elemental human stuff, ever new provinces of the world and the Spirit are raised to form, summoned to divine form."[32] Again, Buber insists that all meeting with God has as its end and aim a true meeting with and entering into the world. Surely, there are decisive, "existential" and ethical issues in which the whole community has the chance to see Christ ("the form of God in the world") and to accept Him by taking the concrete situation which "presents" Him with eschatological seriousness. For (as we have insisted) Christ represents not simply the pattern, norm and method of God's once appearing, but even more the pattern, norm and method of his recurring presence. And "discipleship" to this is as possible for the state today as "walking in the way of the Lord" was for the nation in the days of the prophets.

But, it may be objected, does not this oversimplify the problematic relation of Christianity to the State? Let this be said in reply. First, the New Testament knows nothing of any kind of doctrine or philosophy of Church-State relations such as developed under Constantine, Augustine, Luther or the American pioneers. Second, the New Testament does not suggest that the Church is a place where God finds it invariably a walk-over to get His will done (cf. I Corinthians!): if there is a problem about the State, there is also one about a non-disciple Church. With both Church and State, God is batting on sticky wickets. Third, the remarks of Paul in Rom. 13:1-7 must be seen in their context (as advice to respect police forces) and in comparison with the rest of the New Testament, which represents the State either as evil (Revelation) or else as the purely neutral area in which God battles in Christ for the control of human kind. The state's function is to keep things quiet so that God can get on with the important business of casting out devils and making disciples. Fourth, there is no question of the Church's "interfering" in another "realm." God has not one will for the select few and another will for the nations. He has revealed in Christ His plan for making both human beings and human communities work.[33]

There are, of course, problems if one takes the New Testament or the Sermon on the Mount as a "personal ethic," and tries to apply it willy-nilly in politics. But we have claimed all along that both New Testament and Sermon on the Mount are not to be taken as personal ethics, but as the description of discipleship—as description of the human activities inspired by grace and accepted by God through Christ into ultimate significance. Precisely the same applies in politics. The points at which national policies fit into the pattern of Christ's ongoing ministry are the points at which they also become ultimately significant, and are hence "redeemed" and accepted into the pattern which saves the world. The great problem of Protestant theology today is that it must tackle its "ghetto" spirit, and stop trying to enlarge the ghetto, but rather seek to be where Jesus has His place, beside the men for whom the Gospel is intended. Only then shall we understand the Gospel—in His world, which is not ours, but which must be ours now that He has made it His. Thus Gerhard Ebeling.[34] So far as the Christian is concerned, "the State" does not exist as a separate "realm." It exists as part of *the world,* and as such is part of the whole cosmos, including man, which is to be redeemed.

Can we only speak to the State when we have first converted the Church? We have often assumed so. But let us be frank. If we wait for the Church to be converted to seeing the signs of the times, we shall wait forever. Specific churches and churchmen will be able to make specific acts and recommendations. But there are, in any case, at present so many thinking men not within the Church's discussions who are convinced of the moral issues in the nuclear question, that it is a question of the Church's contribution being made within the organisations already committed to progressive action, such as SANE (National Committee for a Sane Nuclear Policy), Women Against War, and others. Denominational efforts—such as the excellent Methodist "Race for Peace" program—should not attempt to supplant the wider groups.

But now, what have we to say and do? Are there lines of word and deed dictated to us in the present situation by the theological factors we have been considering? Are there things in the so-called "secular" world which God is already inspiring with His grace in line with His incarnation and redemption, things to which His Spirit is seeking to commit the Church which bears that revelation?

OUR NUCLEAR SITUATION

If all this is correct, then it remains for us to suggest ways in which the fivefold commitment of the disciple to the ongoing ministry of Christ might be said to be relevant in our present nuclear situation. For details, I must refer the reader elsewhere.[35]

1. *Servanthood.* Christ is where His deeds are done, and discipleship is "being with Christ." Christ represents truly a whole activity of redemption going on in the world. We must discern "the signs of the times." We must find where Christ is in the whole vast complex of our modern world. Our "world-view" must be determined by the discovery of His presence. This is probably the most urgent task of the Church today. We are all at sea on particular problems because we have no longer any faith that there is any pattern or meaning in history. We no longer believe (if Christians every really did believe) that there are specific means whereby history may receive "the gift of ultimate significance" by being taken into the activity of Christ. We are unclear about the H-bomb, world poverty, birth control, communism, and the rest, because we are unclear about Christ. I have tried to suggest the lines by which Christ may be engaged

in our current situations, lines in which "the finality of Christ" is to be found in "an age of universal history."[36]

First, He is among us as One who serves, and He tells us that the only "lordship" exists in service. That is to say, the test of any disciple is not whether he is "chief," but whether he excels others in the degree of his serving and devotion to others. If this is the test of the disciple, it is also the test of the Church. The Church which is acceptable to God is the Church which is giving itself to its neighbours in costly service: and its neighbours are not simply those "of its own household," but are the poor, the outcast, the halt, the lame and the blind. The acid test of the disciple Church is what it does about the underprivileged and half-starved two-thirds of the world. And is not the same true of governments? The test of any government is not what it does for the standard of living of those already comfortably placed, but what it does for those who cannot care for themselves, who fear to be ill or to grow old. I will be pardoned for saying that if the American churches are to lead their government into this kind of servanthood, they will have to do a good deal of study of the political, social and economic implications of their faith —the kind of things which gave birth to the Labour Party in Britain and the Socialist Movements in Europe. Servanthood can be exercised by the churches so far as mission lands are concerned by unilateral gestures which will cost them dearly but which could be done *before* the government could be persuaded to enter into them. But social service ("socialized medicine" for a start!) will probably have to become a policy acceptable domestically if it is to be advocated as a foreign policy. The danger is, of course, that the government will do the Church's "Peace Corps" job before the churches get round to it. This is no "problem" for God. If the Church, the agent of His love, does not act as servant, then others are raised up.

If Christ is where His deeds are done, then we must beware of any easy alignment of Christ with any country or "power bloc." Certainly, the evil effects of the continued arms race are to be found on both sides.[37] Certainly, the cry of mankind for preservation, peace, security and welfare is a cry heard by the sensitive on both sides in an age in which the common interests of mankind infinitely outweigh their traditional and conceptual differences.[38] Certainly, we have no reason to assume that ministrations to human need which in the West are done by the Name of Christ are necessarily separate from His ministry because they are done in the East by those who do not outwardly profess Him. Unquestionably, if the world were to come together with a common concern for the good of mankind, Christ would be identified with that concern and not with the fissiparous sectarianism which would attempt to ally Him with one side or the other. In the present situation, who can doubt that Christ is a force for unity and reconciliation? He is the Servant of all, pacifists and bellicists. At this crucial time, the question is not one of pacifism but one of peace, and the decisive issue is whether we can discover "the lineaments of a peace program on which those with differing presuppositions can make common cause."[39] It is a constant disappointment to those concerned with making headway in thought about disarmament or peace or progress that the views of those who try to take a reconciliatory attitude are still being praised or condemned from the outworn positions of a decade or two ago—be they pacifist, realist, neo-orthodox or liberal. The same is true of East and West. Some who speak most of "reconciliation" are least willing to be reconciled. A few weeks after I was being regarded as a dangerous "fellow-traveler" in the United States, I found myself in the Soviet Union being dubbed an "imperialist warmonger." It is surely part of the ministry of the Christ who belongs to all but is the possession of none to be prepared to be used for the building of new understanding based on the common humanity of men purchased by and ministered to by the Servant Christ. This is no easy way, but it must finally prevail if hopelessness is to be defeated.

2. *Ministry.* Christ's deeds are ministry, healing, redemption, and the creation of new relationships and communities. These things the disciple also must continue. He must "cast out devils." He must do all he can to advance meaningfulness in the lives of

others. And he will know that this cannot be done in the twentieth century but through the agencies of politics and economics. This is particularly relevant for the Christian of the West. Christ is the Servant of all, including the Communist, as we have seen. But there is a sense in which the fate of Christianity is being decided with the fate of the West. In this situation, the Church must do two things. First, she must herself engage in costly and radical "Peace Corps" work, by the creation of an International Christian Task Force, or the like. Second, she must prove to the East that where Christians are influential in Western nations, they force their governments to adopt progressive policies, which issue in aid for those in need. We cannot all go to Africa (though many more could go than do, and the wrong people often go at that), but we can all engage in specific and radical economic disciplines which would release healing and redemptive ministries in the form of scientific and industrial skills and plant with Christians to man them.

Thus, the main lines of the kind of program outlined in Seymour Melman's *The Peace Race*[40] should be the lines of a policy which the churches acting unilaterally could immediately put into effect. The world has heard us say for long enough that we ought to do something for the underdeveloped nations. What is now needed is for the Church to set about some program which will put this into practice, and will be genuinely "prophetic" by doing before the government does it what is required of the West, and particularly the USA. These are things which any Church seriously regarding itself as the embodiment of the ministry of Christ would set about. There is, we are told, only just time. And these things are vital simply because the name of Christ has a "Western" or American ring about it in the ears of the rest of the world. We all know that, in fact, the West is not Christian. But the East and Africa and South America do not know this. We must not be held back from redemptive action merely because it might be confused politically in the minds of others. As things are at present, the survival of Christianity in the East and in Africa is in jeopardy because of the identification of Christianity with the West. We may not like that identification. But it is a fact. And we must try to *use* it, or at least try to redeem it, not simply disown it.

This, as the nuclear disarmers have always claimed, is to meet the Soviet threat on its own ground. One can hardly do better than quote Mr. Khrushchev:[41]

> "An ideological and political struggle is in progress between two systems. We believe that this struggle should not be projected into a war between the states with different social systems, and that the matter should be settled through peaceful competition. Let every country of the socialist and the capitalist world prove the advantages of its system by peaceful endeavour. The main criteria are: Which system, the capitalist or the socialist, provides greater material and spiritual benefits, higher living and cultural standards for the popular masses, which of them provides genuine freedom for the individual, and ensures the most rapid development of productive forces, culture and science, in the interests of man."

Unquestionably, Krushchev is right when he went on to say that "The system which proves its advantages will win the minds of men," and as anyone who has tried to uphold the Western point of view in Russia will know, there are as yet precious few signs of the advantages of "capitalism" to those not financially committed to it. The question is quite a simple one for Western Christians: How long are we going to allow the desecration and prostration of our world mission at the hands of our governments? To persist with antiquated militaristic concepts (and propaganda ones, we might add) is to allow the real leadership in ministry to slip out of the hands of the West—and, ostensibly at least, out of the hands of Christ.

3. *Mystery.* In this, we have assumed that there is some sense in which the Christian West may be thought of as standing in the relation of discipleship to Christ. We need not repeat the anachronisms in any such notion so far as the West is concerned. But, equally, we cannot oversimplify the possible Christian significance of what is happening in the East. May

not the body and the soul of Christianity have become severed in some sense? Is one to assert the presence of Christ *only* in the Church of Russia, with its traditional *laissez-faire* attitude in social, economic and political matters? On balance, I still feel that the West must not "allow itself to be overrun by Communism," though I do not think the Communists intend this by military aggression. Certainly, the Church must admit the complete fallibility of political and economic deeds so far as their Christian significance is concerned. This, at any rate, is part of the "mystery." One obvious need is for "true ecumenicity," a spirit which will unite the Christians at present severed by their commitment to Western or Communist cultures, and which will make clear that the fate of Western nations and cultures will not be identified with the fate of the Church.[42]

The element of mystery in the ongoing presence of Christ manifests itself more plainly and simply in His unforeseeable self-identification with those who suffer because of the sin of others or because of the absence of ministry. If it is true of a food parcel, it is true of a hydrogen bomb that "Inasmuch as you dropped it on one of the least of these my brethren, you dropped it on to Me" (George MacLeod). Strategists themselves are divided as to the "possibility" or "feasibility" of actually using nuclear weapons. The churches, in almost all their reports, have concluded that the use of nuclear weapons in all-out war, that is, against civilians, and producing world-wide effects, is to be regarded as an atrocity, as something to be avoided at all costs, and as indefensible. The two remaining "last threads" in a nuclear policy are the notions of the Deterrent and the notion of Limited Nuclear War. Both are open to serious objection from the purely practical point of view.[43] From our present point of view, both commit governments to the intention of using (by threat) or the possible use of (in a war which "escalates" from "limited" weapons) a weapon which is on all counts indefensible. At very least, the churches must ruthlessly expose the immorality of either notion, based as it is on a possible desecration of humanity such as history has never seen. But also, the Churches must make their contribution within the agonising areas of political decision. All—including Mr. Khrushchev and the Archbishop of Canterbury, to cite two recent advocates!—are in favour of disarmament. What is needed is the urgency to cut into present discussions with practical and forward-looking Christian suggestions.[44]

4. *Suffering*. The disciple, like his Master, must "take up his cross." Many have seen in this the command to replace all coercion with "passive resistance" and "non-violent techniques." Even if this were on all grounds arguable from the Christian point of view (as I hold it is not, except as a specific situational technique, with specific ends in view), it has so little chance of being accepted as to be virtually a non-starter.

What the category of suffering does teach us is the unavoidability of some element of risk and faith in politics and responsible moral action. Faith itself is willingness to be committed to lines of action the outcome of which only becomes clear when one enters upon them, simply because they are right or simply because they are commanded (cf. Heb. 11). Faith is willingness to take initial steps which might appear foolhardy, in the belief that they will be upheld or justified in what follows. Genuine faith invariably brings with it initial inconvenience, suffering or rejection, until the time of God's "justification" comes. A genuinely serving Church is frequently a persecuted Church. We are not persecuted now, because we never do anything which would merit the world's persecuting us!

Does not all this have something to do with what are called "unilateral initiatives"—gestures and deeds that can be seen by the other side to comprise real acts of denial or withdrawal, and which might be expected to "trigger off" a like response in him, provided the area of such unilateral initiative were seen to be clearly to the initiator's disadvantage?[45] Somehow, the vicious circle of the arms race must be broken. "Stabilized deterrence" cannot be a permanent solution, even if it were militarily feasible. How is the vicious circle to be broken except by some act of generosity, "impolity," or faith that might demonstrate that "Whosoever would save his life shall lose it, but whosoever loses his life for my sake shall find it." It may be that the whole risky adventure of God in the incarnation has a great deal to instruct us here.

5. *Rule.* Christ rules openly and in secret, and the disciple is meant to have a taste of authority even himself. What does this mean? I do not think it means that we may relax into some comfortable doctrine of providence. Almost invariably, the notion of providence is employed by those who politically advocate the support of the *status quo.*[46] One difficulty with providence is that it does not sufficiently differentiate between the methods of God's working in the Old Testament from His methods in the New: that is, it does not normally realise that God's Providence has now been focussed in the person and work of Christ, and in their continued manifestation. That means, of course, that God in Christ is at work *against* the forces of history, as well as in them.

> God has not called us to be dragged like slaves in the wake of history plunging to its doom, but to be messengers and servants of Christ who is the Lord of history and the victor over the demonic forces in it.

This conclusion to an earlier *Church Peace Mission* statement[47] indicates the ground of Christian commitment.

How is it to be done? We must discover specific issues and symbolic gestures whereby the Church may immediately and temporarily manifest the ultimate lordship and supremacy of Christ. This means expediency. We must find areas in which progress can be made at this moment, even if the final solution is rejected. We must find areas of activity—perhaps SANE or party politics—in which the Rule of Christ at crucial points can be demonstrated. The great temptation for some of us is to identify the Rule of Christ with our own culture. The great temptation for others of us is to say that our civilization is not Christian, and that therefore we must contract out of these complicated questions. We shall only resist either temptation, and commit ourselves as faithful disciples to responsible and redemptive involvement, if we have a new understanding of a Christ who even now juggles behind the scenes of history with the inabilities of politicians, and who calls now to His followers to live the new allegiance of the Kingdom in the dangerous and compromising commitments of nuclear politics.

FOOTNOTES

[1] Cf. *Morality and Modern Warfare: The State of the Question,* ed. W. J. Nagle (Baltimore: Helicon Press, 1960), or *Nuclear Weapons and Christian Conscience,* ed. Walter Stein (London: Merlin Press, 1961), both of which have comparatively little to say on the Just War theory as such, and both of which also refer to other Catholic literature in the same direction.

[2] So C. F. von Weizsäcker on the World Council of Churches Commission, *Christians and the Prevention of War in an Atomic Age—A Theological Discussion* (Provisional Study Document, 1958) (Geneva: World Council of Churches 1958), p. 10; printed edition by Sir T. Taylor and R. S. Bilheimer, (London: SCM Press, 1961) p. 11f.

[3] Paul Ramsey, *War and the Christian Conscience: How Shall Modern War Be Conducted Justly?* (Duke University Press, 1961); "The Case for Making 'Just War' Possible," in *Nuclear Weapons and the Conflict of Conscience,* ed. John C. Bennett (New York: Scribner's, 1962), pp. 143-170. This latter work hereafter cited as *N.W.C.C.*

[4] See note 2. The first report emphasizes "discipline," the second "discrimination."

[5] T. R. Milford, *The Valley of Decision* (London: British Council of Churches, 1961).

[6] The title of the Study Seminar of the Church Peace Mission, at which the essays in this volume were first presented, was "Kerygma and Ethos in the Nuclear Age."

[7] Cf. my "Didactic Kerygma in the Synoptic Gospels," *Scottish Journal of Theology,* 10 (1957) 3, 262-73; R. A. Bartels, *Kerygma or Gospel Traditions: Which Came First?* (Minneapolis: Augsburg Publishing House, 1961).

[8] Robert W. Tucker, *The Just War: A Study in Contemporary American Doctrine* (Baltimore: Johns Hopkins, 1960).

[9] James Barr, *The Semantics of Biblical Language* (Oxford University Press, 1961), esp. 288-96.

[10] G. H. C. MacGregor, *The New Testament Basis of Pacifism* (Fellowship Publications, N. Y., 1960), 16-50; Culbert G. Rutenber, *The Dagger and the Cross* (Fellowship Publications, N. Y., 1958), 37-70; John Ferguson, *The Enthronement of Love* (London: Fellowship of Reconciliation, 1958), 25-36.

[11] John J. Vincent, *Christ in a Nuclear World* (Manchester: Crux Press—New York: Fellowship Publications, 1962). Most of the themes of the present paper are dealt with in greater detail in this book. The present paper represents a development of the book in the direction of Discipleship, and confines references to the nuclear discussion mainly to the more recent American literature. My later book, *Christian Nuclear Perspective* (London: Epworth Press, 1963) asks whether there are political and ethical aims, methods and

strategies dictated by Christian revelation, and thus takes the present paper a stage further.

12 For example, T. W. Manson, *Ministry and Priesthood, Christ's and Ours.* (London: Epworth Press, 1958); Anthony T. Hanson, *The Pioneer Ministry* (London: SCM Press, 1960); Paul S. Minear, *Images of the Church in the New Testament* (London: Lutterworth Press, 1961).

13 "Discipleship and Synoptic Studies," *Theologische Zeitschrift,* 16 (1960) 6, 456-69. One might recall, in any case, Dietrich Bonhoeffer's *The Cost of Discipleship* (ET London, SCM Press, 1959) and Eduard Schweizer's *Lordship and Discipleship* (ET London, SCM Press, 1960).

14 *Disciple and Lord*—a development of my Basel dissertation on "The Historical and Theological Significance of Discipleship in the Synoptic Gospels."

15 Cf. George Edwards' paper in this volume, p. 89.

16 Vincent Taylor, *The Person of Christ in New Testament Teaching* (London: Macmillan, 1958); Oscar Cullmann, *The Christology of the New Testament* (ET, SCM Press, 1959), Introduction.

17 Ernst Fuchs emphasizes the importance for Christology and history of the deeds, *das Handeln,* of Jesus. Cf. his *Zur Frage nach dem historischen Jesus* (Tübingen: J. C. B. Mohr, 1960).

18 This may be demonstrated by a comparison of the terms used of Jesus and of the disciples, such as servant, son, "little one," beloved, and possibly terms like steward and poor man. I hope to show this later.

19 So. J. M. Robinson, *The Problem of History in Mark* (London: SCM Press, 1957), who describes "history since AD 30 in Mark" as "a continuation of the same cosmic struggle which Jesus began" (p. 67). Cf. also Konrad Weiss, "Ekklesiologie, Tradition und Geschichte in der Jüngerunterweisung, Mark 8:27-10:52" in *Der historische Jesus und der kerygmatische Christus,* ed. H. Ristow and K. Matthiae (Berlin: Evangelische Verlagsanstalt, 1960). Many of the papers in this most important 650-page work, representing in some cases the "New Look on the Gospels" of the Post-Bultmann school, would support the emphases on the deeds of Jesus and on the disciples. Cf. also now Eduard Schweizer, "Anmerkungen zur Theologie des Markus," *Neotestamentica et Patristica: Oscar Cullmann Festschrift* (Leiden: E. J. Brill, 1962), pp. 35-46.

20 See E. J. Tinsley, *The Imitation of God in Christ* (London: SCM Press, 1960), 106-113.

21 Cf. the exposition of Karl Barth, *Church Dogmatics,* III. 2 (ET, Edinburgh: T. & T. Clark, 1960), pp. 507f.

22 See esp. Ernst Percy, *Die Botschaft Jesu* (Lund: Uppsala Univ., 1953), p. 172, quoting Anton Fridrichsen. Cf. Fridrichsen on "Deny Yourself" in *Coniectanea Neotestamentica* (Lund: Gleerup), II (1936), pp. 1-8.

23 Cf. Oscar Cullmann on the significance of the "salt," in *Revue d'Histoire et de Philosophie religieuses* 37 (1957), pp. 36-43.

24 The command to *love* the enemy takes this a stage further, although William Klassen's characterisation of the enemy as "anyone who allows himself to be used by Satan to destroy the Church" (see p. 153) would accord with the interpretation above.

25 G. H. C. MacGregor, *The Relevance of an Impossible Ideal* (Fellowship

Some Proposed Solutions

Publications, 1960); John H. Yoder, *Reinhold Niebuhr and Christian Pacifism* (Concern Reprint, 1961) (Scottdale, Penna.; Mennonite Pub. House.)

[26] Cf. Yoder, *Peace With Eschatology* (Concern Reprint, 1960), p. 7: "Christ is *agape;* self-giving, nonresistant love." Or Ferguson, op. cit., pp. 25f.

[27] Rutenber, *op. cit.,* p. 46.

[28] Yoder, *op. cit.* Cf. Roland H. Bainton, *Christian Attitudes to War and Peace* (New York: Abingdon Press, 1960), p. 248: "Christian pacifism is not a strategy but a witness." What I am trying to show above is that I find myself in such agreement with so much that is said both by pacifists and by non-pacifists that I must ask whether the set of questions they are both answering is the right one!

[29] Cf. *Christ in a Nuclear World*, pp. 63-66.

[30] Cf. his paper, p. 139. The question we must settle is, whether the Spirit is calling us to such "Messianic License" now. I go on to suggest above that He may be—though it is a "license" which is expedient and not merely self-expression.

[31] Robert McFadden, "The Nuclear Dilemma, with a nod to Kierkegaard," *Theology Today*, XVII (1961) 1, pp. 505-518, p. 518.

[32] Martin Buber, *I and Thou* (London: James Clarke, 1950), pp. 115-117.

[33] These considerations are, I feel, to be urged in view of the "non-interference" with the State to which Clinton Morrison's paper (p. 103) seems to lead us. This whole subject has been very well treated in Part III; "The Christian's Obedience to the State" of Jean Lassère's *War and the Gospel* (ET. London: James Clarke, 1962), pp. 81-163. Lassère's study is easily the most significant from the pacifist side for some time.

[34] Gerhard Ebeling, "Hauptprobleme der protestantischen Theologie in der Gegenwart," *Zeitschrift für Theologie und Kirche*, 58 (1961) 1, pp. 123-36, p. 135.

[35] *Christ in a Nuclear World*, pp. 118-160 on "First Steps in Christian Action" and "God's Purpose in the Nuclear World"; *Christian Nuclear Perspective*, Chapters One to Four.

[36] Cf. the current major study theme of the World Council of Churches Division of Study, "The Finality of Christ in the Age of Universal History," *The New Delhi Report* (London: SCM Press, 1962), pp. 165ff.

[37] See John C. Bennett, "Moral urgencies in the nuclear context," *N.W.C.C.*, pp. 93-121, p. 109 ff.

[38] With, among many, John H. Herz, "International politics and the nuclear dilemma," *N.W.C.C.*, pp. 15-38, p. 37.

[39] Roland H. Bainton, *op. cit.,* p. 253.

[40] Seymour Melman, *The Peace Race* (New York: Ballantine Books, 1961), described as "A program to put America's unemployed men and factories to work to industrialize the emerging nations."

[41] Nikita S. Khrushchev, "General and Complete Disarmament is a Guarantee of Peace and Security for all Nations" (Speech at *World Congress* for *General Disarmament and Peace,* Moscow, July 8-13), (Moscow: Foreign Languages Publishing House, 1962), p. 26. (I was one of 15 official observers from the *British Campaign for Nuclear Disarmament* present.) On Soviet intentions, see Erich Fromm, *May Man Prevail?* (New York: Doubleday, 1961),

pp. 121-188. Present military policies by the West simply make Soviet economic victory more likely: cf. Seymour Melman, *op. cit.*, pp. 39-53.

42 See the section, "The Need for True Ecumenicity," in *The Christian Conscience and War* (New York: Church Peace Mission, 1950), pp. 33-39.

43 Cf. recently D. F. Fleming, *Does Deterrence Deter?* (Philadelphia: Friends Service Committee, 1962), which summarizes much American discussion. The doctrine of counterforce is, of course, essentially a sophistication of the two older doctrines. Cf. *Christian Nuclear Perspective*, Chapter Nine.

44 With few exceptions, one is bound to say that there appear very few possible lines of advance in the thinking of the "experts" on the subject of disarmament. The symposium, *Arms and Arms Control*, ed. Ernest W. Lefever (London: Thames and Hudson, 1962) can hardly be described as a very promising document, for all the enthusiasm of the Institute of Strategic Studies. It seems to have nothing to say at exactly the points where new thinking is required most urgently.

45 See Erich Fromm, "Explorations into the unilateral disarmament position," *N.W.C.C.*, pp. 125-139, esp. p. 125 f; Mulford Sibley, *Unilateral Initiatives and Disarmament* (Philadelphia: Friends Service Committee, 1962). The importance of what might be called "unilateral steps" is implied in two recent statements on Disarmament—that of the World Council of Churches, issued by their Executive (April, 1962), and the *Pattern for Disarmament* of the International Department of the British Council of Churches, April 1962. They urge "calculated risks" and "contributions which can be made by one country (the UK) alone."

46 So T. R. Milford, *op. cit.*, pp. 41-44; also essentially Roger L. Shinn, "Faith and the perilous future," *N.W.C.C.*, pp. 173-188, esp. pp. 181 ff.

47 *A Christian Approach to Nuclear War* (Church Peace Mission pamphlet, 1958), ed. Norman K. Gottwald. The seven conclusions in this document seem to me admirable.

11

A SUMMARY: TOWARD RECOVERY

Paul Peachey

···

THIS SYMPOSIUM was occasioned by the widely deplored lack of integrity in the life and witness of the American churches amidst the claims and the dynamics of our national life. In the introductory essay this writer traced a few of the steps whereby across the centuries the churches came to share deeply in the power structure of Western civilization. Without presuming to judge the wisdom of given choices along the way, we observed that in the end the churches found themselves deeply at the mercy of the civilization they had helped to build. As a result, while by her nature the Church is an *innovating* adventure of faith, in America, it is to be feared, she has become too much merely a culture *ratifying* force.

John Smylie followed this more general introduction with a three-fold outline of the manner in which the American nation has assumed some of the functions of the Church: 1) The nation has become for many Christians the primary agent of God's meaningful activity in history, assuming thus a catholicity of importance which theology attributes only to the Church universal; 2) The nation replaces the Church as the primary society within which Christians find their primary identity; and 3) In the absence of vitality and discipline within the churches, the nation became also the community of sanctification. These criticisms, it must be noted, do not rest on a denial of the rightful place of the nation in the purpose of God, nor of the possibility that the nation might legitimately espouse values or embrace functions which in fact originated in the churches. They are based rather on the awareness that certain functions of the Church are by definition inalienable from her life, if she is true to herself, and that any confusion of roles between the two communities is harmful to both. Smylie's conclusion is compelling: *a recovery or rediscovery of the Church* in our time is mandatory.

We carried this problem to the biblical scholars, not merely because it is a good Protestant "principle" to appeal to the Bible, but because it can be said that in some measure a recovery in biblical understanding has already taken place. In view of the disagreements among our essayists, however, the results at first thought seem disappointing. I am reminded of a breakfast table conversation at a theological conference on war and peace, held in Germany a few years ago. On the third morning, when a great weight of confusion and uncertainty rested heavily on everyone, a German theologian remarked, *"Ich glaub' die Theologen kommen alle in die Hölle"* (I suspect that the theologians will all end up in limbo). If in fact the teachers of the Church can achieve no greater consensus on the biblical word than did our writers, is it surprising if "ordinary" church people, whether lay or clergy, find it simply more commodious to listen instead to the nation?

Nor is our disappointment greatly assuaged when in a few major lines of agreement which do emerge among them we hear echoes of arguments we had long thought were threadbare. There is, for example, their strong and near unanimous insistence on the self-sufficiency of the state over against the Church. God deals directly with the nations, and not necessarily through the redemptive community (Israel or Church), (Whiston, Gottwald, Morrison). The state does not depend on the Church for its legitimation. Civil rulers "are fully capable of carrying out their divinely appointed responsibilities apart from special revelation" (Morrison), for, given God's broad activity beyond the specific scope of redemption, "a wide knowledge of God is available to man without special revelation" (Gottwald). Though these writers espouse no particular view of a "natural law," they clearly suppose the existence of some sort of principles informing the life of the nations which are not first mediated by special revelation or the Church.

A close corollary is the emphasis on the direct nonapplicability of Christian principles to the political order. This is equally true regarding governments in power, and protest or revolutionary reform movements that seek to replace existing governments or policies. "Peace movements" that seek to induce governments to adopt pacifist policies, even when biblically inspired, are regarded as a case in point (Whiston, Morrison, Piper). Christians cannot expect non-Christians to see the same reality they see in the work of God, unless they "become part of the redemptive center, the church" (Gottwald). To move directly into the political arena with the ethical demands of the gospel is to pay too little tribute to God's sustaining work in the world apart from the Church, just as it is also to depreciate his high redemptive activity. One must distinguish between Christ's *lordship* and his *victory*. The locus of the *victory*, contrary to his *lordship*, is not "the cosmos in general," thus also the political powers, but rather the Church. "The powers, sin, and death are defeated in relation to those who believe in what was manifest by God's act in Christ" (Morrison). Christian ethics is for Christians. "A church intent upon legislating the Kingdom of God, or a reasonably accurate facsimile denies its mission. . . . It assumes that the obedience desired can come about another way from the freedom which characterized the new possibility in reconciliation by faith" (Morrison). The gospel ethic cannot be legislated generally; it is rather an new possibility, a "messianic license" (Stendahl). It is Christ's victory in and on behalf of the Church that renders the new ethical orientation possible here where it is not possible in the "world" (Morrison, Klassen). Thus not only can the gospel not be realized by means of political programs, but it can be regarded in some sense as subversive to the political order which by definition follows other "laws" (Stendahl). "We contribute only to a growing confusion in political life, when we advise political leaders to pursue Christian utopias becoming to a sinless world only" (Piper).

On the surface, however, this line of reasoning seems even more distressing than the various disagreements among our writers. Here apparently is the theological program for much of the state of affairs that we deplore. Here it would seem we have, quite intact, the "two-kingdom" theory, that notorious charter of conservative Christianity. Here, too, there is ready-made a theological rationale for the modern absolute state, unrestrained in its Machiavellian impulses. Here is the charter for the quiescent Church, yielding to the nation, drawn inwardly upon herself, content merely to worship and to "save souls." The state is here effectively walled off from the prophetic scrutiny of the Church, while the Church in turn readily becomes subservient to the interests of the classes in power and indifferent to the strivings of the oppressed. In sum, we seem to be confronted anew with the conservative caricature of Christianity that liberals have always lampooned.

To draw a thus simple conclusion from these essays, however, though the danger that we do so is indeed implicit, would be to miss their central thrust. It is essential in any event to view the task of the biblical scholar in proper perspective. Not all the difficulties can be laid at his door nor can we expect him to solve all of them now. Moreover, it is his task to grasp and to present as clearly as possible the content of the biblical witness. In turn, he and we must together listen to that witness, and not simply judge it by our own preconceived criteria. If the foregoing is the actual content of the biblical witness, we need to be told just that. In any case it is of utmost importance to have these arguments, though in a sense negative and secondary, stated clearly at this point. For by so doing, our writers place themselves in center stream of orthodox Christian doctrine. Thereafter they cannot be falsely accused when their main thesis pushes us in a quite other direction.

However varied actual practises in the churches across the centuries, the great creeds have always taken a "realistic" position. The world and the Church are nourished by two different modes of divine activity, though both are held together within the larger purpose of the one God. The world as world cannot be organized in accordance with the inner life of the Church except by the same route of repentance. Attempts to introduce a gospel ethic directly into political programs were always spurned as utopian, visionary, and enthusiast. Characteristically such efforts were limited to the "sects." In our own social gospel movement, however, this view in considerable measure captured the leadership of the major quasi-established denominations. It is the resultant confusion that called forth Reinhold Niebuhr and gave him historic mission. Presumably, however, our essayists derive their "realism" from biblical rather than from analytical grounds.

When we come now to the affirmations of these writers, we sense some accents of faith and thought that are clearly distinguishing when compared to traditional attitudes. As far as biblical sanction is concerned, our writers deliver a clear death-blow to all jingoism, to all nationalism as ideology or idolatry. The nation organized politically in the state is a legitimate but limited instrument placed in the context of the wider humanity which it must serve. This becomes impressively clear in Whiston's treatment of "people" and "nation" in the Old Testament. Nationhood comes under judgment when it militates against the wider humanity it must serve. The unity of God and the unity of mankind, to both of which the Old Testament continuously witnesses, places inexorable obligations and limits upon nations and empires, even quite apart from a consideration of God's redemptive activity.

Moreover, the use of the Old Testament as authority for the military crusade, that perverted amalgam of tribal and chosen people motifs, is clearly without foundation. Nor is this disclaimer based on any effort to read a modern idealism or pacifism back into early Old Testament times. Not only must the Israelites be recognized as children of their time, but more importantly, the accents in the accounts themselves must be left where they are placed. Thus we find that the focus is on the wickedness of the Canaanite nations and on their ripeness for judgment, rather than on the righteousness of Israel. Militarism is not the divinely approved route to national self-realization. Moreover, it is the faithfulness of God rather than the self-interest of the Israelites that is at stake. Israel as nation—and it must be remembered that the monarchy was an ill-fated concession—was subject to the same destiny as all other nations. Her mission to the world was not her nationhood, but her distinction as a covenant people. That she was chosen was not due to her own merit, nor was it for her own benefit as an end in itself. The choice rather was universal in intention. It is only as the Suffering Servant image finally emerges and then flows forward into the Church that the lines of God's purpose become fully clear (Whiston). One looks in vain, therefore, for a counterpart to Israel's military crusades under New Testament auspices, whether in nation or in Church. That a confusion regarding Israel's true destiny should have arisen through her national history is hardly surprising; that it persists in our era, however, must surely be inexcusable.

This line of affirmation is reinforced by a strongly "existential" vein of thought which runs through much of the discussion. "Existential" in the present context refers, not to a vacuous astructural outlook which reduces all reality to a single uncharted moment, but rather to the way the gospel embraces the total man in his total situation, requiring not merely thought or sentiment but his very being. The ethical question is thus built into the very foundation of the faith itself, on Christ himself, and thus also our christology. Following the earliest of the gospels, Edwards insists that the mere Christ of the creeds is not truly Christ. According to the Markan account (ch. 8:34—9:1), "There is, in fact, no 'you are the Christ' without 'take up the cross.'" In this passage, Edwards continues, "the danger of a moralistic ethic uprooted from its religious ground and the danger of a sterile christology which does not touch on the essence of human personhood are both overcome." The liberation of the Christian from the "principalities" of this world does not provide a license for his self-indulgence, but rather the basis for a new possibility of obedience (I Peter 2:16) (Morrison). In our witness among the nations we are "confronted with an either/or dilemma. Are we, as members of an affluent society, going to continue to identify our existence with that of a particular nation? Or, shall we move into the life of the people of God to which we are called? If it be the latter, this means there is to be placed upon us the necessity of suffering for the healing of the nations" (Whiston). Christ's way to meet the enemy is our way (Klassen). It is in the concept of discipleship, of being where Christ is, of being "in" on what he is doing, and not primarily in creed, sacraments, or subjective experience, that we approach the real heart of our faith (Vincent).

Several of our writers likewise affirm deeply the identity of personal and social morality. "No distinction between the individual's cross-bearing and that of the communal (crowd-disciple) one is possible. . . . Despite the notable contributions of Christian existentialists to the theology of the New Testament, it must be affirmed against some of them that 'authentic selfhood' can never be reduced to a private and individual matter, nor can it be seen in some way as removed from economic, political, racial and all other human relationships" (Edwards). "The similarities in the ethical obligation of a Christian in personal relations and the same person in social and political groups are primary and the dissimilarities secondary" (Gottwald). "The prophet insisted on a continuum of responsibility extending from the individual through the corporate realms" (Gottwald). Similarly Klassen concludes that "the concept of 'the enemy' cannot be narrowed down but includes personal, national and religious enemies." New Testament writers can make these exuberant affirmations, since they are confident of the victory of Christ over the powers that otherwise bound them (Morrison, Klassen).

In sum, despite nuances and disagreements, there runs through these essays something of the revolutionary realism—both terms are important—which has always characterized the Christian faith and witness at its best. Our two common escape routes from the high calling are resolutely blocked: on the one hand, the sell-out to the nation, whether in succumbing to the conservative party or to the opposition (though we may still have various tasks to perform within these constellations); on the other hand, the ascetic withdrawal, whether monastic or sectarian (though there may also be tasks to perform within these

220

constellations). Yet to point to these presumably opposite poles is not to suggest that our way lies in a golden or Aristotelian mean, lived under the aegis or judgment of an impossible ideal. If there is a pessimism here regarding the possibilities of love or of the way of Christ in the larger social order, it is not because society is more immoral than the individual, but because it is not consonant with the nature of man and the forces of evil to expect a sudden or general condition of penitence, faith and regeneration to occur. If there is a seeming utopianism about the expectation that the gospel will change men, this is not because of perfectionist illusions, but because the grace of God means genuine possibility, even though men may fail to yield to its full potential.

We are offered here a dynamic, open-ended, and adventurous commitment, a faith and a life that may well be the dismay of moralists in search of paragraphs, of those who seek in "religion" security without risk. Thus the vital Christian may refuse to identify totally with the world or the nation, and participate so thoroughly in it as to transform it (Piper). Though there is neither anarchy nor disregard for order or continuity, the commitment is always one of programmatic openness (Gottwald). Precisely because the "world" and the nation have been broken as absolute powers, the Christian can serve in confidence and freedom within them (Morrison). He labors and struggles in the social arena, not because he shares the utopian illusions of reformists expecting an ideal world, but because in these tasks he is able to serve his neighbor (Piper). Most decisive of all, perhaps, is the fact that in the Church, the community of grace, the victory of Christ over the principalities and powers is already accomplished (Morrison, Vincent). It is here that the healing and reconciliation of men and nations is already being actualized, becoming thus a witness for all to see. It is here, too, rather than in the requirements of a humanity still broken, that Christian conduct is truly shaped.

Given the long and deep confusion in these matters which is our legacy as Western Christians, it would be presumptuous to propose in a word the practical implications of the recovery here suggested, even regarding the crucial questions of nuclear war. Indeed, to rush forward with easy blueprints would be once more to smuggle in the utopian solution. Yet clearly there is "divine atomic energy" in the affirmations of these papers, to use Stendahl's figure. In terms of the best that biblical studies offer us today, there is no return behind the revolutionary realism which they breathe. There is no return to an ethic which exhausts its meaning and determines its limits by the logic of civilization.

Some major questions remain unanswered, however, partly because of what the writers here have said, and partly because of what they have left unsaid. In some respects we stand, as it were, at the foundations of a great archway, not yet built far enough to enable us to project the angle or arc of the finished structure. Thus the eschatological question, not merely as the qualitative difference aeons or spheres, but with reference to the structure, the course and the end of history, remains decisive yet unclear. Where and how do Church and nations meet, intersect, or relate in the events of our time in the fulfillment of the purposes of God? Further, despite the basic claim that the Church is the locus of Christ's victory, these essays, strangely enough, give us little help on the question of the Church. Morrison, who is most incisive at the basic point, is less clear or convincing when he speaks of the political meaning of the Church. In his discussion, how does one escape the reduction of the Church's witness to the mere individual deeds of isolated, politically active church members? Or when the Old Testament scholars rightly stress the broader activity of God among the nations, even when they do not acknowledge Him, does not the Church become politically irrelevant? Is not some universal norm or value among all the nations regardless of their religious outlook far more decisive than a limited church ethic? In the age of "universal history" upon which we have entered, where contradictory value systems must be brought into some coherent order, will not Christianity decrease yet more in its political relevance? Indeed, if one accepts such a definition of "universal history," one might ask whether the whole renewal in biblical theology has more than esoteric Christian value.

Summary: Toward Recovery

Implicitly, John Vincent's essay is addressed to precisely the foregoing question. His proposal to regard discipleship as the "overall category within which we may listen to what the New Testament has to say to us on our present problems" is indeed a fruitful one. We are thus carried beyond mere credal, or sacramental, or subjective conversionistic interests. In the end our obedience, our deeds, express determinatively our faith in Christ. And yet, because of Christ's ongoing activity in the world, and because our responses are rooted in that activity, we are delivered from the legalisms or moralisms which always threaten emphases on Christian deeds. Fertile, too, is the suggestion that expediency is not automatically alien to the requirements of discipleship; indeed that expediency is one test to be applied.

It must be asked, however, whether Vincent has actually carried the logic of this argument through, and whether the "expediency" of Britain's formation of a "non-nuclear club" (which may or may not be feasible) has not gained undue influence over the theological argument. For while early in the paper he espouses a view similar to Morrison's that the Church is the locus of Christ's victory over the powers, the main conclusion of the paper points rather to the demand for the whole society to respond directly to the demands of the discipleship without waiting for the Church. At this point, however, it is difficult to discern the role or relevance of atonement and repentance, of the reality and power of evil in the world. Indeed, in the understandable haste for politically relevant expressions, are we not back again close to the older liberalism, brushing aside once more the church-world distinctions here so tentatively and painfully recovered, or in "pre-Niebuhrian" fashion, expecting the ethics of the sermon on the mount directly to transform political realities? Does the confession that Jesus is Lord obliterate the distinction between the modes of God's dealing with men as determined by their response in faith or in unfaith? Do coincidences between religious and political assessments, of which there will surely always be many, warrant the conclusion that events in the latter domain are therefore endowed with "ultimate significance"?

Some Proposed Solutions

In the end, therefore, we are left with a consensus sufficiently strong to call for a reformulation of the content and meaning of Christian ethics, particularly with reference to inordinate national demands, yet sufficiently tentative to prevent a premature termination to our quest. Much will depend on our response to the biblical witness. In this scientific age, theological paragraphs, biblical concepts, and eternal verities make little impact upon us. We look to religion as to other cultural resources for the realization of what we regard as greater ends, and thus we block our own way to faith. But as Morrison well says, "The prior question is not peace or war, but the will of God." Are we in our time able to comprehend and to accept this affirmation?